The Western American Indian

THE WESTERN AMERICAN INDIAN

Case Studies in Tribal History

Edited with an introduction
by Richard N. Ellis

UNIVERSITY OF NEBRASKA PRESS • LINCOLN

Acknowledgments for the use of copyrighted material appear on pp. vii-viii, which constitute an extension of the copyright page.

International Standard Book Number 0-8032-5754-6
Library of Congress Catalog Card Number 70-181597

Most recent Bison Book printing shown by first digit below:
2 3 4 5 6 7 8 9 10

For R. C. Gorman

Manufactured in the United States of America

Contents

Acknowledgments

Grateful acknowledgment is made to the authors and publishers for their permission to reprint the following selections:

"A Most Satisfactory Council," by Alvin M. Josephy, Jr. Chapter 8 of *The Nez Perce Indians and the Opening of the Northwest* (New Haven: Yale University Press, 1965), pp. 315–32. Copyright © 1965 by Yale University Press.

"'A Lasting Peace'—Fort Laramie, 1866," by James C. Olson. Chapter 3 of *Red Cloud and the Sioux Problem* (Lincoln: University of Nebraska Press, 1965), pp. 27–40.

"The Battle of the Washita, 1868," by George Bird Grinnell. Chapter 22 of *The Fighting Cheyennes* (Norman: University of Oklahoma Press, 1955), pp. 299–309.

"Grant's Indian Peace Policy on the Yakima Reservation, 1870–82," by Robert Whitner. *Pacific Northwest Quarterly* 50 (October 1959): 135–42.

"The Old 'Hand to Mouth Way,'" by Richard N. Ellis. Chapter 10 of *General Pope and U.S. Indian Policy* (Albuquerque: University of New Mexico Press, 1970), 196–211. Originally published in somewhat different form in the *Southwestern Historical Quarterly* 72 (October 1968) and reprinted by permission of the *Texas State Historical Association.*

"A Better Way: General George Crook and the Ponca Indians," by James T. King. *Nebraska History* 50 (Autumn 1969): 239–54.

"The End of Apache Resistance," by Ralph H. Ogle. Chapter 8 of *Federal Control of the Western Apaches, 1848-1886* (Albuquerque: University of New Mexico Press, 1970), pp. 216–23.

"The Struggle with McGillycuddy," by James C. Olson. Chapter 14 of *Red Cloud and the Sioux Problem* (Lincoln: University of Nebraska Press, 1965), pp. 264–85.

"The Decision to Use Force," by Loring Benson Priest. Chapter 18 of *Uncle Sam's Stepchildren: The Reformation of United States Indian Policy, 1865-1887* (New Brunswick, N.J.: Rutgers University Press, 1942), pp. 233–47.

"Federal Indian Policy and the Southern Cheyennes and Arapahoes, 1887–1907," by Donald J. Berthrong. *Ethnohistory* 3 (Spring 1956): 138–48.

"The Genesis and Philosophy of the Indian Reorganization Act," by John Collier. *Indian Affairs and the Indian Reorganization Act: The Twenty Year Record* (Tucson: University of Arizona Press, 1954), pp. 3–8.

"The Role of the Bureau of Indian Affairs since 1933," by William Zimmerman, Jr. *Annals of the American Academy of Political and Social Science* 311 (May 1957): 31–40.

"The Twentieth Century: Santee," by Roy W. Meyer. Chapter 15 of *History of the Santee Sioux* (Lincoln: University of Nebraska Press, 1967), pp. 294–316.

"Indian Tribal Claims before the Court of Claims," by Glen A. Wilkinson. *Georgetown Law Journal* 55 (December 1966): 511–28.

"Termination in Retrospect," by Gary Orfield. Chapter 6 of *A Study of Termination Policy* (Denver: National Congress of American Indians, n.d.), pp. 15–23.

Introduction

Much of the recent history of the Indian tribes of the United States has been determined or heavily influenced by the actions, policies, and attitudes of white Americans. Contact with whites brought drastic modifications in the economic, political, religious, and social lives of the Indian people—changes which in many cases were the direct result of the federal government's dealings with the tribes. This official aspect of Indian-white relations did not become an important element in the lives of the majority of American Indians until the mid-nineteenth century, when white settlers began to move into the trans-Mississippi West in large numbers. By that time most of the tribes were living west of the Mississippi; some eastern Indians had moved beyond the Mississippi by choice, and the official removal policy of the United States government had effectively relocated all but a few of the remaining eastern tribes to the western Indian country.

Until the 1840s relations with the original inhabitants of the West had been limited, although fur traders and explorers had established contact with some of the tribes and meetings with Indians increased after the opening of trade to Santa Fe in the 1820s. Nevertheless, the English-speaking people of North America had had two centuries of experience in dealing with various tribes. Official views of the Indians had developed over the years, and policies for regulating relations with them had evolved. The Constitution and subsequent legislation provided that the federal government was responsible for formulating and enforcing Indian policy and that it alone could treat with Indian tribes and purchase land from them. On the whole policy makers sought to be just and humane, but more often than not they were unsuccessful. During the early years of the Republic the Indian Trade and

Intercourse Acts prohibited the sale of alcohol to Indians, forbade intrusion onto Indian lands, and regulated the Indian trade, but enforcement left much to be desired.

This period before 1850 also saw the gradual bureaucratic growth of the Indian Service. Indian affairs originally fell under the control of the Secretary of War, and in 1824 the Bureau of Indian Affairs was founded in the War Department. Six years later the office of Commissioner of Indian Affairs was created. In 1849, however, the Department of the Interior was established, and the Bureau was transferred to that department, creating a jurisdictional dispute that plagued the successful development and implementation of government policies throughout the remainder of the nineteenth century.

Friction between the War and Interior departments was not the only hindrance to an enlightened administration of Indian affairs. The diversity of the tribes was overwhelming, although many administrators acted on the premise that all Indians were basically alike. The hundreds of different Indian groups speaking hundreds of different languages ranged from the peaceful Pueblos to the warlike Sioux and Apaches; from the Five Civilized Tribes, with highly evolved governments, to the scattered, loosely organized bands which struggled for existence in the hostile environment of the Great Basin; from farmers such as the Mandans and Hidatsas of the Missouri Valley to the Commanche buffalo hunters and sea-going fishermen like the Makahs of the Olympic Peninsula. The Indian population north of Mexico, variously estimated at between 800,000 and 1,153,450 at the time of the discovery of America, had declined precipitously in the East because of disease, warfare, the advance of white settlement, and eventually the removal policy, but government officials could only guess—and guess inaccurately—at the Indian population in the West. Nor could they discern the number of tribes, subtribes, triblets, or bands that existed in that region. Government knowledge of Indian political organization also left much to be desired.

Yet the Commissioner of Indian Affairs was expected to develop and enforce rational policies for these people. In so doing he had to take into account the opinions and requests of western settlers and speculators, eastern humanitarians, the War Department and its political supporters, the Secretary of the Interior and the President under whom he served, and members of Congress who must ratify treaties and appropriate funds. In this mélange of conflicting ideas and demands, Indian views were ignored.

The history of the Indian tribes of the trans-Mississippi West is one of rapid change and cultural oppression. Before the coming of the whites they lived in complete freedom—although this is not to say that they lived in peace, harmony, and economic plenty. Within the space of a few decades, however, their status changed drastically. Anglo-American settlers moved into the West and demanded land; treaties were made; wars were fought; and the tribes were defeated and placed on reservations. White Americans, exhibiting a remarkable degree of ethnocentrism, agreed that Indian culture was unacceptable and insisted that the Indian people conform to the dominant way of life. The government therefore undertook programs to eradicate Indian customs, and despite the New Deal attempts to reverse this policy the misguided insistence on cultural conformity has continued.

The Indians have reacted to forced change in various ways. Some tribes fought the government while others employed passive resistance. Acculturation has undoubtedly taken place, but the Indian people have also demonstrated a remarkable ability to preserve aspects of their culture. Indian leaders have become increasingly vocal in the mid-twentieth century, and organizations such as the National Congress of American Indians, founded in 1944, the National Indian Youth Council, established in 1961, the National Tribal Chairmans Association, organized in 1971, and other smaller groups have provided both the organizational medium for increasing Indian unity and platforms for the expression of Indian views. In the past Indian policy was formulated by white government officials who refused to solicit or listen to Indian opinions. Now Indian leaders demand that they be heard and that they be given voice in the development of government programs and policies. There have been some indications that this will occur, if only because the Indian people insist upon it.

In 1966 President Lyndon B. Johnson appointed Robert Bennett Commissioner of Indian Affairs. Bennett, only the second Indian to hold that position, began to give increased responsibilities to Indian communities. One area, for example, in which Indian leaders have sought more influence is education, and fights for greater representation on school boards in districts with large numbers of Indian students have been common. The creation of the Rough Rock Demonstration School on the Navajo Reservation in 1966 provided Navajos with the opportunity to run their own school, and in 1970 the Navajos at Ramah, New Mexico, assumed control of the local high school. Indians have also moved into the area of higher education with the founding of the Navajo Community College. To alleviate the unemployment on reservations and to stem the flow of young people to the cities, a number of tribes have attracted private industries to their reservations or have established their own tribal business concerns.

Although the Indian people have made some gains in self-determination, they are still engaged in the struggle to protect their interests and control their own affairs. The attack on their land base and water and fishing rights is continuing, and the current controversy over Pyramid Lake in Nevada between Indians who claim water rights and proponents of reclamation projects is but one example of this.

On July 8, 1970, President Richard M. Nixon issued a major policy statement on Indian self-determination. He has since reiterated his pledge to grant tribes a greater say in governing themselves and has promised a reorganization of the Bureau of Indian Affairs, but some Indian leaders have remained dissatisfied enough to demand the creation of a new Indian Department with a cabinet-level director. The next few years will demonstrate the extent of the federal government's commitment to the Indian people.

This book is designed to provide case studies on major topics which illuminate the impact of white settlement, and especially of official governmental policy and actions, on the western tribes in the post-1850 period. It is not intended as a comprehensive history of the western Indians; rather the goal is to provide in-depth treatment of specific issues such as treaty making, warfare, reservation life, allotment, the Indian New Deal, and termination. Most of the selections present illustrative experiences of individual tribes; a few deal more generally with the evolution and application of particular federal policies and laws. If Indian views are lacking, it is because accounts from that perspective rarely exist for nineteenth-century events and although they are more readily available for later developments such as the New Deal, the work of the Indian Claims Commission, and the policy of termination, systematic studies of these materials have not been made. In the interest of economy most of the footnotes have been omitted from the readings. A source note following each selection gives complete bibliographical information for those who wish to refer to the scholarly apparatus in the original article or chapter and explains what editorial changes if any have been made in this reprinting.

Treaty Making

Although European powers claimed the New World by right of discovery and conquest, they established the precedent of negotiating with the original inhabitants and purchasing land from them. Over the years this became a firmly established practice. Negotiations were invariably held when the whites wanted something from the Indians, and it was evident that threats, pressure, trickery, the influence of alcohol, disagreement within the tribe, or merely the weight of time eventually gave them what they wanted. By the middle of the nineteenth century officials of the United States government were quite experienced in dealing with Indians, and in their recent negotiations for the removal of the eastern tribes to the trans-Mississippi West they had used most of the above techniques, especially the exploitation of tribal divisions.

In the 1850s white Americans began to come into contact with the tribes of the trans-Mississippi West on a wide scale. Settlers moved into the Upper Mississippi Valley and to the Pacific Northwest while thousands of people were attracted to California by the discovery of gold. The spread of settlement and increased travel across the West necessitated negotiations with the Indians, and in 1851 the government began to seek concessions from the western tribes. The Fort Laramie Treaty of 1851, with the northern Plains tribes, and the Fort Atkinson Treaty of 1853, with the southern Plains tribes, defined tribal boundaries, pledged peace and friendship, and secured approval of certain roads through Indian country. Two examples of government treaty-making techniques can be seen in the 1855 council at Walla Walla in Washington Territory and the 1866 negotiations with the Sioux at Fort Laramie. Both had widespread and serious ramifications.

The tribes of the interior of the Northwest, including the Yakimas, Spokans, Nez Perces, Cayuses, and others, reflected cultural influences of the plains as well as the coastal region.

They possessed horses and had a Plains type of military tradition. Early contact with white fur traders and missionaries had caused the tribes to split into conservative and progressive factions, which government officials would be quick to exploit.

The creation of Washington Territory in 1853 brought Isaac I. Stevens to the Northwest as governor and superintendent of Indian Affairs, two offices that were often mutually incompatible. Stevens, a former military officer, had been involved in government railroad surveys in the region. As a leading promoter of the Northwest, he wanted to clear title to the land, place the Indians on reservations, and teach them to farm, and he immediately set out to obtain those goals. After concluding a series of treaties with the tribes in the Puget Sound region, he called a grand council of the tribes of the interior. Alvin Josephy has provided an outstanding description and evaluation of the Walla Walla Council of 1855 and has clearly outlined the techniques used by Stevens to secure the treaties that he was determined to have.

Indian resentment of Stevens's methods and of the treaty provisions was quick to develop. Although the treaties were not ratified by the United States Senate until four years later, Stevens announced that the lands of the interior were open to settlement. Whites moved into the area, and almost immediately reports of gold discoveries at Colville caused a small rush across Yakima lands. In the resulting friction a number of whites were killed, and when Major Granville O. Haller marched into Yakima country to put down the trouble, he was repulsed in what was only the first of a series of battles. Before fighting subsided, tribes on both sides of the Cascades turned against the whites, and although the army eventually emerged victorious by 1858, the warfare demonstrated the foolishness of tricking Indians and forcing unacceptable treaties on them.

The Walla Walla Council of 1855

ALVIN M. JOSEPHY, JR.

On May 21 Stevens, Palmer, and their parties reached the council grounds, where an advance group had erected tents, a log storehouse for the Indian presents, and two arbors of poles and boughs, one to serve as a council chamber, the other "as a banqueting-hall for distinguished chiefs, so that, as in civilized lands, gastronomy might aid diplomacy." On May 24 a great part of the Nez Perce nation, some 2,500 Indians of the different bands and villages from the Wallowa Valley to the upper waters of the Clearwater, arrived. When about a mile distant from the council grounds, they halted, and the leading men, including Lawyer, Joseph, old James, Utsinmalikin, Metat Waptass, Red Wolf, and several others, rode forward with [their interpreter] William Craig to be introduced formally to Stevens and Palmer. Then, as the chiefs dismounted and joined the commissioners' party in a reviewing group at the council's flagpole, the rest of the Nez Perces started toward them and circled about the pole. They made a dramatic sight, "a thousand warriors mounted on fine horses and riding at a gallop, two abreast, naked to the breech-clout, their faces covered with white, red, and yellow paint in fanciful designs, and decked with plumes and feathers and trinkets fluttering in the sunshine." They put on a series of equestrian displays for the commissioners, "charging at full gallop . . . firing their guns, brandishing their shields, beating their drums, and yelling their war-whoops," and then, after a war dance, filed off to a location a half mile away that had been selected for their camp. Stevens was pleased by the grand show, but he missed part of its significance. It was the Indians' way not only of according him a salute but of demonstrating that they were strong and unafraid, and expected to be treated as a powerful people.

Still, some of the most important Nez Perces—because of their prowess and leadership in war—were not there. Looking Glass and many of the tribe's ablest warriors and hunters were in the buffalo country. Stevens must have been delighted to receive that information. In the absence of Looking Glass there was less chance of his encountering difficulty with the more tractable head chief, Lawyer, who in his opinion was "wise, enlightened, and magnanimous . . . head and shoulders above the other chiefs, whether in intellect, nobility of soul, or influence."

To the members of the council who were meeting the Nez Perces for the first time, Lawyer and his people were remarkable

Indians. "There is an odd mixture of this world and the next in some of the Nez Perces,—an equal love for fighting and [religious] devotion, the wildest Indian traits with a strictness in some religious rites which might shame those 'who profess and call themselves Christians,'" wrote Lieutenant Lawrence Kip, a member of Stevens' military escort. "They have prayers in their lodges every morning and evening—service several times on Sunday—and nothing will induce them on that day to engage in any trading." Later, after the council began, Kip was impressed when he learned that "two or three of the half-civilized Nez Perces, who could write, were keeping a minute account of all that transpired at these meetings." Nevertheless, there was still a gap between those friendly Indians and the whites. When Lieutenant Archibald Gracie, who commanded the military escort, strove to "test" Lawyer by asking him if he would welcome having Gracie make a brief visit to the Nez Perces' country, the head chief evaded the question and then answered only, "Perhaps so." It was a measure of the narrow line Lawyer was trying to walk between accommodating the whites and retaining his hold over his people, but Lieutenant Gracie did not recognize it.

When the Cayuses, Wallawallas, and Umatillas arrived, they were less friendly than the Nez Perces and "went into camp without any parade or salutations." With them was Peopeo Moxmox, who reflected the deep distrust of those tribes by sending word to Stevens that they had brought their own provisions with them, and did not want any from the whites. Even the Wallawalla leader's messenger refused to accept any tobacco for his chief, "a very unfriendly sign," and rode off muttering, "You will find out by and by why we won't take provisions." Soon afterward, Tauitau, known to Stevens as the Young Chief, and several of the Cayuse headmen rode into Stevens' camp and, refusing to smoke, "shook hands in a very cold manner." Nevertheless, Stevens wrote in his diary, "The haughty carriage of these chiefs and their manly character have, for the first time in my Indian experience, realized the descriptions of the writers of fiction."

Fathers Chirouse of the Walla Walla Valley and Pandosy of the Yakima mission also appeared, reporting to Stevens that all the Indians they knew, except Kamiakin, were well disposed toward the whites. Some Indians had told them, "Kamiakin will come with his young men with powder and ball." Stevens added Kamiakin to his list of potential "malcontents" that now included Peopeo Moxmox and the Young Chief; but when the Yakima leader arrived with Owhi, Skloom, and a number of warriors, he shook hands in a friendly manner and sat down for a smoke, although he refused tobacco from the commissioners.

The day before the council opened, Peopeo Moxmox, having insisted that he, the Young Chief, Lawyer, and Kamiakin do all the talking for the Indians, asked Stevens for more than one interpreter, "that they might know they translated truly." When Stevens agreed to the request, the old chief looked around the area at young Nez Perces who loitered about and said with scorn, "I do not wish my boys running around the camp of the whites like these young men."

The distinction between distrust and hostility was a thin one, but Stevens, the optimist, was still sure that he could win over men like Peopeo Moxmox without using force. Palmer and some of the others were not so sure. And if it came to force, forty-seven troopers were slim security against several thousand Indians. There was always Lawyer, however, and through him Stevens continued to count on the Nez Perces. He cultivated the Nez Perce chiefs and at a banquet for thirty of them piled their tin plates to the brim "again and again." A mess was maintained for them throughout the council, "and every day was well attended."

Before the council started, a number of other Indians arrived, including members of several bands that lived along the Columbia, a headman of the Palouses who reported that his people "were indifferent to the matter," and [the Spokan leader] Spokan Garry, who came as an observer. Altogether, some 5,000 Indians were in attendance. On the morning the council was to begin, the commissioners visited Lawyer, who was in great pain from the old wound he had received at the Battle of Pierre's Hole more than twenty years before. While they were with Lawyer, Utsinmalikin appeared and told the commissioners that Peopeo Moxmox, Kamiakin, and the Cayuses had asked him and two other Nez Perce chiefs to come to their camp for a council. He claimed he had rebuffed them angrily. "Why do you come here and ask three chiefs to come to a council, while to the head chief [Lawyer] and the rest you say nothing?" he reported he had said. The news confirmed to the commissioners that the "malcontents" were already at work, plotting some conspiracy; but it seemed evident also that the friendly Lawyer was still in firm control of the Nez Perces, and there were as many of them as all the other Indians together.

The council began on the afternoon of May 29. The minutes of the proceedings are astounding to read. The transparency of the speeches of Governor Stevens and Superintendent Palmer is so obvious that it is a wonder the commissioners could not realize the ease with which the Indians saw through what they were saying. One can only assume either that their ignorance of the Indians' mentality was appalling or that they were so intent on having their way with the tribes that they blinded themselves to the flagrancy of their hypocrisy. It was so clear to the Indians, however, that it soon placed Lawyer and the friendly Nez Perce headmen in an awkward position, undermining their ability to cope with the Indians who were opposed to selling their lands, and finally even embarrassed Palmer, who, more attuned to Indian reactions than Stevens, suddenly realized the harm that was being done.

The council met in front of an arbor erected near Stevens' tent. Stevens and Palmer sat on a bench, and the Indians gathered around them on the ground in a large circle. The chiefs sat in the front row, with some 1,000 of their people ranged behind them. As the white men spoke, Craig and the other interpreters translated each sentence to Indian criers, who announced it in loud voices to the assemblage. After the interpreters were sworn in on the first day, it began to rain, and the council was adjourned. The next day Stevens opened the proceedings with a speech, praising the individual tribes for their friendship to whites and for their accomplishments so far in adopting the ways of life of the white man. "I went back to the Great Father last year to say that you had been good, you have been kind, *he must do something for you,*" he told the Indians. Getting to what that "something" was took him through a long, circuitous, and tortuous explanation. There were bad white men, he said, who made trouble for

Indians. But east of the mountains, the Great Father had taken measures to protect his Indian children from the bad white men. He had guided "the red man across a great river into a fine country," where he could take care of them, away from the trouble-making white men. He even named the Great Father, Andrew Jackson, but he was on thin ground. Although he omitted references to the coercion, misery, starvation, and deaths of the "trail of tears" that marked the enforced removal of Indians from their homelands east of the Mississippi, some of the Northwestern Indians were not as uninformed as he thought they were. Delawares, Iroquois, and plains Indians had been telling them for fifteen years of what had happened to the eastern Indians. As they sat and listened to Stevens, the governor was already beginning to lose ground.

But he went on. The Great Father had done wonderful things for the Indians whom he had moved to new homes. In fact, they were so happy that Stevens wanted to do the same thing for the western tribes. "This brings us now to the question. What shall we do at this council? We want you and ourselves to agree upon tracts of lands where you shall live; in those tracts of land we want each man who will work to have his own land, his own horses, his own cattle, and his home for himself and his children." Among the Indians who were absorbing this, he was now in trouble. He may have recognized that he was moving too fast, for he checked himself, and switched quickly to a long list of things he wanted to give the Indians: schools, blacksmiths, carpenters, farmers, plows, wagons, saw mills, grist mills, and instructors who would teach them to spin, weave, make clothes, and become mechanics, farmers, doctors, and lawyers. Then suddenly it was out: "Now we want you to agree with us to such a state of things: You to have your tract with all these things; the rest to be the Great Father's for his white children." There must have been an awful pause, for he immediately reverted to a repetition of all the things the Great Father would give the Indians. "Besides all these things, these shops, these mills and these schools which I have mentioned, we must pay you for the land which you give to the Great Father," he summed up, finally saying, "I am tired of speaking; you are tired of listening. I will speak tomorrow."

Palmer must already have sensed that the Indians were not reacting well. He took over for a moment with an explanation: "It is not expected that we can come together with one day's talk; nor do we expect you can understand with what has been said all that we want . . . Sometimes when people have a matter to settle, they commence way off; but as they understand each other they come together. With us, if we commenced way off, I hope we are a little nearer now, and by and by I hope we shall come quite together." The minutes show that the Indians made no reply, and the council was adjourned until the next day.

On May 31 Stevens made another speech, repeating several times the many things the Great Father wished to give the Indians. "We want you to have schools and mills and shops and farms . . . there will be blankets and cloth for leggings . . . we want in your houses plates and cups and brass and tin kettles, frying pans to cook your meat and bake ovens to bake your bread . . . you will have your own smiths, your own wheelwrights, your own carpenters, your own physicians and lawyers and other learned men . . ." He went on, appearing as if he had a compulsion to keep talking about gifts but obviously doing everything possible to postpone coming to the main point — acquisition of the Indians' lands. None of what he was saying could have been helpful to him. Save perhaps for Lawyer and a few other headmen, the Indians had not the slightest interest in abandoning their own ways and adopting the white man's culture. Few of them could have understood the desirability of acquiring all that Stevens was offering them, but they could see clearly that he was bargaining with promises of gifts if they sold him what they did not wish to sell.

Eventually, Stevens changed his tack and told them about his plan to end the Blackfoot menace to their buffalo-hunting parties. The Blackfeet would be friends of the western tribes, but Stevens would want the western tribes to be models for the Blackfeet and teach the Blackfeet how to settle down on prosperous farms like white men. This the western tribes could do to help Stevens.

He then called on Palmer, who spoke as if he did not know what to say. Launching into a discussion of "the course pursued by the government towards the Indians on the other side of the mountains," he gave a long, rambling, and distorted version of the history of Indian-white relations in the East, commencing with Columbus. It was a hodge-podge of colonial and mid-western episodes, showing, if anything, Palmer's ignorance of what he was talking about. However, it led abruptly to a relevant point, which Palmer recognized was worth emphasizing for several moments: There had always been bad white men from whom the Indians had needed protection, and there were bad men now scheming "to get your horses," and do other evil things to the Indians. "It is these men I am told who would rob you of your property," he said, suddenly adding a new idea, "who are giving you advice not to treat with us. Whose councils do you prefer to take? These men who would rob you, or ours who come to befriend you?" These men, he concluded, even married Indian women in order to steal the Indians' horses. "All such men need watching . . . who are your friends, such men, or myself and my brother [Stevens] who have come here to act for your good?" On that note, the council adjourned till the next day.

But the council did not meet the next day, "as the Indians," said Lieutenant Kip, "wished time to consider the proposals." It is obvious that in the private meetings among the headmen the purpose of the white commissioners was clear to all, and Kamiakin and Peopeo Moxmox must have found it easy to muster support for their policy of opposition to the sale of the Indians' lands. The talk of history, presents, and other matters that had clothed the commissioners' central point, their hope that the Indians would give up some of their country, must, in fact, have angered men like Kamiakin who would have characterized it as the glibness of crooked tongues. With the Nez Perces at the council was a Delaware Indian, Jim Simonds, who had lived and traveled with the Sahaptins since 1849 or 1850. Well known both to the whites and Indians as Delaware Jim, he would have been able to give the Northwestern Indians a different version of Stevens' account of Andrew Jackson's removal of the eastern Indians, and the council proceedings later indicated that he did just that.

At any rate, when the council convened again on June 2, Palmer knew that the Indians' opposition was hardening, and he made a more forthright appeal to them, stating that "like grasshoppers on the plains," the white settlers were coming to this country, and no one would be able to stop them. It simply could not be done, any more than one could "stop the waters of the Columbia River from flowing." But the land, like the air, the water, the fish, and the game, was "made for the white man and the red man," and that was why the commissioners wished to have the Indians choose the lands they wanted to keep for themselves before the settlers arrived. "We did not come here to scare you or to drive you away, but we came here to talk to you like men . . . if we enter into a treaty now we can select a good country for you; but if we wait till the country is filled up with whites, where will we find such a place? . . . If we make a treaty with you . . . you can rely on all its provisions being carried out strictly."

When Palmer was done, Stevens announced that the time had come for the Indians to be heard. There was a pause. "We are tired," said Five Crows. Palmer assured him that the whites had nothing more to say, and Five Crows then spoke briefly. He was the Cayuse half-brother of Joseph, who had taken one of the female prisoners to live with him on the Umatilla after the massacre at Waiilatpu, and had been wounded in battle with the volunteers during the Cayuse war. Spalding had converted him and given him the name Hezekiah, but the events of the months after the massacre had destroyed his faith in the white man's religion. The Father in Heaven had made the earth, and had made man of earth, but he had given man no gardens to plow, he pointed out to the commissioners in a reply to Stevens' talk about turning the Indians into farmers.

He was followed by Peopeo Moxmox, who was full of anger. "We have listened to all you have to say, and we desire you to listen when any Indian speaks . . . I know the value of your speech from having experienced the same in California." The memory of his son's death, still unpunished, flooded through his mind, but it would have meant nothing to Stevens or Palmer. "We have not seen in a true light the object of your speeches . . . you have spoken in a round about way. Speak straight. I have ears to hear you, and here is my heart . . . You have spoken in a manner partly tending to evil. Speak plain to us . . . ."

The session ended tensely. The old Wallawalla had been blunt.

Moreover, he had embarrassed Lawyer by stating that he knew that Craig was putting pressure on the Nez Perces for an immediate answer, without giving them time to think. "The whole has been prearranged," he had said.

What happened among the Indians that evening will probably never be clear. Long after the entire council was over, Stevens claimed that Lawyer had come to his tent alone after midnight that night and had told him that he had just learned that during the day the Cayuses had formed a plot to massacre all the whites at the council, and that the Yakimas and Wallawallas were now about to join them. The conspirators did not trust the Nez Perces, he had said, and he had announced to Stevens, "I will come with my family and pitch my lodge in the midst of your camp, that those Cayuses may see that you and your party are under the protection of the head chief of the Nez Perces." Lawyer did move into Stevens' camp, but his story, if indeed that is what he told Stevens, is questionable. Stevens made no mention of it in the contemporary records of the council, and the Indians have always laughed at his later report of the plot. They have insisted that there was no such plan, that Lawyer would not have been so stupid as to move his family to the site of an intended attack, and that more likely the truth of what had happened was that after Peopeo Moxmox's speech many of the Nez Perces had turned against Lawyer, and he had left his people for his own safety.

There is no doubt that Lawyer was in a difficult position, and that he was frightened. On Monday, June 4, when the council reconvened, Stevens called on him to talk. The head chief orated in a confused manner, trying not to offend Stevens, but at the same time attempting not to arouse the ire of the Indians who were listening to him. After posing somewhat as an intermediary, and telling Stevens that the Indians were poor and did not want to lose their lands, he pleaded, "There are a good many men here who wish to speak. Let them speak."

But no one had much to say. Kamiakin stated that he was afraid of the white man; Utsinmalikin said he agreed with Lawyer; Stickus the Cayuse asked Stevens to speak plainly; and Peopeo Moxmox demanded that the commissioners mention the specific lands they were talking about. "You have spoken for lands generally. You have not spoken of any particular ones." Then Tipyahlanah Ka-ou-pu, the Eagle of the Morning Light, or of the Dawn (known to whites variously as Eagle of the Light, Eagle From the Light, and Eagle of Delight), rose to review the history of Nez Perce relations with the white men, telling the commissioners of his "brother," whom the Astorians had hanged many years before "for no offense" at the mouth of the Palouse River. "This I say to my brother here that he may think of it," he said bitterly. He also told them of The Hat, "my Father," whom [the missionary Henry H.] Spalding had sent to the States with [missionary] William H. Gray. "His body was never returned . . . that is another thing to think of." And during the Cayuse war the Nez Perces had remained friendly to the whites, but his chief, Ellis, had gone to the East to look for counsel, "and there his body lies beyond here. He has never returned." He condemned Spalding, who, he claimed, had come to teach the Indians but had stayed to become a trader. "He made a farm and raised grain and bought our stock . . . and I do not wish another preacher to come."

When Eagle From the Light sat down, no other Indian wished to speak, and Stevens rose hesitantly to answer Peopeo Moxmox's question and make clear the specifics of the treaty. Feeling his way carefully, he announced that he had two reservations in mind, one in the Nez Perce country from the Blue Mountains to the Bitterroots and from the Palouse River to the Grande Ronde and Salmon rivers, and the other in the Yakima country between the Yakima and Columbia rivers. On the first reservation he proposed that the Spokans, Cayuses, Wallawallas, and Umatillas move in with the Nez Perces, and on the second reservation he hoped to gather all the tribes and bands along the Columbia River from The Dallas to the Okanogan and Colville valleys far in the north. Both schemes had been carefully worked out and were already delineated on maps which he showed the Indians. He did not, however, tell them his purposes, which were to select lands for them that no white man yet wanted, and to clear all the areas which the settlers were already eyeing or entering, or which he would have to secure for the building of a railroad and highways. Thus he planned to have the Indians vacate regions like the

Umatilla, Walla Walla, and Colville valleys, as well as the Spokan and Palouse countries and the Yakima River valley through which his projected northern railroad would run.

He spent the next two days explaining the reservations more fully, tracing their boundaries on his map, and describing the payments the government would give the tribes for the lands they sold. But he made little headway. With the exception of Lawyer and a few of the Nez Perce headmen whose homelands were untouched by Stevens' proposals, the Indians reacted coldly and with bitterness. "There is evidently a more hostile feeling toward the whites getting up among some of the tribes," Lieutenant Kip noted on one of the evenings, adding that when he and Lieutenant Gracie attempted to visit the Cayuse camp, a group of young warriors stood in their way and motioned them to leave.

In addition to having to surrender their lands, none of the tribes liked the prospect of being forced to live together like a single people. Few of the Columbia River bands that were supposed to move in with the Yakimas were even present at the council, and no one could speak for them. Some of them were Salish and some Sahaptins, but the Yakimas wanted none of them on their lands. Similarly, the Cayuses, Wallawallas, and Umatillas had no intention of moving onto Nez Perce lands, and few of the Nez Perces looked forward happily to welcoming them. Spokan Garry, merely a witness at the council, sat glumly, worrying how to inform his people that they would have to join the Nez Perces, and Joseph and Chief Plenty Bears from the Wallowa and Grande Ronde River districts were concerned that the treaty called for them to sell their parts of the Nez Perce domain.

Nevertheless, Lawyer conferred privately with the commissioners at night and, after ascertaining that he would receive added benefits and payments befitting his position as head chief, he worked on Spotted Eagle, James, Red Wolf, Timothy, and some of the other headmen and won their approval of the treaty. On June 7 he got up in the council meeting and again played the role of politician and diplomat for Stevens, making a long speech about the history of Indians and white men. In the course of it he amused everyone with a recital of the story of Columbus and the egg, which the Spaldings must have taught him, and then inadvertently revealed that Delaware Jim, who was sitting with the Nez Perces, had related to the Indians how the white men had come steadily pushing against the Indians all across the continent, and now "they are here." In closing, he expressed his approval of the treaty, but reminded Stevens that the Indians were poor people, and begged him to "take care of us well."

The spokesmen for the other tribes were smoldering. All of the Cayuses, including Stickus, made known their opposition to abandoning their own country and moving in with the Nez Perces. Tauitau, the Young Chief of the Umatilla Valley, who had already lived through many crises, was angry. What Lawyer could see well, "us Indians" could not see. "The reason . . . is I do not see the offer you have made us yet. If I had the money in my hand then I would see . . . I wonder if this ground has anything to say? I wonder if the ground is listening to what is said? I wonder if the ground would come to life and what is on it? I hear what this earth says. The earth says, God has placed me here. The earth says that God tells me to take care of the Indians on this earth. The earth says to the Indians that stop on the earth, feed them right. God named the roots that he should feed the Indians on. The water speaks the same way: God says, feed the Indians upon the Earth. The grass says the same thing: feed the horses and cattle. The earth and water and grass says, God has given our names and we are told those names. Neither the Indians or the whites have a right to change those names. The earth says, God has placed me here to produce all that grows upon me . . . The same way the earth says it was from her man was made. God on placing them on the earth . . . said, you Indians who take care of the earth and do each other no harm. God said, you Indians who take care of a certain portion of the country should not trade it off unless you get a fair price."

There it was, the Indians' sacred belief in their Earth Mother, a deeply held feeling, already twisted somewhat by some of the leaders who were trying to adjust to white culture. But Stevens could not see it. Five Crows supported the Young Chief; and Peopeo Moxmox, now fighting for the valley of his ancestors, the land where his forebear the great Yellepit had welcomed Lewis and Clark and David Thompson, told the commissioners that they were treating him as if he were a child or a feather. He wanted to go slower, to have time to think. "I request another meeting," he asked. "It is not only by one meeting that we can come to a decision."

Kamiakin, also feeling the pressure that the whites, with Lawyer's help, were beginning to place upon him, had nothing to say. But Owhi reminded the commissioners that God had made the earth and given it to the Indians. Could the Indians now steal it and sell it? "God made our bodies from the earth . . . What shall I do? Shall I give the lands that are a part of my body?" When the Yakima had finished, Stevens again asked Kamiakin to talk. It is possible that Kamiakin was thinking of the many unrepresented Columbia River bands that would be moved onto the Yakima reservation if he agreed to the treaty. He had no right to speak in their names. "What have I to be talking about?" he said to Stevens.

Now Palmer was impatient. He told the Indians he could not understand what more information they needed. He and Governor Stevens had informed them of everything the government would give them. "Can we bring these sawmills and these grist mills here on our backs . . . can we cause farms of wheat and corn to spring up in a day . . . ?" How long would the Indians remain blind? "We don't come to steal your lands; we pay you more than it is worth." Gold had been discovered in the Colville region, he told them. Bad men would soon be coming onto their lands. He and Governor Stevens wanted to protect them. Peopeo Moxmox had asked for another council. But there could not be another council. There was no time. "We want to help you . . . we want to open your eyes and give you light . . . we want to make you a good people. Will you receive our talk or will you throw it behind you?"

The tempo was speeding up, and the Indians could sense the hurry. Howlish Wompoon, a Cayuse, glared at Palmer. "I have listened to your speech without any impression . . . The Nez Perces have given you their land. You want us to go there . . . I cannot think of leaving this land. Your words since you came here have been crooked. That is all I have to say."

For a moment, Palmer tried hurriedly to answer the different objections. Then Five Crows spoke again, looking at the Nez Perces in anger. "Listen to me, you chiefs. We have been as one people with the Nez Perces heretofore. This day we are divided." At that point, Stevens took over, maintaining the pressure on the Indians that Palmer had begun. "I must say a few words. My Brother and I have talked straight. Have all of you talked straight? . . . The treaty will have to be drawn up tonight. You can see it tomorrow. The Nez Perces must not be put off any longer. This business must be dispatched . . . ." The council then adjourned.

That night Lieutenant Kip wrote that in all the Indian camps save that of the Nez Perces there was violent confusion. "The Cayuse and other tribes were very much incensed against the Nez Perces." But the next day the commissioners found that the pressure was working. At the council the Young Chief suddenly began to give in. "The reason why we could not understand you," he said to Stevens and Palmer, "was that you selected this country for us to live in without our having any voice in the matter . . . Wait, we may come to an agreement . . ." He pleaded, however, for more time to consider a division of the country between the whites and the Indians. He did not want to abandon his own homeland—"the land where my forefathers are buried should be mine. That is the place that I am speaking for. We shall talk about it," and his words seemed suddenly almost begging, "we shall then know, my brothers, that is what I have to show you, that is what I love—the place we get our roots to live upon—the salmon comes up the stream—. That is all."

He sat down, but Palmer had good news for him. The night before, as a result of the Cayuse, Wallawalla, and Umatilla opposition to going onto the Nez Perce reservation, the commissioners had changed their plans, and Palmer now offered them a single reservation of their own, centering on the Umatilla Valley. In a long speech aimed directly at the recalcitrant headmen, he made many new promises of things the government would do for them personally if they accepted this reservation: "We will build a good house for Peopeo Moxmox, and a good house for the chief of the Cayuses . . . we will plow and fence ten acres of land for Peopeo Moxmox; we will plow and fence the same for the chief of the Cayuses . . . we will give him [Peopeo Moxmox] . . . $500 in money, we will give him three yoke of oxen, wagon and two plows . . . we give him a salary, and also the chief of the Cayuses $500 a year in money, this to continue for twenty years—the same as is to be given to the Lawyer . . . ." Moreover, "you will not be required to go onto the reservation till our chief the President and his council sees this paper and says it is good, and we build the houses, the mills and the blacksmith shop . . . How long will it take you to decide?"

The new promises had their effect. The Wallawalla, Cayuse, and Umatilla spokesmen were won over, and Peopeo Moxmox promised to go on the reservation as soon as his new house was built. Stevens was delighted, and ordered the treaties prepared for signature. Only Kamiakin and the Yakimas still held out. Suddenly, wrote Lieutenant Kip, "a new explosive element dropped into this little political caldron. Just before the Council adjourned, an Indian runner arrived with the news that Looking Glass, the war chief of the Nez Perces, was coming." It is probable that both Lawyer and Stevens were thrown into confusion. Stevens recovered quickly. "I am glad Looking Glass . . . is coming," he announced. "He is a friend of Kamiakin . . . he has come away from the Blackfeet . . . let his first glance be upon you sitting here. When he is close by two or three of us will go and take him by the hand and set him down by his chief in the presence of his friend Kamiakin. Let us now have Kamiakin's heart."

The Yakima's reply, at last, was one of submission. But it indicated that he had received a dressing down from the chiefs of his wife's people, Te-i-as and Owhi, who had told him that they intended signing the treaty. The significance of what he had to say was apparently not noticed by Stevens and Palmer. Let the Americans settle down by the Yakima Valley wagon route, Kamiakin said. Let them settle about the road so that the Indians may go and see them. "I do not speak this for myself; it is my people's wish. Owhi and Te-i-as and the chiefs. I, Kamiakin, do not wish for goods for myself. The forest knows me. He knows my heart . . . I am tired. I am anxious to get back to my garden."

So Kamiakin capitulated, and after him Joseph, Red Wolf, and Skloom spoke. Joseph appealed to the commissioners to think of the future generations of Nez Perces, and to be certain to include his Wallowa land in the Nez Perce reservation. Red Wolf asked that Craig be allowed to stay with the Nez Perces "because he understands us . . . when there is any news that comes into the country we can go to him and hear it straight." Skloom, Kamiakin's brother, asked merely that the Americans pay what the Yakimas' land was worth. Stevens agreed, and on a note of complete victory announced that the treaties would be signed the next day. Then he adjourned the council.

A few minutes later the Indians hurried off to meet Looking Glass, who came riding onto the council grounds with three elderly buffalo-hunting chiefs and a retinue of about twenty warriors. Their arrival created a commotion. All were in buffalo robes and were painted for war. They had been in fights with the Blackfeet and had got back to the Bitterroot Valley when they had heard of the council. Looking Glass had left most of his band behind to travel slowly, and with the small group that now appeared with him had hastened across the mountains by the Coeur d'Alene route. As Stevens and Palmer came up to meet them, they noticed that one of the warriors carried a staff from which dangled a Blackfoot scalp. Looking Glass received the commissioners coldly. He looked around at the Indians, and launched suddenly into a tirade: "My people, what have you done? While I was gone, you have sold my country. I have come home, and there is not left me a place on which to pitch my lodge. Go home to your lodges. I will talk to you."

All of Stevens' work fell suddenly apart. The 70-year-old war chief—"old, irascible, and treacherous," Stevens called him—whipped scorn that night on the headmen who had agreed to sign the treaty. The next day, June 9, Lawyer told Stevens that Looking Glass would probably calm down in a day or two, but Stevens' determination had now risen, and he had no intention of letting Looking Glass defeat him at the last moment. Before the council started, the Governor met privately with Peopeo Moxmox and Kamiakin and won promises from them to abide by their word and sign the treaties. Then he asked Kamiakin for a list of the tribes over which he had authority as head chief. The Yakima, according to Stevens' secretary, Doty, named the tribes, but the only one other than the Yakimas which Doty recorded at that time was the Palouse.

When the council reconvened, Stevens presented the Indians with finished versions of the treaties for the three reservations, all ready to be signed. With studied indifference to Looking Glass, he reviewed what the treaties said, reminding the chiefs that they did not have to move their people onto the reservations "for two or three years." Certain points were glossed over: Kamiakin, for instance, was to be considered the head chief of a long list of Columbia River bands that were not present but whose people Stevens wished to move onto the Yakima reservation, out of the way of the whites. Stevens was talking quickly, and probably did not even reveal the role he was assigning Kamiakin, for the Yakima would not willingly have accepted it, and it is not likely that the Indian had included those bands in the list he had given Stevens and Doty earlier that morning. All of them had their own headmen, and Kamiakin had nothing to do with their affairs.[1]

1. The introduction to the text of the Yakima Treaty read, in part, "Articles of agreement . . . between . . . the United States, and the undersigned head chiefs, chiefs head-men, and delegates of the Yakima, Palouse, Pisquouse, Wenatshapam, Klikitat, Klinquit, Kow-was-say-ee, Li-ay-was, Skin-pah, Wash-ham, Shyiks, Ochechotes, Kah-milt-pah, and Se-ap-cat . . . who for the purpose of this treaty are to be considered as one nation, under the name of Yakima, with Kamiakin as its head chief, on behalf of and acting for said tribes and bands, and being duly authorized thereto by them." This was an old trick, almost standard operating procedure since the time of General Anthony Wayne, for American officials who wanted to acquire title to Indian land quickly. Often a venal chief, for a bribe, would claim that he spoke for other tribes and would then sell their lands without telling them anything about it. This had been a common practice in the Ohio Valley and the Southeast. The difference here was that Kamiakin was honest and turned down American offers of payment. It is extremely doubtful that he knew he was being made a tool, because it appears that Stevens did not even read the treaty aloud to him, either before or during the council. It is unlikely, also, that Stevens had misunderstood Kamiakin during the private meeting in the morning, and had actually thought that the Yakima could speak for those Chinookan, Salish, and Sahaptin bands. The assumption ran counter to the strongest Indian traditions: Kamiakin never before or afterward posed as spokesman for those bands that had their own councils of headmen. If he had done so at Walla Walla, he would have known that he had committed a crime against other Indians.

But Stevens brushed past the point and kept talking. He offered to read the treaties, article by article, but told the Indians they had already heard everything in them, "not once but two or three times." Then he asked if anyone still wanted to be heard.

That gave Looking Glass his chance. He did not tell white men where to go, he snapped at Stevens angrily, and if anybody was going to tell his people where to go, it would be he, not a white man. "I am going to talk straight," he said. He looked around, pointing to the other headmen. "I am not like those people who hang their heads and say nothing." He paused a moment, and the Young Chief suddenly said, "That is the reason I told the Governor to let it be till another time . . . ." Stevens patiently cautioned the Young Chief to let Looking Glass finish. The old war chief suddenly ran his finger along Stevens' map, outlining the borders of the Nez Perce lands. That was the reservation he wanted for the Nez Perces. It was the stratagem that Kamiakin, Peopeo Moxmox, and Looking Glass had originally devised. They would designate all their land as reservations, and there would be no country to sell. Then he asked for a second council, later on. One of the Nez Perces, a follower of Lawyer named Billy, called out that that was just putting it off. He was answered by Metat Waptass, the Three Feathers: "Looking Glass is speaking. We look upon him as a chief."

"I thought we had appointed Lawyer our head chief, and he was to do our talking," Billy replied.

Stevens and Palmer both tried to argue with Looking Glass, but to no avail. The war chief argued for *his* line, not the one defined in the treaty. Stevens turned away from him to ask the tribes if they were ready to sign. "What the Looking Glass says, I say," said the Young Chief. "I ask you whether you are ready to sign?" Stevens repeated. "The papers are drawn. We ask are you now ready to sign those papers and let them go to the President."

". . . to the line I marked myself. Not to your line," Looking Glass insisted.

Stevens faced the old war chief. "I will say to the Looking Glass, we cannot agree."

"Why do you talk so much about it?" Palmer snapped angrily at the Nez Perce.

"It was my children that spoke yesterday, and now I come . . . ," said Looking Glass.

Stevens sat back resignedly, as Palmer argued with the old man. It did him no good. "I am not going to say anymore today," Looking Glass said. Stevens finally adjourned the council, urging Looking Glass to think the matter over and talk to the other Nez Perces.

After the meeting, Peopeo Moxmox signed the treaty for the Wallawallas. Stevens maintained that Kamiakin also signed, having "yielded to the advice of the other [Yakima] chiefs." But Kamiakin later insisted that he only made a pledge of friendship by touching a little stick as it made a mark. Later in the evening Lawyer came to see Stevens, and told him that he should have reminded Looking Glass that he, Lawyer, was the head chief, that the whole Nez Perce tribe had said in council that he was the head chief, and that the tribe had agreed to the treaty and had pledged its word. Stevens, he said, should have insisted that the Nez Perces live up to their pledge.

"In reply," Stevens wrote, "I told the Lawyer . . . your authority will be sustained, and your people will be called upon to keep their word . . . The Looking Glass will not be allowed to speak as head chief. You, and you alone, will be recognized. Should Looking Glass persist, the appeal will be made to your people. They must sign the treaty agreed to by them through you as head chief . . ." Lawyer then went to the Nez Perce camp, and in a stormy council that lasted through most of the next day managed to muster enough support to reaffirm his position as head chief. Looking Glass, the war leader of Asotin, apparently accepted his position as second to Lawyer in the council, and the headmen drew up a paper that pledged the tribe to honor its word to Governor Stevens.

Early on the morning of June 11 Stevens told Lawyer that he was about to call the council. "I shall call upon your people to keep their word, and upon you as head chief to sign first. We want no speeches. This will be the last day of the council."

Lawyer assured him that that was the right course, and it was the way it finally happened. The council convened, Stevens reminded the Nez Perces that they had all originally agreed that Lawyer was their head chief and spokesman, and that Lawyer had given his word to the treaty. "I shall call upon Lawyer the head chief, and then I shall call on the other chiefs to sign. Will Lawyer now come forward."

Lawyer signed. Then Stevens called on Looking Glass and Joseph, and both of them stepped up and made their marks without a word. The other Nez Perce headmen followed in a line, and after them, the Cayuses signed their treaty.

"Thus ended in the most satisfactory manner this great council," Stevens wrote in his journal.

Originally published as Chapter 8, "A Most Satisfactory Council," of *The Nez Perce Indians and the Opening of the Northwest* (New Haven: Yale University Press, 1965), pp. 315–32. Bracketed insertions except those in direct quotations added. All footnotes omitted except one.

Isaac Stevens wanted a treaty, and he was in a hurry. His actions at Walla Walla were not uncharacteristic of government negotiations with Indians, and similar events occurred at Fort Laramie in 1866. Government negotiators there were also in a hurry to arrange a treaty with the Sioux and to announce that peace had returned to the northern plains.

In 1862 the Santee, or Eastern, Sioux in Minnesota had revolted and been defeated, and in 1863 and 1864 military expeditions were sent against the Western Sioux in Dakota Territory, who had been warring on emigrant parties. In the following year the army sought to subdue the Sioux with a massive, coordinated effort known as the Powder River campaign. Results were negligible, however, and the Indians went into winter camp confident that they had driven the soldiers from their country.

Despite the military failures of 1865, the government inaugurated a peace campaign while the troops were in the field, and during the autumn several treaties were negotiated with the friendly Sioux along the Missouri River. Preparations were made to hold additional councils on the Missouri and at Fort Laramie in the spring, but the goal of peace was not so easy to attain with the more hostile elements of the tribe. Red Cloud, a leader of the Western Sioux, displayed a total lack of interest in treaty talks, and it was only with great effort that he was finally persuaded to meet with government agents. Edward B. Taylor, the government negotiator, was less than candid with the Indians. He wanted approval of unhindered use of the Bozeman Trail, a short cut to the Montana gold regions that traversed the heart of the Powder River country, one of the last great undisturbed hunting grounds of the Sioux. During the talks United States troops arrived to guard the road, and Red Cloud and his followers marched out of the council, warning that all travelers on the Bozeman Trail risked their lives.

Red Cloud's abrupt exit removed the primary obstacle to a treaty, but it also meant that the one man whose approval was essential was not a party to it. Taylor was heard to say that he would have a treaty even if only two Indians signed, and he concluded an agreement with the friendly bands who had no direct interest in the Powder River country—whereupon it was announced that peace had been made with the Sioux. Red Cloud, true to his word, resisted the fortification of the Bozeman Trail. The resulting conflict, known as Red Cloud's war, saw the soldiers locked in their forts in a state of seige, the massacre of a command of eighty men under Captain William J. Fetterman, and other dramatic battles. In the end the government conceded its mistake and concluded a new treaty with Red Cloud in 1868 by which it abandoned the Bozeman road.

"A Lasting Peace"—Fort Laramie, 1866

JAMES C. OLSON

The hope that the Powder River Sioux would come in and that peace might be secured set everyone atwitter. On January 16, 1866, [Maj. Gen. Grenville M.] Dodge [commander of the Department of the Missouri] telegraphed [Bvt. Maj. Gen. John] Pope [commanding the Military Division of the Missouri]: "Big Ribs has returned with a large delegation of Sioux Indians to Fort Laramie. The prospects of peace with the Sioux Nation good." Later that same day he got off another wire to Pope. "Please telegraph me what you consider I should say to the Sioux, what to promise them and what to demand from them," he asked. "They want to hear from me and demand to treat with a soldier. If we manage this matter right, we will settle all troubles in the North. . . ." The next day Pope advised Secretary of the Interior James Harlan that he had instructed Dodge to arrange with the Sioux Indians to meet in council early in the spring, with commissioners appointed by the President, for the conclusion of a final treaty of peace.

It seemed, indeed, that a miracle was about to happen; that the Sioux, who the year before had frustrated General [Patrick E.] Connor's efforts to open the Powder River road, were willing to call it quits and come in for a conference; that the "successes" of the Edmunds Commission on the upper Missouri were to be repeated on the Platte.

The Army had taken the initiative in the events that had led up to this happy prospect—and it had done so even though most high-ranking officers on the plains had been opposed to a treaty with the Indians until they had been soundly punished and made to feel the power of the government. The reason for the abrupt change in attitude can be found in the Army's impossible position vis-à-vis the Indians: It had been unable to defeat them with the forces available in 1865, and now even those forces were to be reduced. As Pope wrote Bvt. Maj. Gen. Frank Wheaton, assigned to command the District of Nebraska (which included the Platte and Powder River country), it was hoped that Connor's campaign would bring an end to hostilities, but "In any event . . . it is the purpose to return to a purely defensive arrangement for the security of the overland routes . . . and I desire especially, General, to impress upon you the absolute necessity of the strictest economy in your expenditures. It is essential that you return without delay to a peace basis, and to the economical arrangements which obtained before the rebellion. . . ."

In a sense, conditions were about what they had been fifteen years earlier: with the Army unable to coerce the Indians, the only hope for peace and security lay in persuading the tribes themselves to keep the peace. Accordingly, when General Wheaton visited Fort Laramie in October he ordered Col. Henry E. Maynadier, commandant of the post and of the West Sub-District of Nebraska, to send messengers to the hostile Sioux "to inform them that other tribes were making peace and an opportunity would be offered them to do the same." The prospects of success were not very bright; the mission was so dangerous that no white man could be found who would try it. Maynadier, however, had finally persuaded Big Ribs, one of the "Laramie Loafers," and four others to undertake the mission. After three months, during which Maynadier despaired of ever seeing his envoys again, they returned. They brought the great news that had so excited Dodge: Red Cloud would soon be in with some two hundred and fifty lodges. They also brought Swift Bear and his band of Brulés.

Maynadier was elated. He told Swift Bear that his people could have peace if they wanted it—and peace would mean presents and the right to camp where they could get game and live quietly. All they had to do was to abstain from hostilities and commit no more depredations on the whites. Swift Bear was ready. He had wanted peace all along, but his people had been afraid to come into the fort for fear of being killed. Now they were glad to be able to come and get something for their women and children, who were naked and starving. After reporting all this to the Commissioner of Indian Affairs, Maynadier wrote:

> As soon as I have completed all arrangements with the Brules and Ogallalas, I will direct them to go to the Black Hills, 80 miles north, and establish their camps until Spring. This is their favorite ground, but for three years they have not been permitted to occupy it.

The Sioux were not the only ones with whom peace would be secured: "The band of Northern Cheyennes affiliate with the Sioux and I have good reason to suppose that they will ask to be allowed to come in." The Arapahoes were on the Big Horn and the Yellowstone, some seven hundred miles away, and could not be communicated with until spring, but, "If they should continue to be hostile, the aid of the Sioux can be obtained next summer to chastise them."

All that spring the plains were bathed in hope. E. B. Taylor, head of the Northern Superintendency [the Indian Bureau], who had been appointed president of the commission to treat with the tribes, busied himself at Omaha in preparation for the trip to Fort Laramie, where the final treaty was to be concluded. And from Fort Laramie good news arrived steadily. On March 3, couriers from Red Cloud reported that he was on his way, and that he wanted the Northern Cheyennes and the Arapahoes to join the Sioux in making peace. A few days later there was word from Spotted Tail, chief of the Brulés. He had had long association with the whites and for the most part had been friendly; alienated by mistreatment, however, for the past several years he had been with the hostiles. Now he had with him the body of his daughter who had died from disease and exposure and who had begged to have her grave among those of the whites. Would Colonel Maynadier permit it? Maynadier, seeing an opportunity to bring Spotted Tail back into the fold, not only replied that he would permit it but rode out to meet the sorrowing chief and personally escorted him to his headquarters. He was honored that the great chief would entrust to him the remains of a daughter whom he knew Spotted Tail deeply loved. Everything would be prepared to have her funeral at sunset, "and as the sun went down it might remind him of the darkness left in his lodge when his beloved daughter was taken away; but as the sun would surely rise again, so she would rise, and some day we would all meet in the land of the Great Spirit." Maynadier also talked of peace, saying that in a few months commissioners from the Great Father would come to treat with the Indians and that everything would be settled on a permanent basis of peace and friendship. Spotted Tail was overwhelmed. Tears fell from his eyes, and as he grasped Maynadier's hand, he said:

> This must be a dream for me to be in such a fine room and surrounded by such as you. Have I been asleep during the last four years of hardship and trial and am dreaming that all is to be well again, or is this real? Yes, I see

that it is; the beautiful day, the sky blue, without a cloud, the wind calm and still to suit the errand I come on and remind me that you have offered me peace. We think we have been much wronged and are entitled to compensation for the damages and distress caused by making so many roads through our country, and driving off and destroying the buffalo and game. My heart is very sad and I cannot talk on business; I will wait and see the counsellors the Great Father will send.

Maynadier was quite overwhelmed, too. The scene was "one of the most impressive" he ever saw, and its ramifications could hardly be overemphasized. "I attach great importance to this ceremony as rendering beyond a doubt the success of the efforts I have made to restore peace," he concluded. "It satisfies me of the entire trustiness of Pegaleshka, who is always with Red Cloud, and they two rule the nation. . . . The occurrence of such an incident is regarded by the oldest settlers, men of most experience in Indian character, as unprecedented, and as calculated to secure a certain and lasting peace."

But this was not all that augured for peace. On March 12, four days after the funeral, Red Cloud himself arrived. He, Spotted Tail, and two hundred warriors were escorted into the fort with great pomp and ceremony for a council with Maynadier and Vital Jarrot, agent for the Indians of the Upper Platte. This was to be no ordinary conference. Maynadier would use the talking wires so that the chiefs could counsel with the man whom the Great Father was sending to Fort Laramie. At first, Red Cloud refused to enter the telegraph office, but finally his objections were overcome, and between the chiefs at Laramie and Taylor at Omaha, the telegraph carried messages of peace and good will. Taylor sent the following message to Red Cloud:

The Great Father at Washington has appointed Commissioners to treat with the Sioux, the Arapahoes and Cheyennes of the Upper Platte, on the subject of peace. He wants you all to be his friends and the friends of the White Man. If you conclude a treaty of peace, he wishes to make presents to you and your people as a token of his friendship. A train loaded with supplies and presents cannot reach Fort Laramie from the Missouri River before the first of June and he desires that about that time be agreed upon as the day when his commissioners shall meet you to make a treaty.

The message was interpreted to the Indians and they seemed to approve. Taylor's next concern was whether peace would be imperiled by delaying the conference until June 1. Maynadier thought the chiefs would consent to wait:

> Red Cloud says now our horses are very poor and the Indians are scattered and will take some time to gather up all the Indians. Will do it as soon as possible. He will stay and hear what we have to say for two months and all will be quiet and peaceable.

To protect himself, Taylor stated that June 1 was the earliest possible date, and that he could more certainly have the presents with him if the conference were delayed until June 30. The chiefs apparently were agreeable. Maynadier reported, "Red Cloud says he will be five or six days going to his village but he will tell them how he has been received and will assemble all the Indians to come in here at the time the commissioners will be here. He knows now that everything is right and they can be better to wait and get traps and beaver between now and the first of June."

Taylor was jubilant. That same day he wrote D. N. Cooley, Commissioner of Indian Affairs: "There is every reason to hope and no cause to doubt that a lasting peace will be easily effected with the hitherto hostile tribes of the Upper Platte, including the Sioux, Arapahoes and Cheyennes."

That hopeful phrase, "a lasting peace," seemed to be the watchword on the plains during the spring of 1866. Apparently it was based solely on the supposition that with the disappearance of buffalo and other game the Indians had become so destitute that they were willing to agree to anything in return for presents and subsistence. Of their desperate condition, there was ample and heart-rending evidence; Maynadier wrote of Red Cloud's people: "Nothing but occular demonstration can make one appreciate their destitution, and near approach to starvation." Of their willingness to agree to anything, the evidence was not quite so clear, although Maynadier thought them "thoroughly subdued" and believed that "the wildest spirit will only have to remember last winter to make him forgo any depredations."

The critical question, of course, was the willingness of the Indians to permit the use of the Powder River road to Montana.

Swift Bear and other friendlies had said that they would not object if they were paid for it. This was a foregone conclusion; the friendlies had never really objected. The important consideration was the attitude of Red Cloud and others who had carried on the war during 1865. Apparently, no one bothered to find out what it was. At least, there is no record to show that at any time during the pre-conference parleys Taylor, Maynadier, or Jarrot intimated to Red Cloud that a condition of peace and presents would be the maintenance of the Powder River road. Subsequent events would indicate that the failure was no mere oversight, but that it was based on the assumption that the best policy was to keep the Indians content with presents until the Commissioners could reach Fort Laramie, and then hope that their situation really was so desperate that they would agree to anything and could be held to that agreement with a minimum force.

The Army certainly operated on the assumption that a minimum force would be sufficient, and its plans for protecting the Powder River road consisted almost entirely of an administrative reorganization. In April, the Department of the Platte was established, with headquarters at Omaha, to afford, as Maj. Gen. William T. Sherman [commander of the Division of the Mississippi] stated, "the best possible protection to . . . the region of Montana, and the routes thereto." Almost simultaneously, Col. Henry B. Carrington was placed in command of a newly created "Mountain District" and ordered to take the Second Battalion of the 18th Infantry from Fort Kearny to occupy it. No fighting was expected. Carrington was a garrison officer with no experience in Indian warfare, and his little force consisted almost entirely of raw recruits—but more of that later.

Meanwhile, in Omaha, Taylor busied himself with plans for the conference, and out at Fort Laramie, Maynadier and Jarrot tried to keep the Indians content until the Commissioners could arrive. It was not an easy task.

After the conference of March 12, Maynadier gave his visitors a small amount of powder and lead and urged them to go off and hunt until the council was called. By May 8, however, they were all back at Fort Laramie, desperately in need of provisions. Maynadier wrote Cooley that they were "grateful and patient and have implicit confidence in promises made them," but Jarrot wired Taylor that the chiefs were very impatient and that if he wanted to meet with them he had better arrive by the twentieth or they would all have dispersed. That, Taylor replied, was impossible, although he would try to reach Laramie by the twenty-sixth. Jarrot and Maynadier would have to explain the whole matter to the chiefs and hold them together if possible.

Somehow—largely through issuing rations and making promises—the two men managed to keep the Indians in the vicinity of Fort Laramie. Taylor and his associates finally arrived on May 30, and on June 5 the conference that was to bring "a lasting peace" formally opened.

Taylor was pleased at the prospect. Red Cloud, Red Leaf, Man-Afraid-of-His-Horse, and Spotted Tail were all there, and many of their people were with them. There was also a small representation of Cheyennes and Arapahoes. Taylor told the assembled Indians that "it was not the desire of the government to purchase their country, but simply to establish peaceful relations with them and to obtain from them a recognition of the rights of the government to make and use through their country such roads as may be deemed necessary for the public service and for the emigrants to mining districts of the West." Taylor was not being altogether candid. E. B. Chandler, who was sent to Fort Laramie in December, 1866, to investigate Indian problems there, wrote that Taylor had intimated to the Indians that travel on the Powder River road "should be confined strictly to the line thereof, and that emigrants and travellers generally should not be allowed to molest or disturb the game in the country through which they passed." This impossible promise, Chandler charged, "was well calculated, and . . . designed to deceive" the Indians.

The next day, Red Cloud, Spotted Tail, Red Leaf, and Man-Afraid-of-His-Horse responded for the Sioux. We have no direct translation of their speeches, but Taylor—apparently lacking candor in his reports to his superiors as well as in his representations to the Indians—wrote that they

> were marked by moderation and good feeling; and at the conclusion of the council, these chiefs expressed the opinion that a treaty could and would be made and asked for time to bring in their people who are encamped in

large numbers on the head waters of White River, some fifty or sixty miles distant from Fort Laramie. . . . The general feeling of all these tribes is very conciliatory and friendly and I have no doubt that satisfactory treaties will be effected with each and all, if their attendance can be secured.

Taylor, of course, had the chiefs who really counted, and while it was a truism of Indian negotiations that you had to get common consent of all to make an agreement binding, it is difficult to see how much more authoritative representation could have been achieved than was already present. Nevertheless, he agreed to adjourn the council until the thirteenth, meanwhile persuading Colonel Maynadier to issue supplies to the chiefs for the trip to White River and keep on issuing rations to the Indians who remained behind.

On the thirteenth the council convened again—and immediately exploded. The charge was unwittingly detonated by the arrival of Colonel Carrington who for the past several weeks had been plodding up the Platte bringing troops to provide protection for travelers who would use the road that was to be opened by the peace commissioners at Fort Laramie.

There are many stories as to just what happened on that fateful day; and, in the absence of a detailed, official report, various writers have accepted uncritically one or another of the yarns. Perhaps the most spectacular account is Cyrus Townsend Brady's. Brady has it that Carrington approached in advance of his troops and was introduced to the members of the council. "Red Cloud, noticing his shoulder straps, hotly denounced him as the 'White Eagle' who had come to steal the road before the Indian said yes or no. In full view of the mass of Indians who occupied the parade ground he sprang from the platform under the shelter of pine boughs, struck his tepees and went on the warpath." This story is to a degree confirmed by Frances C. Carrington, who wrote:

Red Cloud himself, it is officially reported, when he saw Colonel Carrington at his visit to the council, upon his arrival threw his blanket around himself, refused an introduction, and left with this announcement of his views, pointing to the officer who had just arrived, "The Great Father sends us presents and wants us to sell him the road, but White Chief goes with soldiers to steal the road before the Indians say Yes or No.

Frances Carrington was then the wife of Lt. George W. Grummond of Colonel Carrington's command. She arrived at Fort Laramie after Carrington, and was not an eyewitness of the events she described, but she included in her story a reminiscence of William Murphy, an enlisted man in the 18th Infantry who apparently was an observer:

> Our expedition reached Fort Laramie on June 13, in time for Colonel Carrington to participate in the council being held with Red Cloud, Man-Afraid-of-His-Horses [*sic*], and other Indian chiefs to secure the Indian's consent to the construction of a road and the erection of the promised forts, the Indians protesting vigorously against this.
>
> Red Cloud made a dramatic and effective speech. He claimed that the Peace Commissioners were treating the assembled chiefs as children; that they were pretending to negotiate for a country which they had already taken by Conquest. He accused the Government of bad faith in all its transactions with Indian tribes.
>
> In his harangue to the Indians he told them that the white men had crowded the Indians back year by year and forced them to live in a small country north of the Platte and now their last hunting ground, the home of their people, was to be taken from them. This meant that they and their women and children were to starve, and for his part he preferred to die fighting rather than by starvation.
>
> Red Cloud promised that if the combined tribes would defend their homes they would be able to drive the soldiers out of the country. He said it might be a long war, but as they were defending their last hunting grounds they must in the end be successful.
>
> The powwow continued for some time, until finally the hostile Sioux under Red Cloud withdrew, refusing to have any further counsel or to accept any presents.

Margaret I. Carrington, who was with her husband, describes the council chamber, but writes only in a general way of Red Cloud as protagonist, saying that he and Man-Afraid-of-His-Horse "made no secret of their opposition," and that Red Cloud, "with all his fighting men, withdrew from all association with the treaty-makers, and in a very few days quite decidedly developed his hate and his schemes of mischief."

Finally, there is the tale that when Red Cloud was informed that the soldiers had come to open the Bozeman Road, he "leaped from the platform, caught up his rifle, saying, 'In this and the Great Spirit I trust for the right.' "

Whatever happened—and Murphy's story seems to be the most viable—it was apparent that with the withdrawal of Red Cloud, the great council at Fort Laramie was not going to bring peace to the plains. Later, officials of the Indian Bureau would blame Carrington's arrival in the midst of negotiations for the failure of the treaty,[1] but Taylor went ahead as though nothing had happened; he had been heard to say that he had been sent by the Government to make peace and it should be accomplished if made with but two Indians. Treating the departure of Red Cloud and Man-Afraid-of-His-Horse as of no consequence, he busied himself with signing up the friendly chiefs. They were not a very impressive lot: Big Mouth and Blue Horse, of the Laramie Loafers; Swift Bear, who had been with the hostiles only against his wishes; and a few others of even less importance. The biggest catch of all was Spotted Tail, but even he had a long history of friendship with the whites. Moreover, his people, preferring to live south of the Platte, had little interest in the Powder River country. Essentially, of course, what it boiled down to was that those who had no stake in the Powder River area were perfectly willing to sign a treaty granting a right-of-way through it. The inducements, it might be noted, were substantial: annuities in the amount of seventy thousand dollars a year for twenty years. Taylor also managed to sign up a few Cheyennes—they were to get fifteen thousand dollars a year for twenty years—and on June 29 he triumphantly wired the Commissioner of Indian Affairs: "Satisfactory treaty concluded with the Sioux and Cheyennes. Large representations. Most cordial feeling prevails."

1. Carrington's arrival was unfortunate, and it undoubtedly triggered Red Cloud's flare-up. It is difficult to believe, however, that Red Cloud was prepared at this time to sign a treaty permitting a road through the Powder River country—notwithstanding the hopeful estimates of the effect of the winter's privations on the spirit of the Sioux. Moreover, Taylor and Cooley were fully aware of Carrington's proposed movement and there seems to be no record of any protest on their part against it. Carrington probably would have been beyond Fort Laramie when the council began had not his departure from Fort Kearny been delayed by General [Philip St. George] Cooke [commandant of the newly created Department of the Platte and Carrington's immediate superior] because of the weather and the condition of his command.

It was not long, however, before disturbing rumors began to filter back to Washington. The Indians, it seemed, were as hostile as they had been before the treaty, and travel on the Powder River road was as hazardous as it had ever been. The Commission, back in Omaha, telegraphed President Johnson: "Satisfactory treaties of peace have been concluded with the Upper Platte Sioux and Cheyennes at Fort Laramie. Contradictory reports are without foundation." Still the rumors would not down. The *Omaha Herald,* which was frequently quoted by eastern papers on Indian affairs, wrote on July 27:

> Much doubt prevails concerning the late so-called Treaty with the Indians at Fort Laramie. From all we can gather we do not believe it will prove of the least value to our interests. Long-winded speeches and the deal out of powder and lead, bogus kinnikinnick, small trinkets, rations, and other similar traps, to a set of blind and antiquated Indian chiefs, amounts to nothing. . . . We have ceased to hope anything from the Laramie abortion. . . .

By August 22, Cooley was calling on Taylor, now in Washington, for a special report. Taylor had a ready answer. There had been depredations, but these were the work of "about two hundred fifty Bad Faces, composed of Oglalas and desperate characters of various tribes of Sioux . . . [who] refused to recognize the authority of the tribe." The depredations would not lead to a general war, and alarmist news to the contrary could be attributed "to the fertile imagination of some enterprising gentleman who cares more for army contracts than the public peace."

Taylor continued to play on this theme. In his report as president of the treaty commission, he wrote that "although the Indians, as might naturally be expected, were reluctant to allow the proposed road to pass through the best of their remaining hunting grounds, yet when informed of the wishes of the government, and of our disposition to give a liberal equivalent, they acquiesced in our request in a full council. . . ." Those who were trying to cast doubt on the permanence of the treaty were "evil-disposed persons, actuated by malice or cupidity." In his annual report as head of the Northern Superintendency, written October

1, he took cognizance of the difficulties with Red Cloud, but hardly in a way to describe what had actually happened:

> A band numbering perhaps three hundred warriors, headed by Red Cloud, a prominent chief of the Ogalallahs, refused to come in. They are known as Bad Faces, and are composed of the most refractory and desperate characters of the tribe, who, having committed some serious infraction of the internal policy of the tribe, have congregated themselves together, and refuse to be governed by the will of the majority.

They were of no consequence, because "at least seven-eighths of the Ogalallahs and Brulés" had signed the treaty.

Moreover, it soon appeared that even these "refractory and desperate characters" would be brought to terms. On October 18, M. T. Patrick, who had succeeded Jarrot as agent for the Indians of the Upper Platte, wired Taylor that Red Leaf's band was on the way to Fort Laramie to make peace, and that Red Cloud himself was coming in to sign the treaty. On November 19, Patrick solemnly announced that he was "about to move Red Cloud, Red Leaf and Man-Afraid-of-His-Horses, Sioux bands of Indians, now north of Powder River, to Mr. Bordeaux Ranche, nine miles east of this place, and there negotiate a peace treaty with them." Taylor, the same day, advised his superiors in Washington that all hostile bands of Sioux wanted to sign the treaty.

This continuing optimism evidently made an impression at the highest levels of government. On December 5, President Johnson, in his annual message on the state of the union, assured the country that the Indians had "unconditionally submitted to our authority and manifested an earnest desire for a renewal of friendly relations."

A little more than a fortnight later, these same Indians inflicted upon Colonel Carrington's command the worst defeat the Army had yet suffered in Indian warfare.

Originally published as Chapter 3 of *Red Cloud and the Sioux Problem* (Lincoln: University of Nebraska Press, 1965), pp. 27–40. Bracketed insertions except those in direct quotations added. All footnotes omitted except one.

Plains Warfare

While Red Cloud and his warriors were embarrassing both the army and the Indian Bureau, other Plains tribes were also in conflict with the government. In 1864 raids by the Kiowas and Comanches of the southern plains provoked a military expedition led by Colonel Kit Carson. At the same time serious Indian difficulties broke out in Colorado Territory and western Kansas. In the eyes of Colorado officials the Cheyennes were guilty of depredations on white settlers, and on November 29, 1864, Colonel John Chivington of the Colorado Volunteers launched a brutal surprise attack on a village at Sand Creek that was under the control of the peaceful chief Black Kettle. The Sand Creek massacre precipitated widespread warfare as the Cheyennes and their allies retaliated, and many Cheyennes joined the Sioux forces during the Powder River campaign of 1865.

During the autumn of 1865 while negotiations were underway with the Sioux along the Missouri River, the government also sought peace with the Kiowas, Comanches, and Cheyennes, concluding the Treaty of the Little Arkansas in October. It was a short-lived treaty, for sporadic violence continued, and in 1867 warfare again erupted on the southern plains. During the spring General Winfield S. Hancock precipitated the conflict by burning a Cheyenne village. His unwise actions brought massive retaliation and after considerable loss of life ultimately led to a new peace offensive by the government. The large military escort that was needed to protect the government agents and newspapermen who attended the talks did not bode well for the future. The Medicine Lodge Treaty was signed in October 1867, but hostilities soon broke out again.

When veteran Civil War cavalryman Philip Sheridan failed to defeat the Cheyennes during the summer of 1868, he instituted an innovation in Plains Indian warfare that would cause the Indians to surrender. Ignoring the pessimistic advice of westerners, Sheridan prepared for a winter campaign in an effort to strike the hostiles when least expected and when Indian ponies were weak from lack of grass. In November, Lieutenant Colonel George Custer marched out of Camp Supply, Indian Territory, in a snowstorm and soon picked up a trail that led him to the Washita River. There, in the early dawn of November 27, he attacked the village of Black Kettle, long an advocate of peace, who had attempted to restrain the young men of his tribe during the summer and on November 20 had appeared at Fort Cobb to state that his camp wanted peace. Black Kettle was one of those killed.

Custer's controversial attack, the first blow of the winter campaign, was followed by continued fighting which soon persuaded the Kiowas and Comanches and many Cheyennes to surrender. During the following summer the hostile Cheyennes under Tall Bull were defeated at the Battle of Summit Springs in Colorado, bringing the campaign to an end.

George Bird Grinnell, an ethnohistorian who began to work with the Cheyennes in the late nineteenth century, drew heavily upon Indian testimony, and his history of the Cheyennes therefore reflects the Indian viewpoint as well as the official government version of events. The use of Cheyenne sources makes his account of the Battle of the Washita especially valuable.

The Battle of the Washita, 1868

GEORGE BIRD GRINNELL

The peace commission appointed by Congress in July, 1867, made its report January 7, 1868. An interesting conclusion which it reached was that in all cases investigated by the commission of difficulties which existed with Indians at the date of the commission's creation, and for some years previous, the cause of the difficulty was traced to the acts of white men—either civilians or soldiers.

The treaties made at Medicine Lodge Creek were not ratified by the Senate until July, 1868, and were not proclaimed by the President until August, 1868—the treaty with the Sioux not until February, 1869. The delay in ratifying these treaties put it out of the power of the authorities to do anything to locate the Indians on the lands arranged for them to occupy under the treaty stipulations. Besides, the Cheyennes and Arapahoes objected to settling down on the reservation selected for them because of the bitter water of many of the streams, it being in the gypsum belt between the southern line of Kansas and the Cimarron River. It did not help the Indians—and they did not know of it—that by the Act of July 20, 1868, Congress appropriated $500,000 to be expended under the direction of General Sherman in carrying out treaty stipulations; that is, in preparing homes, furnishing provisions, tools and farming utensils, and subsistence for those tribes with which treaties had been made and not yet ratified. General Sherman assigned Generals [William S.] Harney and [W. B.] Hazen to the two military districts which he had established, the latter being given control of the Cheyennes, Arapahoes, Kiowas, and Comanches, and perhaps other bands. To the use of General Hazen $50,000 was allotted.

Meantime there was some disorder on the plains, and some raiding by young men who had started north on the war-path against the Pawnees and had committed some outrages on the Saline River.

The invasion of the country by white people had driven off the buffalo, and, according to Colonel Wynkoop, the Indians were starving. At this time the massacre of the Cheyennes and Arapahoes at Sand Creek was less than four years distant, and was still fresh in their minds, while the attack on the village on Pawnee Fork and its destruction by Hancock was only a year old. General Sherman and General Sheridan, neither of whom had been enough in contact with Indians of the plains to know anything about them or their methods of thought, seem to have determined that they must be punished. This was a common feeling in those days, the military officers seeming to forget that before Indians could be punished they must be caught, and that before they could be caught they would have every opportunity to commit enormous injuries in the way of killing people and destroying property.

About the middle of October, General Sheridan was authorized to go ahead with his proposed work of punishing the Indians, and about the 6th of November, 1868, he left Fort Hays to join his forces at Bear Creek. It was reported that a million rations had been provided for the troops, and a large supply of extra horses taken along. At that time a large number of Indians, all of them at the time peaceful, were camped on the Washita River, not very far from old Fort Cobb. The village of Black Kettle—about seventy-five lodges—was the farthest west of these camps on the Washita. Below him was a large village of Cheyennes and Arapahoes, and below them the Kiowas and Comanches. Before this the governor of the State of Kansas had declared that Kansas would do her part in punishing the Indians, and the militia regiment, known as the Nineteenth Kansas, had been enlisted for this purpose.

At Camp Supply, which Sheridan reached November 21, he found General [Alfred] Sully engaged on the work of the post, but the Kansas militia had not made its appearance. The weather was tempestuous, very cold and snowy, but the horses of the Seventh Cavalry were in good condition, and that regiment was ready for service. On the morning of November 23, General Sheridan ordered General Custer to set out, with the idea of looking for Indians. A few days later took place the Battle of the Washita—commonly spoken of as a great victory.

The story from the point of view of the troops is told in General Custer's report to Sheridan, which has been printed many times. It is claimed that one hundred and three warriors were killed and fifty-three women and children captured. As usual, there were many women and children killed. An Indian was an Indian and always good to shoot at. The village was captured and burned. The troops lost Major Elliot, Captain Hamilton, and nineteen enlisted men killed, three officers and eleven enlisted men wounded. The Indians from the lower camps came up toward Black Kettle's village, perhaps to fight, perhaps with the purpose of saving the women and children, but Custer scarcely waited for them, and withdrew without a collision with this larger force. Ben Clark, who was in the fight, stated that when the first people appeared from the lower villages General Custer ordered Major Elliot to take a few men, and disperse those Indians. Elliot set out to do this, but found the Indians too many to disperse, and was soon driven up a side ravine. Here his force was surrounded, and the men turned loose their horses, and got into a hollow where they lay in tall grass so that the Indians could see only the smoke from their carbines. Before long they were all killed.

The Indians say that from Camp Supply, whence Custer's command started, it went up Wolf Creek to a point about eighteen miles above Supply. From Wolf Creek Custer crossed over by way of the Antelope Hills to the South Canadian River, following the trail made by a war party that had been raiding on the Smoky Hill River. The snow was nearly two feet deep and the trail was easily followed from the point where the Osage scouts had found it on Wolf Creek. As the soldiers travelled along, they found buffalo along the South Canadian, and some were killed for the uses of the command.

The Indians whose trail Custer was following had passed along only the day before. Some of the Cheyennes were going to Black Kettle's village on the Washita, and some to other Cheyenne villages which were down below. When they reached the Canadian one party crossed, and went on south by the Antelope Hills, while the other party kept on down the river, each group wishing to go directly to the village where each belonged.

Bear Shield and his party, who had gone down the river, camped five or six miles below the Antelope Hills, and the next morning when about to start on they heard shooting up the river. One of the party, named Wood, said: "One of you men had better go up on that hill and look back and see what you can see. To me those guns sound like the guns of soldiers." "No," said Red Nose, "it must be that other party. They have stopped somewhere, and have found buffalo, and are killing some." So the Indians did not take the trouble to go up on the hill to look back to see who was doing the shooting. Bear Shield and his party went on, and that night reached the village on the Washita below Black Kettle's village.

The party with which Crow Neck was went on over toward Black Kettle's village. They struck the Washita about fifteen miles above the village, and seeing where the camp had just moved down the river, followed the trail, and reached home that night. At the point where they reached the Washita, Crow Neck left a worn-out horse, and the next afternoon, thinking that by this time the animal would be rested, he went back to get it. When he had come almost to the place where he had left the horse, he saw something coming over the hills, a long line of people or animals, and being afraid that these were soldiers he turned back to the village without getting his horse. When he reached the camp he said to Bad Man, in whose lodge he was stopping: "I believe I saw soldiers going over the hill to the river when I went to get my horse. They were either soldiers or buffalo; at all events, I was frightened and did not get my horse. You will do well to get in your horses this afternoon, and to-morrow morning to move away. I am afraid that perhaps soldiers are coming." Bad Man got in his horses, as advised.

What Crow Neck had seen was Custer's command marching over from the Canadian to the Washita. It was during that night that Custer made the march through the snow and cold, and the next morning he attacked the village.

When the firing began many of the women and children rushed out of the village and down into the bed of the stream, and tried to hide there. Black Kettle and his wife were killed close together in the village. The Indians who could do so hurried down the stream or crossed it, and sought refuge in the hills. Most of those killed were shot in the valley of the stream, close to it, and practically all the women and children who were killed were shot while hiding in the brush or trying to run away through it. Many women and children ran into the river, and waded down through the water, waist or breast deep, and by keeping close under the banks escaped the shots of the soldiers, who were riding along the bluffs, and on the bank above them. The weather was bitterly cold, and the people half froze, but in view of the greater danger of the soldiers, they thought little of that discomfort. Perhaps two miles below Black Kettle's village was a horseshoe bend of the Washita, about which the water was deep for the whole width of the stream, and it was impossible for a person to walk, even close under the banks. The Indians knew about this and warned the women and children of it, telling them, when they got to the beginning of this bend, to leave the river, and cut across the point, and then re-enter the water below. This they did.

Among those who waded down the river was a large party of women and children behind whom followed three men ready to fight, a Kiowa and two Cheyennes named Packer (Stō kó wo) and Little Rock (Hō hăn ĭ no ó). When these people emerged from the water they were seen by Custer's command, and these may have been the Indians that Major Elliot is said to have been ordered to attack and disperse. Elliot went down toward them with his force of fourteen or fifteen men. Farther down the river a number of Indians were gathered on the south side of the stream, and the orders may have referred to them. When Elliot got near to these women and children, the three men who were with them stopped behind to fight.

About the middle of this cut-off across the point, Little Rock, who had a rifle and powder-horn, stopped and fired back at the soldiers and killed a horse under one of them. Almost at the same moment he himself was killed. The Kiowa jumped back to his body, snatched from him his rifle and powder-horn, and as he retreated began to load and fire. Packer and the Kiowa escaped and are alive to-day [1915].

A little farther along Buffalo Woman (Wó ĭsta) with three children became exhausted and stopped and sat down. When the soldiers came up, Elliot detailed the man who had been dismounted to take these prisoners back to the command. As they were going back toward the command a number of Indians were beginning to come in from the south. The woman saw them, and said to the soldier: "Wait a moment; these children's feet are pretty nearly frozen; let me wrap some rags about them, to protect them." Of course, it is not to be supposed that the soldier knew what she was saying, but he saw her tear pieces from her dress and bind up the feet of the children. While she was doing this, the Indians who were coming in had time to creep around and get between her and the command. Then, when she and the soldier started on, the Indians, who had recognized her, charged on them, and killed the soldier and took the woman away. Little Chief, of the Arapahoes, counted coup on the soldier with a hatchet.

When the party of women and children, and the two men with them, had reached the bank of the river they climbed down and continued to wade through the water under the high bank. From time to time, as the Kiowa finished loading his gun, he crept up the bank and fired a shot at the soldiers. Once while he was doing this he saw a great crowd of Indians coming toward him from down the river, and a moment after saw Elliot's men turn off from the stream and ride up toward the hills. The Kiowa called to Packer, who also crept up on the bank, and just then they saw a crowd of Indians coming down the stream—Little Chief and his party who had cut off the soldier and rescued the woman and the three children. Then the Kiowa called out to the women and children and said: "They are charging from both sides. You can come up on the bank now."

Meantime the Indians had surrounded Elliot's party. His men let their horses go and all lay down in the high grass to fight. Those who were looking on from a distance could see nothing but smoke and confusion. The shooting by the soldiers was constant. The Indians who had surrounded them crept closer and closer, and presently they could see that the soldiers were apparently not taking any aim, but were holding their carbines up over the grass and shooting wildly. Meantime Packer, the Kiowa, and many of the women and children hurried to the place where the fight was taking place, but when they reached it the shooting was all over and the soldiers were dead. The fight must have been short.

Among the Indians there was a difference of opinion as to who it was that counted the first coup on Elliot's men. Some people declare that it was Roman Nose Thunder, a Cheyenne, who rushed in among the troops and was shot in the arm, and others that it was an Arapaho, who also rushed in and was killed. Opinion seems to favor the Arapaho, who was the only man killed by Elliot's force in the final battle. His name was Tobacco. He was the owner of a flat war club similar to the one owned by the Arapaho who was killed in the big fight with the Kiowas in 1838. A man who carries one of these war clubs feels obliged to perform some great feat. Another Arapaho, Single Coyote, was mortally wounded here and died some time after.

The Indians all say that the soldiers lay flat on the ground and did not rise up above the grass to take any aim. They seemed to depend for safety on concealment rather than on defense; and while they fired many shots these shots were not directed toward their enemies. Roman Nose Thunder, who rode close to and around them, could see them in the grass and shooting, but to him they appeared to be shooting upward and not toward the Indians. The Arapaho, who with many has credit for counting the first coup, rode immediately over them and was shot in the breast by an upward-directed ball.

A number of the older and more prudent Indians thought that they would crawl up the ravine and get close shots at Elliot's men and began to do this. They moved slowly, on hands and knees, and before they had come near the troops the Indians made a charge and almost ran over them.

In the killing of Elliot's men Cheyennes, Arapahoes, Kiowas, and Apaches took part, so there was a great counting of coups, each tribe being at liberty to count the coups allowed by its own customs. In that way twelve coups might have been counted on each one of Elliot's men.

It has been stated on supposed Indian authority that Elliot held the Indians off for two days, but this is clearly a misunderstanding of what the Indians said, for the fight was very short, probably much less than an hour.

The people of Black Kettle's village who survived went down to the other villages below, in many cases being taken there by friends who came up with horses for their transportation. Custer very prudently made no move to attack the villages below, and the Indians thought that if he had done so his whole command would have been wiped out. It was not until about two weeks after the battle that Custer's command returned to the scene to look after the remains of Elliot and his party, who were found close together at the place where they were killed.

After the Washita fight the tribes which had been camped together there withdrew to the Red River, and most of them camped on the north fork of the Red River. The captured women and children were taken to Fort Hays, Kansas, but before long an old woman named Red Hair was sent out to find the Cheyennes. About this time Little Robe, a Cheyenne, and Black Eagle, a Kiowa, went into Fort Cobb to see what terms they could get if their people surrendered and to procure news of the Cheyenne prisoners. They saw General Hazen, who talked with them and advised them to wait for the coming of General Sheridan, who reached there a few days later. Sheridan told the Indians that they must give up the white prisoners they had; that he would send Custer to the Cheyenne camp for the prisoners, and that the chiefs must go back and warn their people that Custer was coming, so that the Indians would not fight him. He told them that the Cheyenne prisoners would be given up in the summer at Fort Supply, and advised the Cheyennes and Arapahoes to go in there and surrender.

Custer's story is somewhat different. He says the Indian woman and an Apache chief named Iron Shirt were sent to the Cheyennes; that Iron Shirt returned alone and said that two chiefs would soon be in to talk. A few days later Little Robe and Yellow Bear, "second chief of the Arapahoes," came into Fort Cobb and said their people were talking of coming in and would send a runner with the news of their purpose in a few days. Custer says he waited but no messengers came, so, with forty men, he and the two chiefs set out. They went to the Arapaho village and persuaded that tribe to come in, but the Cheyennes did not come. In March Custer, with eleven troops of the Seventh Cavalry and ten of the Nineteenth Kansas Cavalry, set out to look for the Cheyennes. He moved from the neighborhood of Fort Cobb, where the troops had been nearly all winter, toward the Red River, and striking a trail followed it to the north fork of the Red River, where in the middle of March he found the Cheyennes on a timbered stream. Custer rode out ahead of his command with an orderly and was met by some chiefs, including Medicine Arrow. The Indians say that Custer was brought into the camp and to the medicine arrow lodge, where he sat down under the medicine arrows, and the keeper of the arrows lit a pipe and held it while Custer smoked, and while Custer was smoking Medicine Arrow told him in Cheyenne that he was a treacherous man and that if he came there with a bad purpose—to do harm to the people—he would be killed with all his men. Then the arrow keeper with a pipe stick loosened the ashes in the pipe and poured them out on the toes of Custer's boots, to give him bad luck.

The Indian was not far wrong as to Custer's intention, for Custer says that while he was smoking this pipe he was planning how to surround the camp and attack or capture it. However, he now learned that there were two white women in the camp, so he did not dare attack until he could secure them. Custer says that when his troops approached the Indians fled from their village and made toward Little Robe's camp, which was some distance off. He says that he caused to be seized Big Head and Dull Knife, Dog Soldier chiefs, and two other men, whom he held as hostages. He then sent word to the Indians to return and take away their lodges if they chose, and many did so. After waiting here a few days for the delivery of the white prisoners, he told them that if the prisoners were not given up on the following day, he would hang the Cheyennes he held. The following afternoon the women were given up.

Bent says that while the Indians were making a friendly visit to Custer's camp they heard the officer give a loud command, and the soldiers all seized their guns and attempted to surround the Indians. All got away except three, whom Custer held and sent to Fort Hays, where they were imprisoned with the Cheyenne women. Afterward two of these men, Slim Face, eighty years old, and Curly Hair, fifty, were killed by the guards. There seems to be some confusion about the men who were captured. They are the three who were photographed and whose picture has been printed in a multitude of books on the early West, with a great many captions. . . . Ē hyōph́ stā tells the same story as that given by Bent. These three men, she says, went in to make peace. They were surrounded by the soldiers, captured, and their pictures were taken. Afterward they were killed.

Custer, with the two rescued white women and the "three chiefs" he had captured, marched back to Camp Supply. Soon after this the Cheyennes came in and settled down at Supply. In the South there was no more fighting between the Cheyennes and the whites, until 1874.

In Black Kettle, White Antelope, and Yellow Wolf, all old men, who were killed by the whites, we have three examples of high patriotism. These men were constant workers among the Indians in behalf of peace with the white people. They did this not because they loved the white people, from whom they had received nothing good, but because they loved their own tribe, and wished to guide it in paths that would be for the tribe's greatest advantage. White Antelope and Yellow Wolf were killed at Sand Creek, and Black Kettle four years later, when Custer attacked his village on the Washita. Black Kettle was a frank, good man, who did not hesitate to expose himself to any danger if he thought that his tribe might be benefited thereby. Notwithstanding the attacks made on different parties of Cheyennes by troops in Colorado, Black Kettle was quite willing to visit Governor Evans in Denver. Before and after Sand Creek he consistently talked and acted for peace, and his last words in this behalf were spoken to General Hazen only a few days before he was killed in the village on the Washita. He was the first of the Cheyenne chiefs to dare to attend the meetings of the peace commission at the treaty of Medicine Lodge, in 1867. Taught by past experience—at Sand Creek and on Pawnee Fork—the other Cheyennes feared to present themselves at a place where there was a large number of troops and where they might be attacked without warning.

Black Kettle was a striking example of a consistently friendly Indian, who, because he was friendly and so because his whereabouts was usually known, was punished for the acts of people whom it was supposed he could control.

President Grant's Peace Policy

Continued fighting with western and southwestern tribes during and after the Civil War and events such as the Sand Creek massacre of 1864 and the Fetterman massacre of 1866 focused national attention on the Indian problem and stimulated interest in United States Indian policy. Both the Sand Creek and Fetterman massacres brought government investigations, while Congress studied general difficulties with the Indians. In 1865 a committee under Senator James R. Doolittle conducted a broad inquiry into the condition of the Indians, seeking opinions from army officers, Indian agents, and other concerned persons. Two years later Congress created the Peace Commission to continue the investigation of the Indian problem and to negotiate peace treaties with the western tribes—although, unfortunately, the creation of such commissions did not ensure peace.

Listed among the members of both the Doolittle committee and the Peace Commission were men who were sympathetic to the Indians and critical of government policies, and after the Civil War, humanitarian groups demonstrated an increasing interest in the American Indian. Religious organizations, too, reflected a growing concern for the welfare of the Indians, although some individuals such as Episcopalian Bishop Henry Whipple of Minnesota, had been critics of federal Indian policy for some time. The growing pressure from religious groups, the recommendations of government investigators, and the knowledge that corruption was widespread in the Indian Bureau ultimately led to reform during the administration of President Ulysses S. Grant.

Even before his inauguration Grant had made a commitment to reform. Influenced by Quakers who deplored the prevalence of corruption and inefficiency in the Indian Bureau, Grant offered to allow them to nominate men for bureau positions in certain areas in the West. The success of this experiment prompted Grant to include other religious denominations, and eventually the superintendencies and agencies were divided up among various churches. In 1869 Congress took a further step to eliminate graft in the Indian Service by creating the Board of Indian Commissioners, a group of ten unpaid philanthropists who were to oversee government contracts and offer recommendations for policy changes. The board never lived up to its full potential, but it can be considered part of the so-called Quaker Policy, the administrative policy regarding appointments in the Bureau of Indian Affairs.

At the same time the Grant administration also developed the Peace Policy—separate from the Quaker Policy, although the distinction was rarely made in the nineteenth century—which embodied the government's official aims vis-à-vis the tribes. It sought to place the Indians on reservations, by peaceful means if possible, but by force if necessary. There they would be cared for by the government and receive instruction in the ways of white civilization until they could be assimilated into the predominant American society.

The two policies met with varying success. The Peace Policy did not guarantee peace, and the Quaker Policy did not eliminate graft and inefficiency, although it did generally raise the level of the Indian Service and reduce corruption. Robert L. Whitner describes the successes and failures of these policies on the Yakima Reservation.

Grant's Indian Peace Policy on the Yakima Reservation, 1870-82

ROBERT L. WHITNER

The Indian problem, which from the colonial period had faced the whites in America, became particularly acute following the Civil War, as the pace of the westward movement was speeded up. The reservation system, already begun before the Civil War, was considered to be the basis of the solution. It kept the Indians out of the way, and it provided a means whereby they would be taught to live like white men. Grant's peace policy was intended to be an improvement on the reservation system, calling generally for the use of peaceful means rather than force—locating all the tribes on reservations with eventual individual allotments, expanding the education program and facilities, providing food and clothing for the Indians until they could become self-sufficient, and improving the quality of the agents.

Of all the features of the peace policy, the unique and most interesting—and the one emphasized here—was the new system for selecting agents. Thirteen of the larger churches were invited to submit to the Commissioner of Indian Affairs their nominations for agents, and the seventy-odd agencies were divided among the churches for this purpose. It was intended that the churches, or their missionary societies, should nominate agents for those reservations on which they were then supporting missionary work or were willing to do so.

The Indian Office knew relatively little about Indian missions as such, and the first distribution of the agencies was followed by correction and modification, though not to the satisfaction of every participating church, particularly the Roman Catholic, which had been contributing more than half of all the money spent for Indian missionary work, but was assigned only seven agencies. The largest church, though not one of the most active in Indian work—the Methodist Episcopal—was invited to nominate the most agents, for fifteen reservations in all.

It is not the purpose here to analyze or to explain the distribution of the agencies, but it should be noted that the system was planned and assignments were made by Protestants, including some prominent laymen, a fact which Catholic publications frequently mentioned. After the final adjustments were made, the Methodists, through their Missionary Society, nominated agents for four reservations in Montana Territory, three each in California and Washington Territory, two each in Oregon and Idaho Territory, and the Mackinac agency in Michigan.

In December, 1870, President Ulysses S. Grant, in his annual message to Congress, announced the new method for selecting agents and hopefully predicted the results

> I determined to give all the agencies to such religious denominations as had heretofore established missionaries among the Indians, and perhaps to some other denominations who would undertake the work on the same terms—i.e., as a missionary work. The Societies selected are allowed to name their own agents . . . and are expected to watch over them and aid them as missionaries, to Christianize and civilize the Indian, and to train him in the arts of peace. I entertain the confident hope that the policy now pursued will in a few years bring all the Indians upon reservations, where they will live in houses, and have schoolhouses and churches, and will be pursuing peaceful and self-sustaining avocations. . . .

It must be said that these goals were generally not realized. Though the interest of the Roman Catholic Church in Indian work remained high during this period—in fact, its activities increased considerably—that of many of the Protestant sects did not. By 1870 the Methodists, in particular, had come to feel that the greenest mission pastures were in Africa and Asia, and their greatest efforts and most of their appropriations were expended on the heathen of the Old World. Their meager efforts among the Indians were rationalized by an enthusiastic acceptance of social Darwinism, no better expression of which can be found than in the editorial columns of the *Christian Advocate*, the organ of the Methodist Episcopal Church. Though the *Advocate* rejected Darwin's theory of evolution, it applied his principles to the American Indian.

> It is a law of human society, and among the races of men not less effective in its workings or certain in its results than plants and irrational animals,

that the stronger must overcome the weaker, and either exterminate or subordinate them, unless, indeed, there shall be found in the inferiors a capability of assimilation and absorption by the superior . . . all ethnological evidences go to prove that even . . . [when white men first came to America the Indians] were but the remnants of a decaying and vagrant race. Beyond almost every other people they have shown an inaptitude and distaste for improvement. The whole race seems to have been so smitten with a deep-seated depravation of character that their redemption was impossible, and so divine wisdom and goodness decreed their extinction, and the bestowment of the continent upon a better race.

It is not surprising, then, that the Methodist Episcopal Church and its Missionary Society took little interest in the peace policy other than to nominate agents. Methodist agents not infrequently complained that the Missionary Society made no effort to convert its Indians. The Society's aid to Indian education and missionary work consisted largely of occasionally appointing a missionary to a reservation where he was employed as a teacher and paid by the government. Late in the life of the peace policy the Society did take over a contract boarding school at Fort Peck in Montana, but it did so primarily because the Catholics wanted to.

Not only did the Methodists do little about education and missions, the Missionary Society generally failed to select agents who improved the service. This is not to say that some good choices were not made, for some of the Methodist agents were excellent, but rather that a satisfactory method of testing and screening was never developed to insure the nomination of good men. From incomplete records it has been determined that thirty-three agents were nominated by the Methodist Missionary Society from 1870 to 1882, and that nine others were possible if not probable Methodist nominees. Seven of this total of forty-two were outstanding agents, seventeen were clearly poor, being either incompetent or dishonest or both.

Most of the characteristics of the Methodist administration of the peace policy can be seen on the Yakima reservation. Though the Yakimas received more missionary and educational support from the Society than did most other Methodist Indians, the appropriations were extremely meager. No missionaries were supported by the Society among the Yakimas during the period of the peace policy. The Methodists had a tendency to nominate clergymen as agents—eleven of the forty-two—and one of them was the Yakima agent, James H. Wilbur. As far as the quality of agents selected by the Missionary Society is concerned, Wilbur was outstanding, and he was one of the Society's happier choices. His principal fault was the same as that of several other Methodist agents, as well as that of his Church and Missionary Society—his religious intolerance and bigotry.

The Rev. James H. Wilbur, a New Yorker, was appointed to the Oregon mission in 1846 and began his work near Oregon City the next summer. In 1860 he went to the Yakima reservation as superintendent of teaching. In 1864 he was appointed agent for the Yakimas, a position he held until 1869, when he was replaced briefly by an army officer. He was restored to duty in April, 1870, by the Indian Office, and was nominated for the position by the Board of Managers of the Missionary Society in June. He remained at Yakima until his resignation in 1882, the only Methodist agent whose tenure spanned the entire period of the peace policy. He was considered by his superiors, both lay and clerical, to be an outstanding agent, and Yakima was regarded by many as the model agency of the service.

The statistical tables in the annual reports of the Commissioner of Indian Affairs show considerable material improvement during Wilbur's administration as a Methodist nominee. The Yakima reservation showed appreciable increases in the acreage cultivated, agricultural production, and the output of the agency mills. It must be noted, however, that Wilbur was not wholly responsible for this, for the Yakimas had the good fortune to be on a reservation blessed with abundant resources—a large proportion of arable land, good grazing land, and plenty of timber on the western hills and mountains. With Wilbur's encouragement, teaching, and example, the Yakimas made good use of their resources. Many farmed individual plots, lived in comfortable houses, and owned their own farm machinery. Several Indian wives had sewing machines.

Wilbur promoted the self-sufficiency of the Yakimas to a considerable degree. In 1878, for example, some 300 or 400 head of cattle were sold in order to buy farm machinery and additional stock. Agency mills provided all the flour and lumber needed by the reservation. In 1876 the value of the steam sawmill and the shingle mill, both of which had been built without expense to the government, was at least $12,000. They had been paid for with grazing fees earned from leased range lands. In 1877 a planing mill and new equipment were purchased with money also obtained from grazing fees. Work on the reservation provided an important source of employment for the Indians; in fact, all the agency work was done by Indians with a minimum of white supervision.

Wilbur's honesty and integrity in the management of the temporal affairs of his agency were never questioned, though in 1881 an inspector charged him with using improper accounting practices which made it impossible to determine the use and disposition of annuity goods and money. Though his bookkeeping was irregular, there is no doubt that the material condition of the Yakimas was greatly improved during his years of service.

One of Wilbur's chief interests throughout his years with the Yakimas was the reservation boarding school. His constant problem was the inadequate physical plant, and he exerted great effort to expand the facilities so that more children could be accommodated. Despite his efforts, he was never able to provide for all those of school age, but he did have some success in that direction. In 1873 only forty to fifty children, about one-tenth of the school-age population, were all that could be handled, and this number remained fairly constant until 1880, when alterations to the school building nearly doubled its capacity. Facilities were again expanded in 1881, but, because only two teachers were available, the enrollment was limited to 120, and scores of prospective pupils had to be turned away.

During the summer of 1882 Wilbur completed a new schoolhouse large enough to accommodate the children of the Piutes and Bannocks who had been brought to the Yakima reservation in 1879 following the wars in southern Idaho Territory and Utah. Though the physical facilities at Yakima were inadequate throughout the period of the peace policy, they were better than those enjoyed at agencies where offices, mills, granaries, barns, and slaughterhouses were sometimes made to serve as schoolrooms, dormitories, and teachers' quarters.

Wilbur had one difficulty faced by all agents—getting and keeping teachers. Salaries were low, living and teaching conditions poor, the work discouraging, progress slow, and those who were queasy about dirt and vermin found much to endure. Wilbur attempted to solve this problem in the same way as did most other agents. He used people already on the reservation, that is, missionaries, wives of agency employees, and Indians; even Wilbur's wife was on the payroll occasionally. The records indicate that most of the teaching was done by Methodist missionaries paid by the government. But the agent also depended upon the Indians, one of whom, George Waters, was an ordained minister who worked as a house-painter when he was not serving the minds and the souls of the Yakimas.

In terms of the advancement of Indian education, Methodist participation in the peace policy was generally ineffective. The statistical tables in the annual reports of the Indian Commissioner show only slight progress in the facilities provided, and on most reservations they were still inadequate by 1882. The situation at Yakima, though better than at the average agency, reflected the conditions on all Methodist reservations.

The effectiveness of the educational program was also typical. Though Wilbur received warm praise for his work from the Missionary Society and the Indian Office, some were dubious about the results. Wilbur's successor, the Rev. Robert H. Milroy, Superintendent of Indian Affairs for the Territory in the early 1870's, and one of Wilbur's admirers, noted in 1885 that the young men and women who had completed the prescribed courses could read reasonably well, but were not sure what they were reading. Most could write a fair hand, but their compositions defied understanding. Several of the young men had been tried as interpreters, but none of them had performed satisfactorily. It was not for another ten years after Milroy made these observations that the first eighth-grade commencement was held on the reservation.

The worst feature of Wilbur's administration and of Methodist participation in the peace policy was intolerant sectarianism. One important characteristic of late 19th-century America was Protestant antipathy toward Catholicism. Already strong by 1870, it was intensified by the peace policy. The Methodists found in the Yakima reservation a battleground against the Catholics, and in Wilbur an able tactician. Catholic spokesmen undoubtedly had Yakima in mind when they charged that the peace policy was perverted by the Protestant churches into a crusade against Catholic missionary work with the support of a Protestant-dominated Indian Office.

Catholic priests established the first mission among the Yakimas in 1847–St. Joseph's, located outside the boundaries of the reservation as defined eight years later in the treaty of 1855. Closed during the Yakima War, it was reopened and rebuilt in 1865. In the meantime, Wilbur came in 1860 as teacher and missionary, and in 1864 was appointed agent.

That Wilbur disliked the reopening of St. Joseph's is clear. Always alert to keeping priests off the reservation, he also attempted to prevent Indians from leaving to visit the Catholic mission. Lt. James Smith, who replaced him in 1869, charged that he also discriminated against Catholic Indians in the distribution of agricultural implements. Though Wilbur may have been guilty of this charge, no other account of such discrimination has been found. However, his attitude toward Catholic priests and his efforts to prevent their building a church on the reservation are well documented.

In 1873 the Bureau of Catholic Indian Missions was given permission to construct churches on the Nez Perce (a Presbyterian agency) and Yakima reservations. Wilbur's response epitomizes the theocratic tendencies of Methodist participation in the peace policy.

The two reservations referred to have been assigned by the President, under the new Christian policy, to two Protestant denominations . . . with the expectation on the part of all Protestant Christians that, so far as the religious instruction of these tribes is concerned, those respective churches were to have entire jurisdiction without the interference of other denominations, most of all without the interference of the Catholic priesthood.

Wilbur was supported in his opposition by Superintendent Milroy—also a Methodist minister and the man who succeeded him in 1882. Such permission, Milroy said, was a violation of the Yakima treaty of 1855, which prohibited any white men from coming on the reservation without the consent of the superintendent, the agent, and the Indians. He, the superintendent, and Wilbur, the agent, were opposed to the coming of the priests. This line of reasoning not only seemed valid to Milroy, but it was also accepted by Wilbur, by Secretary J. M. Reid of the Missionary Society, and eventually by the Commissioner of Indian Affairs. Before the Catholics could react to the granting of their request to build a church, Secretary of the Interior C. Delano withdrew the Department's permission on the grounds that the Indians did not want it.

In August, 1875, the request was renewed by the Commissioner of the Catholic Bureau, Charles Ewing, who informed Delano that Catholic priests had gone to the Yakimas in 1847 with their consent, and had continued to work among them until Wilbur became agent, from which time he had kept the priests off the reservation. Once again the request was not granted. The refusal was justified in a letter from Commissioner of Indian Affairs E. P. Smith to the Secretary of the Interior.

> Remonstrances having been made by Dr. J. M. Reid of New York, Missionary Secretary of the Methodist Church, to the erection of any buildings on this reserve by the Catholic church, no authority, in my judgment can be given to the Catholic or any other denomination to build churches, schools, or parsonages within that reservation, without the permission of the tribe, and the Agent.
>
> Dr. Reid states that the agent J. H. Wilbur, has forwarded his protest and remonstrance. . . .
>
> In addition to the objection urged because of treaty obligations, I believe that inasmuch as this reservation is now in the care of a religious organization its protest should be allowed due consideration. . . .

Again in 1876 Ewing renewed his petition, and again it was not granted. In 1877 Father J. B. A. Brouillet, on behalf of the Catholic Bureau, asked the Commissioner of Indian Affairs for $1,500 from the Yakima incidental fund for the support of a boarding school in Yakima City, about one mile from the reservation boundary. It must have been no surprise when the money was not forthcoming. The Commissioner sent a copy of Brouillet's letter to Wilbur, who answered with a vigorous protest.

In spite of the original grant of permission for a church, none was built on the reservation. The records of the Indian Office contain no letters from the Catholic Bureau on this subject after 1877. Indeed, there seemed little point in further efforts, for the agent, the Methodist Missionary Society, and the Indian Office were not interested in religious toleration for Indians. Not until 1880 did the Interior Department again permit all denominations access to all reservations. Wilbur was clearly instrumental in keeping the priests off his reservation and in preventing the construction of a Catholic church, but it is most probable that he could not have done so had not the peace policy given him and the Missionary Society justification for claiming a monopoly of religious instruction on the Yakima reservation.

Wilbur's effectiveness in keeping the Catholics off the Yakima reservation and the strong support he received from the Missionary Society suggest that the Methodists' nomination of so many ministers as agents was, at least in part, a deliberate weapon against Catholicism. Some remarks Wilbur made in 1881 at a meeting of the Board of Indian Commissioners with the heads of the missionary societies are especially significant in the context of his battle against the priests. The Rev. John O. Means, secretary of the American Board of Commissioners for Foreign Missions, said to Wilbur, "I suppose your position as agent gives you a great deal of authority among the Indians, so that when you are speaking to them as a spiritual guide it comes with a certain authority." Wilbur replied,

> Yes, sir. I think that in governing the Indians of an agency where a man has the commission from the President, and where he is recognized as having communion with the Father of Spirits, and where his life corresponds with that, it gives him additional power in the management of an agency. The two together give a man a great deal more influence over the Indians than if he had simply the paper from the President.

Means continued, "Does not the fact that he has the paper from the President also make it much simpler and easier for him to lead them in spiritual directions?" "Yes, sir," admitted Wilbur; "they receive it with greater authority."

This dual function, however, was not without some difficulties, and these were noted by Inspector E. C. Kemble in 1873, the year in which the Catholic Bureau was given permission to build the church on the reservation. Kemble believed that Wilbur's responsibilities as missionary added too heavily to his work as agent, but this was not the paramount consideration.

> What is of special importance, particularly in view of the possible incoming of another religious establishment here, it would dissociate him from that part of the work which prevents a full and impartial exercise of the authority, or which, at least subjects his authority to criticism and (doubtless unjust) complaint. It is not unlikely, moreover, that the reluctance of some of the Indians belonging to this Reservation, to remain upon it, and come under the good influence of the agent in secular things, is owing to their indisposition to receive and follow a particular form of religious belief. It would be overcome perhaps in many instances if the agent were to go to them and teach them their secular and moral duties apart from the office of preacher.

Because Inspector Kemble was one of Wilbur's most enthusiastic admirers, this statement is valuable evidence of the agent's intolerance.

In conclusion, it must be said that, except for his strong sectarianism, Wilbur was a good agent who took his responsibilities seriously and was of real service to his charges. The Methodists, however, cannot take full credit for him, for he had already served as agent for six years before the peace policy went into effect, and he had already been restored to duty in 1870 before he was nominated by the Missionary Society.

What effect, then, did the peace policy have on the Yakima reservation? There was only one important result, only one development which would not have taken place had the peace policy not been adopted. It appeared both to Wilbur and to the Missionary Society that the federal government was allied with them in their fight against the Roman Catholic Church. Another area was found in which the Methodists could carry on their warfare with the enemy. Another weapon was added to their arsenal, for it seemed to them that they had legal sanction for their denial of religious freedom to Catholic Indians. Neither Wilbur nor his church was concerned with freedom of conscience for those who did not believe as they did or with the principle of the separation of church and state. It must be concluded, therefore, that the Methodist administration of the peace policy on the Yakima reservation was generally unsuccessful in terms of the goals expressed by Grant in 1870. But more than this, to the never-ending struggle against bigotry and intolerance the Methodists lent not aid, but hindrance.

Originally published in *Pacific Northwest Quarterly* 50 (October 1959): 135–42. All footnotes omitted.

The Peacetime Role of the Military

If the charges of some nineteenth-century critics of the frontier army are to be believed, American soldiers of all ranks were glory hunters who eagerly sought combat to accelerate their own promotions. They were insensitive to the feelings and problems of the American Indian, according to the detractors, and unhesitatingly shot down women and children in battle. There unquestionably were soldiers who fit this stereotype; there were battles that should have been avoided; some officers were primarily concerned with their own careers; and Indian women and children were killed by soldiers (it is not surprising that the My Lai massacre of 1968 has been compared to the Sand Creek massacre of 1864). Nevertheless, there were many officers and men who sympathized with the Indians and who did their best to avoid conflict while also attempting to improve the lot of the tribes. John Pope and George Crook were two such officers, but they were not alone. Others from the rank of general down shared their views in varying degrees.

The frontier army was a peacekeeping force entrusted with the security of white settlements. Many officers realized that there was little glory to be gained from fighting Indians, and they were aware that military activity in the West was subject to criticism from several groups: frontiersmen often charged that the troops were ineffective and did not punish hostile Indians, while eastern humanitarians usually complained that the soldiers were too harsh. Such criticism ignored the fact that many frontier officers did their best to maintain peace and force hostiles to surrender while at the same time they attempted to remove or minimize the causes of conflict. Some officers served with the Bureau of Indian Affairs as acting Indian agents; some commanded companies of Indian scouts; and others encouraged the Indians to become economically self-sufficient.

Generals Pope and Crook directed or led expeditions against hostile Indians when the need arose, but they acted on the assumption that their primary task was to avoid warfare. Both men shared with eastern humanitarians and reformers the goal of civilizing the Indians, and both were concerned with the general welfare of the tribes, although they were critical of the Indian Bureau and urged military control of Indian affairs.

General Pope, an experienced officer, had directed the campaigns against the Sioux from 1862 to 1865. He participated in the Red River War with the Kiowas, Comanches, and Southern Cheyennes in 1874 and 1875, and after the defeat of those tribes he watched over them and aided them. He protested repeatedly that the Indians were not receiving enough food; occasionally he violated government regulations to provide military supplies to hungry Indians; and in time of crisis he arranged for local cattlemen to supply meat to the reservations. Pope also helped start sheep and cattle herds among the Kiowas and Comanches and encouraged them to become herdsmen.

George Crook engaged in similar activities in Arizona. Under his direction irrigation systems were developed; wood, hay, and other products were purchased from the Indians to promote their self-sufficiency; and Apaches were enlisted into the United States Army. Crook's concern and involvement can also be seen in the case of Standing Bear *vs.* Crook. *James T. King provides an excellent description of the events that led to the celebrated case involving the Ponca Indians. His evaluation of Crook destroys the old stereotype of frontier army officers, for Crook supported the case against himself and after the trial was over continued to work on behalf of the Ponca tribe.*

The concern of Crook, Pope, and other officers for Indian welfare was genuine, and their activities demonstrate that the duties of the army were not limited simply to fighting Indians. The army could and did play an active role in helping the Indian people.

General Pope and the Old "Hand-to-Mouth Way"

RICHARD N. ELLIS

The Indian campaign of 1874 did not settle the Indian problem on the southern plains although it did teach the Kiowa, Comanche, and Southern Cheyenne respect for the power of the government. The defeat of the three warlike southern tribes brought peace to the region, but Pope feared that hostilities might begin again. During the remainder of his tour of duty in the Department of the Missouri, he did his utmost to keep the peace and in so doing once again found himself embroiled in a major controversy with the officials of the Indian Bureau.

Even before the conclusion of the military campaign, Pope began to criticize the Indian Bureau. In October 1874 while military operations were at their height, Commissioner of Indian Affairs Edward P. Smith gave permission to 400 Pawnee to hunt buffalo in Indian Territory. Pope protested immediately. To send unsuspecting Indians into an area where troops were under orders to attack all Indians who were not at the agencies was unthinkable. "When it is considered," he wrote, "that the Indian Territory is everywhere now the theatre of active hostilities, and that troops, as well as hostile bands of Indians, are to be met anywhere, this action of the Indian Department seems most extraordinary." It was "extraordinary," but as time passed, such decisions no longer surprised the protesting general.

With the arrival of winter Pope became increasingly concerned about the conditions at the Indian agencies at Fort Sill and Darlington. The peaceful Indians were nearly starving, and when Pope met with Sheridan in December to discuss the military campaign, he discussed their condition and raised the question of treatment of the friendly Indians. Sheridan was appalled. "The peaceful Indians have behaved so admirably," he wrote, "that they should not be allowed to suffer."

The friendly Indians did suffer because the Indian Bureau was unable to care for them, a situation not limited to the agencies at Fort Sill and Darlington. All across the West the Bureau was confronted with the specter of starving Indians. Early in January 1875 agents throughout the Central Superintendency were forced to give the Indians permission to leave the reservations to hunt so that they could feed themselves. Because he could not feed them, Agent [James] Haworth sent some Kiowa and Comanche out to hunt, and soon thereafter Superintendent [Enoch] Hoag gave permission to the Osage tribe to follow suit.

Pope responded angrily to these developments because the Kiowa and Comanche were permitted to hunt while the peaceful Arapaho, who had remained at the agency during hostilities, were starving. He was not surprised that the Arapaho were dissatisfied and feared that they might be forced to depredate to avoid death by starvation. It was a question, he said, of whether they would die of hunger on the reservation or at the hands of soldiers, militia, or citizens off the reservation. There was no doubt, he wrote, that the peaceful Indians should be kept at the agencies and fed sufficiently during the campaign. The friendlies were in a serious condition, he explained, and "in their cases, certainly, keeping the peace has paid badly."

As time passed, the problem intensified. Jonathan Richards of the Wichita Agency was forced to send his Indians on a hunt despite protests by the military; and far to the north in Sioux country, Custer reported that Indians at the Standing Rock Agency had been on half rations for two months and would soon be without any.

Sending hunting parties into the war zone was extremely dangerous, since troops were likely to strike them at any time. There was also the possibility that the hunters might join their hostile comrades. In fact, when the Cheyenne and Arapaho were sent on a hunt west of the agency in January, 1875, they did meet the main group of hostile Cheyenne and camped with them, but only for a time.

As the new year progressed and large groups of hostiles continued to surrender, the problem of feeding them reached crisis proportions. In February, Pope received orders from Washington to cease issuing supplies to Indians who had surrendered as prisoners of war, but he protested that if he did not feed them, they would starve. He could arm them and send them into the war zone, he commented, but he did not think the government desired this. When Stone Calf and the Southern Cheyenne surrendered, Pope pointed out that as prisoners of war humanity demanded they be fed and clothed until the question of their future status was settled.

The question of feeding and caring for the Indians remained a major issue during the time that General Pope commanded the Department of the Missouri. Pope insisted that it was the duty of the Indian Bureau to care for the Indians, but the Bureau was failing in this task as it had failed to enforce the Peace Policy before the outbreak of hostilities in 1874.

Officials of the Interior Department were not pleased with Pope's criticisms. Commissioner Smith complained that Pope gave the wrong impression when he said that the Indians were forced either to starve or be hostile. The blame, Smith said, rested with Congress because sufficient funds had not been appropriated. Congress had, in fact, repeatedly refused to deal with specific problems regarding Indians and Indian policy, but the Interior Department had also failed to meet its responsibilities. The department had made no preparation for the return of peace, and steps that were taken to secure funds to care for the Indians were inadequate.

Conditions at agencies in the Central Superintendency did not improve. In April, Colonel Edward Hatch reported that Indians at Fort Sill complained that they were suffering from hunger. He investigated and found the complaint accurate. He explained that the ration had been established when the Indians were in a position to supplement it by hunting, and no provision for issuing a full ration had been made. There was no flour or sugar, and the beef was "shamefully bad." Beef was issued on the hoof, but the animals often broke down before they had been driven the few miles to the camps. Conditions were abominable at the Wichita Agency where the agent was absent and the Indians were killing their horses for food, and they were little different at Darlington where Agent [John] Miles reported that he had four head of cattle but no sugar, coffee, bacon, tobacco, or salt for over 3,000 Indians.

Pope endorsed Hatch's report and immediately forwarded it

through channels to Washington in an attempt to stir up some action. He did not expect the Indians to stay on the reservation and starve. "So long as this maladministration of affairs with these Indians exists," he wrote, "the military authorities cannot be, and will not consent to be, held accountable for any outbreak which may occur on their part." The Indian Bureau did not permit these charges to pass unchallenged, and Agent Haworth questioned the validity of the report. Despite the fact that the acting agent had told Hatch the only available beef was "unfit for food" but was all he had, Haworth insisted that the Indians had received ample rations and that the beef was of good quality. He admitted that the regular ration was inadequate and that he lacked flour and sugar, but he also said, "at my agency I do not think that there has been any severe suffering."

It was inconceivable to Pope that Indians should be forced to suffer once they had been driven to the reservations, and he feared that starvation would cause a renewal of the war. "Who can blame them," he wrote, "if, rather than starve to death and see their women and children suffering the pangs of hunger and in slow process of starvation, they break away and get food for them in any manner and as soon as they can." When no improvement occurred, he wrote directly to Sherman and urged the War Department to assume the government's obligation to feed the Indians.

Indian agents in the field also reported the lack of supplies and begged for action. In September 1875 the only food available at Darlington was beef, but the Commissioner of Indian Affairs was remarkably unconcerned. The Indians, he said, had no treaty claims on the government for supplies, and what they did receive was "gratuity." Since the Indians were thoroughly humbled, the Commissioner had no fears that they would go on the warpath. The Secretary of the Interior, however, lacked the confidence of the Commissioner and requested that the army give the agents any supplies they could spare. The whole problem led Sherman to propose that "if the military commanders can have control over the supplies needed by these Indians as they now have over their persons, I am convinced by a recent visit that a condition of peace can be maintained."

Pope kept a watch over affairs in Indian Territory, and he was constantly startled and angered by what he discovered. In November 1875 Agent Miles sent his charges on a buffalo hunt and asked the army to supply the Indians with ammunition. "I would be glad to know where and from whom these Indians procured the fire arms. . . ." he told Superintendent Hoag. "Is it the purpose of the Indian Bureau to furnish to these Indians another supply of fire arms to replace those surrendered to the troops, and thus enable them again to commence a war which has only just been brought to a close?" Pope protested vehemently and said that the Indians could kill what buffalo they needed with bows and arrows. If arms and ammunition were furnished by the Indian Bureau, "that Bureau must alone be responsible for the consequences."

Pope's protests that the Indians were suffering produced no results, but the southern tribes managed to avoid starvation by spending the winter months on a hunting expedition although game was scarce. Pope also recognized the fact that failure to feed the Indians delayed their assimilation, for while they were absent on hunts, teachers, missionaries, and farmers could not work with them.

The dangers inherent in this situation became apparent in 1876 when Pope feared that hunger might cause the Southern Cheyenne to join the Sioux. "It is very unfortunate," he wrote to Enoch Hoag's replacement, William Nicholson, "that at this time and in the face of the troubles with the Northern Indians, the Indian Bureau should be unable to buy or otherwise to supply these Southern Indians with food absolutely needed to keep them from starving."

As war swept the northern plains during 1876, Pope was especially concerned with the situation at the Darlington and Fort Sill agencies, for he did not have enough troops to handle emergencies. After the Custer massacre, eighteen companies of cavalry and ten companies of infantry were hurriedly called north, and although Pope was given some artillery companies as replacements, his forces were seriously weakened.

Pope was not the only man to make an issue of the failure to care for the Indians. Although they did not appreciate the tone of his complaints and criticisms, the agents at Darlington and Fort Sill echoed Pope's complaints. They sent their charges out to hunt; they seized cattle by forced sale; and they welcomed supplies received from sympathetic army officers. But their efforts were not enough to prevent hunger.

Supplies of various commodities were either short or missing most of the time, and agents were forced to allow the Indians to leave the reservations to hunt. Hunting parties were often absent for six months at a time, and in November 1877, Agent Miles reported that 3,400 of the 5,000 Indians at Darlington were hunting in the western part of Indian Territory. Game on the southern plains was disappearing so rapidly, however, that the hunters themselves often suffered from hunger. Pope reported that the Cheyenne and Arapaho managed to eke out a bare subsistence during a six-month hunt in 1877, but that on their return the supplies ostensibly for the entire year were barely sufficient to furnish them with half rations for the remaining six months.

Year after year, the agents repeatedly declared that rations were inadequate and begged for a larger appropriation, but Congress refused to provide funds. In 1881 the Kiowa-Comanche agent reported that the yearly appropriation provided supplies for only eight months and that the Indians went hungry for two to three days each week. In 1882 the agent wrote, "There is no doubt that there is actual suffering among these Indians, that they are without anything to eat during a part of each week." The Indian Bureau was forced, however, to issue orders to the Southern Cheyenne, Arapaho, Kiowa, and Comanche agents that the beef ration must be reduced by one-third.

That last order brought Pope into the struggle once more, and he angrily warned Washington, "The Indians cannot live on this amount of beef." Rations were barely sufficient to prevent starvation, and to reduce them further was unthinkable. "Are they expected to suffer the pangs of hunger in the midst of plenty without complaining?" he asked. "Will they refrain from satisfying their absolute needs by levying by force, or otherwise, on the herds around them?" Pope fully expected the Indians to slaughter beef from cattle herds in and around the reservations to provide their families with food, and he requested orders to clarify the duty of the army on this matter. Were the troops "to be used to compel these hungry wretches to submit to hunger and suffering in such a manner and for such reasons?" he asked. Pope's anger was aroused. "I can state with full conviction that I have never known a case in which Indians have been so plainly or so unnecessarily driven to do wrong," he wrote. He had no desire to order his troops to perform the "hateful duty" of forcing the Indians to starve. It was "unreasonable and indefensible," he said, that five thousand peaceful Indians should be driven to hostilities by the lack of food costing such an insignificant sum, and "almost any responsibility ought to be assumed to prevent it."

Pope had a deep and honest concern for the welfare of the Indians, and as no department in Washington seemed willing to assume the responsibility for preventing trouble, he knowingly exceeded his authority to provide a temporary solution. "Indians, like white men, are not reconciled to starve peacefully," he declared, and ordered the post commander at Fort Reno to supplement the rations for the Southern Cheyenne and Arapaho for one week. He also arranged for cattlemen who had large herds in the vicinity of the agency to furnish beef on a weekly basis without guarantee of payment. All Pope could promise was that he would use every influence to see that they were paid. A similar arrangement was made by the Kiowa-Comanche agent, and another crisis passed without depredations and bloodshed.

When Indians were absent from the reservations for long periods of time, the process of assimilation was retarded. In 1876, Agent Haworth had protested, "If Congress fails to furnish the necessary means and the old 'hand to mouth way' has to be continued, no matter how good the management or how faithful and earnest those who work among them may be, they can accomplish but little." Haworth's successor very quickly reached the same conclusion. Some of the Indians had acquired herds of cattle, but when hungry, they slaughtered their cattle to feed their families despite the protests of the agent. He attempted to stop this practice by prohibiting the traders from purchasing any hides which did not have the brand of the Indian Department, but the

Indians were quite ingenious in circumventing this. One tribesman, who learned to read and write while a prisoner in Florida, simply forged the brand.

To keep the Indians, especially tribes with warrior traditions such as the Kiowa and Comanche, on the edge of subsistence was a dangerous practice. There was, however, surprisingly little trouble in the years following the hostilities of 1874 and 1875. The military campaign impressed upon the Indians the power of the government and its determination to keep them on the reservations and punish them for their crimes, but the precautionary measures which Pope took also helped to prevent trouble. He maintained strong garrisons in Indian Territory and constructed new military posts at strategic locations. Fort Reno near the Cheyenne-Arapaho Agency, Fort Elliott in the Texas Panhandle, and a cantonment on the North Fork of the Canadian River did much to control the Indians.

In preparing for any emergencies, Pope also gave orders to his post commanders in Indian Territory to supersede the agents and take any action necessary to prevent an outbreak. His primary desire was to disarm and dismount the Indians, but this he was unable to accomplish because they had to supplement their meager rations by hunting. If the Indians were well fed, they could be disarmed and required to remain near the agency, and thus be in a position for assimilation. The fact that the Indians were forced to hunt, however, kept Pope and his troops constantly on the alert. "No man can tell," he said, "whether they will hunt buffalo or people." Pope did urge the warriors be given muzzle-loading muskets in exchange for their rifles. Muskets were adequate for hunting, and he saw no reason why the Indians should have large quantities of the newest repeating rifles.

Hunger, when added to other causes of discontent, could be serious as the case of the Northern Cheyenne, who had been removed to Indian Territory in 1877, demonstrated. Pope gave orders that the Northern Cheyenne be disarmed and dismounted before they were turned over to the agent at Darlington, but this order was suspended because of promises made to them before they had been sent south. The Northern Cheyenne had many reasons for discontent: short rations, sickness, and the desire to return to their homeland. In September 1878 Dull Knife led about 300 Indians from the reservation and began the long flight to the north. When Pope learned of the escape, he ordered his troops in pursuit. But his department had been stripped of cavalry during the Sioux war in 1876, and infantry units and the few available cavalry troops were unable to prevent their escape.

The Northern Cheyenne who remained in the Indian Territory continued to be troublesome and dissatisfied, constantly threatening that they, also, might attempt to return to the north. Pope, on the one hand, ordered the troops at Fort Reno to seize the warriors at the first hint of flight, but, on the other hand, he also suggested that the government permit them to return home. They disrupted life at the agency and hindered the progress of the other Indians, but the Indian Bureau insisted that they remain at Darlington.

In 1881 this decision was reversed, but only part of the tribe, those under Little Chief, was permitted to move to the Sioux Reservation at Pine Ridge. In 1883 the remainder of the tribe followed, and the disturbing influence of the Northern Cheyenne was finally removed.

Time and again during the 1870s and the early 1880s Pope pondered over the disposition of his troops, studied the Indian problem, and worked for improvement in the government's treatment of the Indian. On the frontier for years, he had watched policies change, suggested numerous reforms that had been disregarded, and still saw no solution. He exhibited a humane attitude and a desire for justice for the Indian, and he earnestly sought to improve their lot and prevent suffering. His primary goal, like that of the humanitarians and the officials in the Indian Bureau, was assimilation, and he offered knowledgeable suggestions as to how this could best be accomplished, but his words made no impact. The Indian Bureau and its humanitarian supporters had made up their minds that the Indians must become farmers and ignored the advice and criticism of the men in the field—like Pope—who offered wiser solutions.

General Pope was an expert on the plains region, having led exploratory and survey parties across the region in the 1850s and having served long years in the West before, during, and after the Civil War. He had always had strong doubts regarding the prospects of agriculture in the dry and barren plains region, and although he watched the settlers surge westward after the Civil War and observed them spreading along the river valleys in Kansas, he still doubted that farming would be successful without water.

At the conclusion of the military campaign of 1875, Pope proposed that the Indians, the Southern Cheyenne in particular, be moved eastward where they could be fed at low cost. He pointed out that the savings in transportation costs alone would enable the government to feed them adequately. Sheridan at first opposed the proposals, but when he understood the relationship of hunger to hostilities, he changed his mind. In 1876 he saw starvation drive many of the reservation Sioux into the hostile camp, and with the conclusion of the Sioux war he fought to have the Sioux reservations located on the Missouri River where transportation costs would be insignificant.

Pope never ceased making suggestions to improve the lot of the Indians, and with his knowledge of the plains and the character of the nomadic Indians, he opposed their conversion into farmers. "These Indians cannot be made self-supporting within any calculable time," he reasoned, "and the sooner that fact is recognized the sooner will the management of them be made to conform to the commonest dictates of humanity." The process of teaching them to support themselves and of preparing them to take their place in white society would be long and difficult, he maintained, and the first step should be to convert them into a pastoral people rather than into farmers.

The Indian tribes, he further explained, were not "precisely alike" and should not be treated as such. "Among tribes so diversely employed we must of course expect to find diversity of life, of habits, and of ideas," he wrote, "and it seems to me essential to any success in civilizing the wild tribes, that a careful study of such matters be made for each tribe, so as best to determine the kind of occupation most suitable, and which would be least at variance with former habits of life." The nomadic plains tribes had a strong warrior tradition, and they were hunters with no interest in agriculture. "It would be (as, indeed it has been found) as difficult to force the nomadic Indians . . . to undergo the daily toil of such plowing and hoeing and reaping as are necessary for the cultivation of a farm," he said, "as it would be to force an Arab or a Tartar to adopt so artificial a mode of life."

Teach them to be stock raisers, he urged, and the first significant step toward assimilation would be accomplished. Those reservations that are unsuited for agriculture could support large herds of animals, and the Indians would soon discover that herding was profitable. In time, he pointed out, they would be able to support themselves, and in so doing would develop an understanding of property ownership which they lacked.

For several years, officials in the Indian Bureau failed to grasp the wisdom of Pope's suggestions, and humanitarian groups in the East never did take cognizance of Pope's experience or heed his advice. The humanitarians were determined to transform warriors who had fought under such great chiefs as Lone Wolf, Stone Calf, Dull Knife, and Red Cloud into peaceful farmers and landowners, and they expected to accomplish this in a few years. The politicians who ran the Interior Department and the Indian Bureau concurred in these views, and for over two decades they fought for legislation which would authorize the allotment of land to individual Indians.

With a notable lack of success, the Indian agents on the reservations did their best to teach the nomadic tribes to become farmers. As time passed, they agreed with Pope. James Haworth, for example, commented in his 1877 annual report, "Five years' experience and observation satisfy me that this is not a good agricultural district, and cannot be relied upon for farming. . . ." As drought and crop failures followed year after year and the Indians who tried their hand at farming gave up in disgust, Haworth's successors and the agents at Darlington echoed his views. "The Indians, as also myself," reported John Miles in 1881, "have become completely discouraged in their efforts to obtain a living from the cultivation of the soil." A year earlier the Kiowa-Comanche agent had remarked that he was convinced that even experienced farmers would have been discouraged after the past three seasons.

The problem was not limited to the agencies in Indian Territory, but was common to all the reservations on the semi-arid high plains. Explorers labeled the Great Plains the "Great American Desert," and after years of repeated crop failures it is probable that most of the agents in the region would have agreed. The outspoken agent at Pine Ridge, V. T. McGillycuddy, had some hard words to say about farming on the high plains. "White men well trained in farming have tried to till the soil in this vicinity in Northern Nebraska and have lost all the money invested, and have not produced enough to pay for the seed. I can confidently venture to state that, if the experiment were tried of placing 7,000 white people on this land, with seed, agricultural implements, and one year's subsistence, at the end of that time they would die of starvation, if they had to depend on their crops for their sustenance."

Pope's ideas on how best to teach the Indians to be self-supporting and how to prepare them for assimilation were not heeded despite similar recommendations from the Indian agents in the field, but the termination of hostilities on the southern plains in 1875 presented Pope with an opportunity to test his theory on a small scale. During the campaign and with the surrender of the hostiles, the army confiscated large numbers of the Indians' ponies. Some were given to Indian scouts who served with the troops; some were returned to their owners, and some were sold at auction. Since the ponies did not sell at their true value, the income from these sales did not amount to much, but the use which Pope made of this money was significant. Some of the funds were used to purchase supplies for the Indians while they were held by the army as prisoners of war, and he turned some over to the U. S. Treasury Department. At the Kiowa-Comanche Agency, however, Pope and [Colonel Ronald S.] Mackenzie also put some of the money to yet another use. About 10,000 animals taken from the hostile bands of the Kiowa and Comanche had brought in about $29,000, and approximately $3,500 of that sum was turned over to the Treasury Department. The remainder, $25,500, was used to purchase livestock for the two tribes.

Mackenzie, who had come under Pope's command with the

addition of Fort Sill to the Department of the Missouri, purchased several thousand sheep in New Mexico Territory and distributed them to the Indians in 1875. This experiment was disastrous because the warriors discovered they did not like mutton and the women had no inclination to become weavers. In the following year Mackenzie purchased cattle rather than sheep, and the Indians willingly began to care for their livestock. The experiment was a remarkable success. Agent Haworth praised the army for its work and, noting the "peculiar fitness of the Indians for stock-raising," secured even more cattle for the tribal herd. Although the army made a start in teaching the Indians to become stockmen, it was on a small scale. Despite the desire of the agents to expand the herd, little was done to purchase a sufficient number of cattle to prevent the warriors from having to slaughter their animals in time of need. The agents attempted to impress upon them the value of maintaining their herds, but when hungry women and children cried, the Indians thought only of feeding their families.

When Pope left the Department of the Missouri to command the more prestigious Division of the Pacific in 1883, the condition of the Indians had improved little. During the thirteen years which Pope served in the Department of the Missouri, he waged a continuous battle with the Indian Bureau over the treatment of the Indians. In the early years of the 1870s Pope sought to make the Indians uncomfortable when they were absent from the reservations and to have them punished for their crimes. At the conclusion of hostilities in 1875 he struggled to make them comfortable when they were on the reservations. He begged and borrowed to provide them with food, and he spent nine years writing letters of criticism and suggestions.

Originally published in slightly different form in the *Southwestern Historical Quarterly* 72 (October 1968). Reprinted from chapter 10, "The Old 'Hand to Mouth Way,'" of *General Pope and U.S. Indian Policy* (Albuquerque: University of New Mexico Press, 1970), pp. 196-211. Bracketed insertions added. All footnotes omitted.

"A Better Way": General George Crook and the Ponca Indians

JAMES T. KING

Early in May, 1879, Judge Elmer S. Dundy, United States District Judge for Nebraska, handed down a decision which was hailed at the time—albeit somewhat optimistically—as a revolution in the treatment of the Indian by the white man. The case was popularly known as "Standing Bear vs. Crook," and involved General George Crook, commander of the military Department of the Platte at Omaha, and Standing Bear, a ranking chief of the Ponca tribe. Dundy's decision stated that Crook had illegally arrested and confined Standing Bear and a small group of Ponca Indians, and that the General was therefore ordered by the court to release the Indians from custody.

On the face of it, the affair seems to coincide quite well with popular notions about the role of the Army in the West. According to the theme hallowed by generations of writers of novels, movie scenarios and television plots, "Standing Bear vs. Crook" should have been simply another example of the Army's brutal and relentless attempts to exterminate the Indian. If the scenario writer were to continue the story, Crook and his blue-coated henchmen would presumably slink back to their fort to plot the next assault on the Indians. Even reputable historians help to perpetuate the hoary legends. One, for example, has recently written of "frontier army commanders like Generals Crook and Custer [who] had frankly followed a 'surrender-or-be-slaughtered' policy."

In fact, however, the old stereotype simply is not true. The regular Army officer in the West often found himself sympathizing with the Indian rather than with the government, and there were few officers indeed who could support a "surrender-or-be-slaughtered" policy as a key to peace in the West. Although the occasions on which a soldier might be able to translate his sympathies into action were rare, when such occasions did arise, the results could be startling. "Standing Bear vs. Crook" is a case in point. George Crook was one officer who was both able and willing to take advantage of such a situation, and the results in this instance had both immediate and long range significance. Far from playing the "heavy" in this drama, General Crook not only sympathized with Standing Bear, but evidently was instrumental in arranging the case against himself. Furthermore, once the trial was over, Crook gave active and continuing support to civilian efforts to rectify the injustices suffered by the Ponca.

At the time of the Ponca dispute, George Crook was already one of the best-known soldiers of his day. His acquaintance with the frontier had begun almost immediately upon his graduation from West Point in 1852, when he joined his regiment in California. There he participated in most of the Pacific Coast Indian wars of the 1850's. Upon leaving the frontier for service in the Civil War, he carried with him the conviction, born of his experiences, that the Indian was more often sinned against than sinning. He rose to the rank of major general in the volunteers during the Civil War, and in 1866 he re-entered the regular Army as a lieutenant colonel of infantry with a brevet commission of major general. His service on the frontier resumed at once, and he was sent first to the Pacific northwest to engage in campaigns in Idaho, Oregon, and California. Then, in 1871, he was given command of the Department of Arizona, where he earned a brigadier general's star by putting down the Apache uprising with an effective combination of firmness and justice. By the time of his appointment in 1875 to command the Department of the Platte, the General had already become fond of asserting—and with some justification—that he had "had as much experience in the management of Indian affairs as any man in the country," and his official reports had already become his forum for urging a humane and enlightened Federal Indian policy.

Previous to his coming to Omaha, Crook's ideas on Indian policy were restricted almost entirely to his official reports. As late as 1871 he had written to his close friend Rutherford B. Hayes that—although he had "expressed myself officially to the War Department" in opposition to aspects of government policy —he felt it would be an "impropriety" for him to take a public stand. After having taken command of the Department of the Platte, Crook evidently came to the conclusion that his official reports were doing little good. In 1878 he spoke out openly against injustices which had driven the Bannock and Shoshone to rebellion. Early in 1879, after the affair at Fort Robinson which claimed the lives of a number of Cheyenne, Crook publicly took the side of the Indians against the government. In his earlier years of service, Crook had had little to do with civilian reformers who wished to "uplift" and civilize the Indians, and he tended to regard them all as meddlesome, impractical visionaries. Yet in 1879 there developed a situation which not only would bring Crook again openly into conflict with government policies, but also would bring him into alliance with the very group of reformers whom he had so long mistrusted.

The matter at issue was the plight of the Ponca tribe. Two years previously the government had moved the quiet, friendly Ponca tribe from their Niobrara River reservation on the Nebraska-Dakota border to a new reservation in the Indian Territory (present Oklahoma). The action was necessary, Secretary of the Interior Carl Schurz later explained, because the Ponca reservation had been given over to their ancient enemies, the Sioux, and the former residents had to be moved for their own protection—this despite the facts that the Ponca owned their land in fee simple, that the Sioux did not want the reservation, and that the two tribes had recently exchanged pledges of friendship. The following year was one of unrelieved misery for the Ponca tribe. The combination of the hard overland journey, the sudden change of climate, a lack of shelter and inadequate food took a heavy toll of human life; of the original 700 Ponca Indians who had started from Nebraska, 158 were dead within twelve months of their departure. The tribesmen had been forced to leave their homes, their farms, and their agricultural implements behind, and —as Judge Dundy later put it—found themselves suddenly in a "country in which they can see little but new made graves opening for their reception."

At last, early in 1879, Standing Bear and about thirty of his people left the new reservation and made their way back to Decatur, Nebraska. There they were welcomed by their old neighbors, the Omaha, and given shelter and provisions. As soon as the arrival of Standing Bear's party was confirmed, Secretary Schurz notified the War Department that the Ponca had left Indian Territory "without permission," and requested that "the nearest military commander be instructed to detail a sufficient guard to return these Poncas to the Agency where they belong."

"The nearest military commander" was General George Crook. The General sent a detachment of troops to arrest the Ponca, and the Indians were placed in detainment at Fort Omaha on March 27. The post commander, Colonel John H. King, reported that serious illness among the Ponca and the weakness of their horses would make it impossible for the Indians to return to Indian Territory at once. It is barely possible that the delay may have been more Crook's idea than King's. Whatever the case, that delay provided time for several important developments.

The first development was the establishment of contact between Crook and the assistant editor of the Omaha *Herald*, Thomas H. Tibbles. Crook had been acquainted with Tibbles for at least a year, or perhaps longer. It was the *Herald*, in fact, which had provided the place for Crook's early ventures into public pronouncements on federal Indian policy, and it was Tibbles who rendered the General's ideas into the form of a personal interview. Now, in a way which still is not entirely clear, Crook again entered into an alliance with Tibbles.

The two men were a study in contrasts. Crook was dour and withdrawn, reticent to the point of severity. Tibbles was effusive, bombastic, and loquacious. Crook had spent his entire adult life in one profession, the military. Tibbles, by his own testimony, had "a strange history." He described himself as a man who "had been born on the frontier, never had had any raising, and did not pretend to be civilized." He was a thorough newspaper man, and had held positions as an editorial writer on several leading papers. He had the medical, legal, theological, turf, stage, and musical terms at his "tongue's end." He had "commenced life," he related, "by enlisting in Jim Lane's company in Kansas in 1856," and—often in company with John Brown—had participated in "every prominent fight" in the Kansas civil war. He had been a preacher, a Pullman-car conductor, and had lived with the Indians as a member of the Soldier Lodge. Now, after years of wandering, he had arrived at Omaha as editorial writer for the *Herald*.

There is some question about the way in which Tibbles was told of the Ponca difficulties. In an account written in 1880,

Tibbles speaks rather vaguely about an unidentified city editor who came into the *Herald* office late one evening to report Crook's arrest of the Ponca. Many years later, however, after Crook's death, Tibbles was much more specific. It was not a newspaperman at all, he asserted in 1905, but Crook himself who had borne the story of the Ponca troubles. Moreover, Tibbles related, Crook had appealed to him for help, and the newspaperman now presented their conversation in detail.

"During twenty-five or thirty years that I've been on the plains in the government service," Crook is supposed to have said, "I've been forced many times by orders from Washington to do most inhuman things in dealing with the Indians, but now I'm ordered to do a more cruel thing than ever before." Tibbles quotes the General as stating that "I would resign my commission," if that would keep the order from being carried out, but that he knew it would not. He would appeal to Washington, except that Washington "always orders the very opposite of what I recommend." Therefore, he had come to see whether Tibbles, as an editor of "a great daily newspaper," would take up the matter.

Tibbles would appear to have no reason to fabricate this story, and although the words may be Tibbles', the sentiments are certainly characteristic of Crook. If the sense of the story is accurate, as it very possibly is, the two men confirmed their alliance after hours of discussion in the editorial offices of the *Herald*. No doubt taking some dramatic license to give the conversation its proper Victorian heroics, Tibbles has himself say that, once in the fight, "I should never give up till I won or died." Crook is made to reply, just as heroically, "If we can do something for which good men can remember us when we're gone, that's the best legacy we can leave. I promise you that if you'll take up this work, I'll stand by you." Whoever the participants and whatever the nature of the conversation that night, Tibbles did take up the cause, and Crook staunchly stood by him. A quarter of a century later, Tibbles could write that "at long last the outcome of General Crook's appeal to me was that our government reversed its hundred-year-old policy towards a whole race of people."

The next day, March 31, 1879, brought a second important development in the Ponca situation. General Crook, accompanied by his staff and several other officers, formally interviewed Standing Bear and several of his tribesmen. The only civilian white man present was "Mr. Tibbles of the 'Omaha Herald.'" Although the other Ponca Indians wore ordinary white men's clothing, Standing Bear had arrayed himself for the occasion in the full dress of a Ponca chieftain. Captain John G. Bourke, the General's aide-de-camp, was impressed by "this noble looking Indian, tall and commanding in presence, dignified in manner and very elegantly dressed."

Invited by the General to speak, Standing Bear recounted the unhappy story of the Ponca's enforced removal. His speech was almost a model of Indian eloquence. They had built their farms on the Niobrara, the chief said, and had hoped to adopt the white man's ways. But, Standing Bear related, "then some power took hold of me, as by the arm, and made me stand up and told us to go south. They took us to a very bad place." He told of the illness which had ravaged the tribe like "some unseen force" which "came down upon us and crushed us to the earth." The chief then made a moving appeal to all who were present. "My brothers," he said, "it seems to me as if I stood in front of a great prairie fire. I would take up my babies and run to save their lives; or as if I stood on the bank of an overflowing river, and I would take my people and move to higher ground. Oh! my brothers, the Almighty looks down on me, and knows what I am, and hears my words. May the Almighty send a good spirit to brood over you, my brothers, to move you to help me."

Standing Bear's oratory had its desired effect; the audience was deeply moved. Crook remarked quietly that "I have heard all this story before. It is just as they represent it. It has long since all been reported to Washington." But the General took the only position he officially could. He had a direct order and he would have to obey it: "It is," he said, "a very disagreeable duty." He assured the Indians, however, that they could stay a few more days until they were better able to travel. Captain Bourke was as unhappy as the General, but his reactions were less restrained. This affair, he wrote in his diary, was an example of "the cruel and senseless way in which [the] Government of the United States deals with the Indian tribes who confide in its justice or trust themselves to its mercy," and he observed bitterly that "our Government's good intentions are always in the inverse ratio of its power [over the Indians], as we become stronger we become more and more indifferent to our obligations."

While Crook watched over the Ponca at Fort Omaha, Tibbles was working feverishly. He telegraphed the story of the interview to eastern newspapers and wrote a heated editorial for the *Herald*. He quickly enlisted the support of the ministers of leading churches in Omaha, and they in turn sent a telegram to Secretary Schurz imploring that the removal order be reversed. Tibbles then roughed out a court case based in the Fourteenth Amendment and took it to his friend John L. Webster, a young lawyer, and to A. J. Poppleton, the chief attorney of the Union Pacific Railroad, both of whom agreed to handle the case without a fee. The three of them then drew up a writ of *habeas corpus*. Judge Dundy was contacted and he agreed to hear the case at Lincoln. According to Tibbles, Crook was well aware of all this activity and was "the most anxious person I ever saw to have a writ served on him." On April 8 the writ was served and, for the time being, the Ponca were safe. They could stay at Fort Omaha until the disposition of their case.

On April 30, 1879, Judge Dundy's gavel signalled the opening of the case of the *United States ex rel. Standing Bear vs. Crook*. The trial lasted two days, and since it had attracted national attention, Tibbles was careful to contribute his share in making all the details available to the American public. Crook, who habitually wore civilian clothing, made one of his rare appearances in the dress uniform of a brigadier general, and he headed an equally glittering military delegation. Chief Standing Bear appeared once again in his tribal regalia. The government's case was simply that an Indian was neither a person nor a citizen within the meaning of the law, and therefore could bring no suit of any kind against the government.

The case for the Ponca stated that, first, in time of peace there is no existing authority for transporting Indians from one place to another without their consent, nor is there authority to arrest or confine Indians for the purpose of moving them; and, second, that the Indian is indeed a person within the meaning of the *habeas corpus* act, and when it can be shown that he is deprived of a liberty, which is "a natural, inherent and inalienable right," then he is entitled to sue out a writ of *habeas corpus* in the federal courts.

The trial hit a slight snag when Crook found that the government had inserted over his signature a statement to the effect that the Ponca had not been leading a civilized life, that they had violated the law by going to the Omaha reservation, and that they were not being restrained illegally. Crook protested formally through the Judge Advocate of the Department of the Platte, Major Horace B. Burnham, that the government's case did not require that he sign a statement which he believed to be untrue. Dundy tried to explain that as commanding general Crook was signing it, not personally, but as a government official. Despite the General's continued protest, the court placed the offending paragraph in the body of the return, and the trial proceeded.

Whatever the merits of the case presented by Poppleton and Webster, it is likely that Standing Bear himself had considerable influence on the outcome of the trial. After both cases had been presented, Judge Dundy permitted the chief to address the court in his own behalf. If anything, Standing Bear was more eloquent than he had been at Fort Omaha. The chief rose slowly, extended his hand and, after several long moments, looked up at Judge Dundy. "That hand is not the color of yours," he said, "but if I pierce it, I shall feel pain. If you pierce your hand, you also feel pain. The blood that will flow from mine will be of the same colour as yours. I am a man. The same God made us both." Then, in a narrative heavily laden with allegory, he described himself as facing a rushing, rising river, with apparently impassable, perpendicular cliffs behind him. Then he finds a path to safety. "But," Standing Bear concluded, "a man bars the passage. . . . If he says that I cannot pass, I cannot. The long struggle would have been in vain. My wife and child and I must return and sink beneath the flood. We are weak and faint and sick. I cannot fight." The chief's head was bowed. Then he looked up at Judge Dundy. "You are that man."

According to Tibbles, "there was silence in the court as the chief sat down. Tears ran down the judge's face. General Crook leaned forward and covered his face with his hands. Some of the ladies sobbed." Suddenly the silence was broken by cheers and the crowd rushed forward. Crook was the first to grasp Standing Bear's hand. Tibbles was the second.

Several days later, Dundy rendered his decision. "I have never been called upon," the judge stated in his preliminary remarks, "to hear or decide a case that appealed so strongly to my sympathy as the one now under consideration." It was to General Crook's everlasting credit, Dundy believed, that "he has no sort of sympathy in the business in which he is forced by his position to bear a part so conspicuous." In his decision Dundy maintained that if the Indian must obey the laws of the land, then he must also be afforded the protection which those laws provide; that the term "person" in legal terms was meant to exclude no one, whether citizen or foreigner, Indian or Caucasian; and that the *habeas corpus* suit was valid, the Ponca were being illegally detained, and they must be freed.

For the first time the right of the Interior Department to do whatever it would do with the person of an Indian had been challenged, and the challenge had been successful. However pleased the Ponca may have been to know that they were now "persons" in the eyes of the law, they were still left without their homes in the north. The next step, therefore, was to restore to them their ancestral lands on the Niobrara.

Tibbles writes that "General Crook, Mr. Webster and I talked long and often about which move to make next." It was decided that Tibbles would resign his position at the *Herald* and lead a national campaign in behalf of the Ponca. In June, 1879, he left Omaha for the east. He carried with him many documents—the transcript of the trial, endorsements by prominent clergymen and a letter from the Governor of Nebraska, for example—but perhaps one of the most significant was a long letter from George Crook.

The letter is important for several reasons. First of all, it provided Tibbles with some potent ammunition in his war with the Department of the Interior. Tibbles quoted portions of it in his speeches and in his book *The Ponca Chiefs,* and it was featured prominently in its entirety in the national press. The letter is also the first of what would be many similar letters to persons in the Indian Rights movement, and it both summarized his thought and experiences to that time and suggested his future course of action.

Crook's statement was clearly designed for publicity purposes. Formal in tone, it ranged widely over the entire question of United States Indian policy and its shortcomings. Like other Nineteenth Century reformers, Crook was convinced that the Indian's best hope—indeed, with the disappearance of game animals, his only hope—lay in settling down to a peaceful agricultural existence, with the expectation that he soon would be absorbed into mainstream of American life. "The leading chiefs," Crook wrote to Tibbles,

> thoroughly understand the changed condition of affairs;—they see that they can no longer depend upon game for their support, and are anxious to obtain cattle, seeds and implements and to have their children educated. They see the necessity of adopting the white man's ways and of conforming to the established order of things. But, I am sorry to say, they have, to a very great degree, lost confidence in our people and their promises. Indians are very much like white men in being unable to live upon air.

Crook believed that a fundamental problem was the Indian's lack of protection either in life or property. "Keep white thieves from plundering him," Crook wrote, "let him see that *Peace* means *Progress;* that he has a market for every pound of beef, every hide and every sack of grain, and, my word for it, he will make rapid advances." Although Crook acknowledged the good work of "conscientious, able men" already being done, he believed that some kind of systematic national effort was necessary. "Between the advocates of the theory that an Indian is incapable of good," he wrote, "and the supporters of the antipodal idea that he will never do wrong, the red man is in danger of annihilation;—of starving to death in the centre of a country which is feeding the world with its exuberant harvests, or being killed for trying to defend rights which the Negro or Mongolian are allowed to enjoy." This, then, would become the core of Crook's theory of Indian management—the protection of the Indian's human rights as he developed into an agrarian capitalist and earned his place in the American democratic system. These ideas were more closely defined and put into broad practice several years later when Crook returned to his old command in the Department of Arizona. And it was these same ideas which helped to bring him into his famous conflict with General Philip H. Sheridan, resulting in his resignation from the Department of Arizona and return to the Department of the Platte.

Upon arriving in the East in the summer of 1879, Tibbles had thrown himself eagerly into his campaign in behalf of the Ponca. He had been joined by Standing Bear and by an attractive, well-educated Indian girl, Susette La Flesche. Susette was better known by her Indian name, Bright Eyes, and soon would become Mrs. Thomas H. Tibbles. The eloquence of Standing Bear, the beauty and intelligence of Bright Eyes, and the enthusiasm of Tibbles proved to be an electric combination. The trio gained the hearty support of such humanitarians as Helen Hunt Jackson, Henry Wadsworth Longfellow, and Boston's Mayor Frederick O. Prince. Tibbles succeeded in obtaining money, sympathy and a pledge from the Department of the Interior that the Ponca were welcome to their old reservation if they wanted it. He did not succeed, however, in his hope to have Standing Bear vs. Crook carried to the Supreme Court. Fearful of a ruling which might remove his control over any Indian who might leave a reservation, Schurz halted appeal proceedings, and there was no longer anything for the Supreme Court to consider.

Towards the end of 1880, the Ponca question grew more heated and less illuminating. Secretary Schurz steadfastly refused to accept responsibility for what he admitted was an unjust situation, and he attempted to shift the blame to others, who promptly shifted it back. President Hayes, convinced that "a great and grievous wrong has been done to the Poncas," decided to establish a commission which could thoroughly examine the situation. Perhaps it was simply chance that General Crook was in Washington in December, 1880, and that he had visited with his friend the President. In any event, the day after that visit Crook was appointed to the Ponca Commission. "My only wish in the affair," the President wrote, "is that the investigation may be thorough and fair, to the end that complete justice may be done to the Poncas for the wrongs they have suffered, preferring rather to go beyond than to fall behind full redress."

Crook was joined on the Commission by General Nelson A. Miles, by William Stickney of the Board of Indian Commissioners, and by Walter Allen of Boston. By any evaluation the investigation fulfilled the President's wish that it be "thorough and fair." The Commission began its hearings in Washington, then took testimony at the new Ponca reservation in Indian Territory, and ended its investigation by interviewing the Ponca in Nebraska. The Commissioners reported to the President their belief that the removal of the Ponca "was not only most unfortunate for the Indians, resulting in great hardships and serious loss of life and property, but was injudicious and without sufficient cause." To the Commission's surprise, however, the southern tribesmen had decided to remain in Indian Territory. The Secretary of the Interior in recent months had sincerely been trying to make amends, and he had expedited the construction of homes and barns for the southern Ponca. The improved conditions may have contributed to the willingness of the southern Ponca to remain on the new reservation; the Commission suspected that it was due rather to their despair of ever regaining their rights in the north.

But the Ponca in Nebraska, the Commission reported, "pray that they may not again be disturbed." Therefore, both groups of Ponca should be permitted to remain where they were, a cash indemnification should be made for the hardships they had suffered, and "prompt action" should be taken to provide for schooling, agricultural implements, stock, and seed. On March 3, 1881, Congress fulfilled the Commission's recommendations with an appropriation of $165,000. The case of the Ponca was closed. Its significance, however, lay far beyond the limits of that small tribe. One historian has suggested that "as a direct outgrowth of the enthusiasm aroused" by the Ponca controversy, "the Boston philantropists continued to work for the betterment of the Indians; the Board of Indian Commissioners received new vigor, and earnest men and women organized the Indian Rights Association."

Originally published in *Nebraska History* 50 (Autumn 1969): 239–54. All footnotes omitted.

Pacification of the Southwest

When the United States won the Southwest from Mexico in 1846, General Stephen Watts Kearny promised the inhabitants that their lives and property would be protected from marauding Indians. Neither Spain nor Mexico had been able to provide peace and security, however, and Kearny failed also. In succeeding years federal policy in the Southwest was inconsistent and included a combination of military expeditions and negotiations. Between 1854 and 1861, for example, the army undertook a dozen major offensives against Apaches, Navajos, and Utes but without notable success. During the Civil War, General James Carleton sent Colonel Kit Carson against the Navajos and Apaches, and although the roundup of the Navajos in 1864 and their temporary incarceration at the Bosque Rendondo, a reservation in the Pecos Valley, brought peace with that tribe, the Apaches remained unconquered.

In the eyes of the Western Apaches of Arizona and southwestern New Mexico, the whites were the aggressors. In 1861 United States troops seized Cochise of the Chiricahuas for a crime he did not commit and killed several warriors after the chief escaped. Two years later soldiers murdered Mangas Coloradas of the Warm Springs band after he had surrendered. Anglo migration into New Mexico and Arizona after the Civil War also caused friction and contributed to sporadic warfare. Hostilities were highlighted by the Camp Grant massacre of 1871 when citizens of Tucson took matters into their own hands and slaughtered peaceful Apaches living under military surveillance at Camp Grant and enslaved many of the children.

The government attempted to construct a just and workable Indian policy for the Southwest but failed on both counts. Vincent Colyer of the Board of Indian Commissioners and General Oliver Otis Howard, Civil War veteran and head of the Freedman's Bureau, were sent with extraordinary powers to treat with the Apaches in 1871 and 1872 respectively. Both men were sympathetic to the Indians—too much so, thought many frontiersmen. New Mexicans ridiculed Colyer as "that old philanthropic humbug" and expressed the wish that he had never come to the territory. Howard, despite his military background, had become known as the "Christian Soldier" because of his humanitarian work with the less fortunate segments of American society. Neither Colyer nor Howard was able to restore permanent peace, however, and General George Crook was ordered to punish the hostiles.

Armed with a sound knowledge of the Indians and their methods of warfare, Crook conducted a whirlwind campaign, coaxing or forcing the Apaches to their reservations. He restored peace to Arizona, but he was transferred to the Department of the Platte in 1875 and conditions deteriorated rapidly in his absence. When the bewhiskered general returned to Arizona in 1882, he again resorted to a mixture of firmness and conciliation. He did his best to eliminate the causes for discontent, encouraged the economic endeavors of the Apaches by purchasing their products, and used every power available to force hostile groups to surrender.

Ralph Ogle describes Crook's policies and explains the conflict between the army and the Indian Bureau that existed in Arizona as well as in most other areas of the West. Despite his considerable abilities, Crook was not fully successful, and the last portion of his service in Arizona was devoted to the pursuit of Geronimo, who finally surrendered to General Nelson Miles in 1886.

The End of Apache Resistance

RALPH H. OGLE

General Sherman's inspection of the Apache country in April, 1882, resulted in his making suggestions for a general military reorganization of the troubled area. A new Department of the Border to embrace Arizona and New Mexico was proposed, but the plan was dropped when General Crook was reassigned to the Department of Arizona.

Crook arrived from the Department of the Platte on September 4, 1882, and began his work of peace at once, for he saw that the Indians were demoralized almost to the point of desperation. Made sullen and distrustful by enigmatical officials, malicious rumors of attack, intrusions on their lands, disarmament and removal plans, they were more than disposed to think the warpath the solution to their evils. Crook brought all his old tact into play. In a series of extended and enlightening powwows near Fort Apache, he convinced the disaffected leaders that war was just what their enemies desired and that peace was the tribe's only salvation. He convinced them of the wisdom there was in the reestablishment of his former system of strict discipline with its careful censuses and frequent roll calls in which every warrior could be identified by the metal tag he wore. They also accepted his plan for a reorganization of the reserve policy whereby native scouts under the command of Captain Emmet Crawford and Lieutenant Charles B. Gatewood were to be scattered among their own bands to observe and report upon affairs. Perhaps a greater step towards peace was his promise that the mountain bands would be returned from the arid Gila Valley to their old home near Fort Apache.

Crook reissued his general orders no. 13 of April 8, 1873, and thus indicated that his original Apache policies would prevail again. But his issuance of supplemental orders, in which "justice to all," "strictest fidelity," "no division of responsibility" and "strict accountability" were emphasized, indicated that a humanitarian policy was to prevail to even a greater degree than before.

Prospects for a speedy success were greatly heightened when

the new San Carlos agent, P. P. Wilcox of Denver, evinced a friendly attitude of cooperation. He quickly fell in with Crook's plan for a military policing of the reservation, abolished the subagency at the general's request, and permitted nearly seven hundred Coyoteros to return to the Fort Apache region where, under the exclusive control of the military, they were to live on a self-supporting basis. His progress in instituting reforms was slow, however, for the supplies that poured in to fill contracts left by former Agent [J. C.] Tiffany were as worthless as those that already filled the warehouses. Besides, he found it almost impossible to get competent employees to replace the unscrupulous henchmen of his predecessor. In an effort to stamp out the graft and illicit liquor traffic which seemed to emanate from the agency store, he discharged the Tiffany holdovers and appointed his son-in-law to the lucrative post. This action, he felt, would insure honesty in all Indian trading.

The magnitude of the agent's task should have produced complete cooperation; instead, violent antagonism soon arose when Crook in an effort to insure regular daily counts moved several pacific bands back to the agency. Thus irked, Wilcox enlisted the aid of the Indian Office, put pressure on Crook, and over Sherman's strong opposition, succeeded in stopping the counts. This early rift was a dangerous one, however, for the agent was already exerting himself to keep rations at a minimum; nevertheless, cold weather during the winter and Captain Crawford's efficient policing kept the Indians quiet. In fact, a total saving of ten per cent in rations was effected.

Amenable as the reservation Indians proved to be, neither Wilcox nor Crook lost sight of the fact that the Chiricahuas remained unreduced in Mexico. Both men were confident that no permanent program of control could be successfully carried out unless these irreconcilables were brought to the reservation. Accordingly, Crook attempted to open communication with them in October, 1882. When his efforts came to naught he became more convinced than ever that devastations might be expected at any time. Again he prepared for war. His troops and pack-trains were reorganized, the reserve Indians were enlisted in a program to bring in the Chiricahuas, and Captain Crawford with his Apache scouts was sent to the border to establish a patrol and to engage in spy activity.

Nothing happened for several months although Crawford's spies found that the hostiles had penetrated more deeply into the Sierra Madre Mountains than had been supposed. Finally in March, 1883, just at the time the Mexicans started operations, the Chiricahuas left their stronghold in two bodies—the one under Gerónimo to raid in Sonora and capture stock, the other under Chatto to raid in Arizona and secure ammunition. Chatto, with twenty-six warriors, crossed the border on March 21, and scattered into small parties difficult to trace. Confirming Crook's view that they were "the worst band of Indians in America," the hostiles while losing only one man, raided for six days in Arizona, killed twenty-six persons, traveled over 400 miles and without being seen by any of the commands dispatched to intercept them escaped back into Mexico.

General Crook, meanwhile, received instructions from Sherman authorizing him to destroy the hostiles even if it were necessary to disregard departmental or national lines. Thus encouraged, he completed arrangements for an expeditionary force to penetrate into Mexico after the hostiles. He next secured the promise of cooperation from General Mackenzie of New Mexico, and then he visited the civil and military authorities of Sonora and Chihuahua who cordially assured him of every possible aid. All details completed he left the border at San Bernardino Springs on May 1 with a small force of men and officers and a command of 193 Apache scouts under Crawford and Gatewood, equipped to stay in the field for sixty days.

Rapid progress was made across a ravished and depopulated region to the south, but the necessity of night marches in the area bordering the Sierra Madre greatly discouraged the scouts. Fortunately, the discovery of an abundance of hostile "sign" fully restored their energy and confidence. The terrain—ideally suited as a place of refuge—now became the roughest imaginable. Ten mules that slipped from the precipitous trail were crushed to a pulp in the deep canyons below. But after several days of such travel the enemy stronghold in the Sierra Madre was reached. The hostiles, however, were not there, although the indications were strong that they were not far away. The pack train was therefore left in the fortress while the scouts under Crawford were sent on to scour the region. Three days later the camps of Chatto and Bonito were discovered, but a premature attack provoked by some chance gunfire allowed the main body of the hostiles to escape.

To pursue the fugitives in that rough country was as impossible as it was futile. Crook had two alternatives. He might either accept their proffered surrender on the best terms he could secure or retire from the country and wait till he could surprise them again. The idea of peace prevailed, and as soon as Gerónimo, Chatto, Bonito, Loco and Nachee could be brought together, a lengthy powwow followed in which it was agreed that all past offenses were to be forgotten and the hostiles were to return to the reservation. Gerónimo promised that if the troops moved slowly he would round up his straggling warriors and overtake the procession at the border. But this he failed to do, and when Captain Crawford reached San Carlos on June 23 with fifty-two men and 273 women, the only prominent chiefs in the group were Nana, Loco and Bonito.

Gerónimo in the meantime decided that he would not be able to command a position of respect at San Carlos unless he had gifts to present to his old friends, so he spent the next several months in Mexico, satiating his thirst for blood and plunder. Finally, during the first few days of March, 1884, he arrived at the border with over eighty followers and a herd of 350 cattle. Demanding the protection of a military escort, he was conducted back to the reservation to the intense disgust of the civil officers and the settlers.

All through the winter and spring preceding the expedition into Mexico, Agent Wilcox and General Crook had given each other reasonable support. Crook especially supported Wilcox against the henchmen of former Agent Tiffany, who in their efforts to expropriate the reserve mineral land and control the Indian trade had carried their fight to President Chester A. Arthur. Wilcox apparently approved Crook's program, but when the Chiricahuas surrendered he concluded that their return to the reservation would undo all the success that had been achieved with the peaceable Apache bands. His arguments won the support of Secretary [of the Interior] Henry M. Teller, and Secretary [of

War Robert T.] Lincoln was informed that, since the Department of the Interior would not agree to the incorporation of the hostiles with the peaceable Apaches, the War Department would have to hold them apart as prisoners of war. Crook remonstrated that any perfidious act on the part of the government would destroy all chances of ever controlling the Chiricahuas by a program of peace, but that if he were allowed to manage them in his own way, he was confident of a permanent peace. The result of the matter was that Secretary Lincoln ordered Crook to Washington for a conference.

The two departments moved quickly, and on July 7, 1883, the entire police control of the reservation was vested in the War Department. The Chiricahuas were to be kept and cared for by General Crook according to his discretion, but they were to be kept at the agency only with the agent's consent. The War Department was also to keep peace, administer justice and punish Indian offenders; otherwise the duties of the agent were to remain unchanged. Within a short time Captain Crawford was officially charged with the execution of the military's part of the new agreement.

Three years before, in 1880, Secretary Schurz had noted two widely urged and antagonistic solutions to the Indian problem. The first, held mainly by distant philanthropists, urged the almost immediate canonization of the noble red man. The opposing view, most frequently found in the Indian country, favored keeping the Indians in a state of barbarism for the purpose of accelerating their extinction. To the secretary a more moderate solution was possible. It consisted in preparing the Indian for ultimate citizenship through the ownership of land in severalty, the encouragement of agriculture and stockraising, the use of Indian police and the general dissemination of education.

The plan followed by General Crook closely resembled the middle-ground policy outlined by Schurz although it had some original features, part of which might be looked upon as idealistic or visionary. The general began with the assumption that just treatment and a paternal attitude toward the Indians would solve the problem. Such just treatment would involve, in his estimation, their ownership of lands in severalty, the right to be tried by their own juries, policed by their own people, and even conquered by Indian troops. They must be permitted to bear arms, and their removal from their homes was to him unthinkable. Last and most extreme, he advocated their early if not immediate enfranchisement. This, he believed, would arouse the whites' interest in the Apaches' concerns and save the tribe from complete degradation.

He defended his system with vigor and intelligence. To disarm the Indians, he said, would not only be an injudicious expression of the whites' fears, but also a folly especially on a frontier infested with white criminals. Besides, the Indians' habit of caching arms would make their disarmament almost an impossibility. Equally foolish to him would be their removal. It would start them towards ultimate extinction, and completely destroy their confidence, which factor, Crook knew, was absolutely necessary to retain if they were to be adjusted to white civilization. Worse yet, he predicted that such a step would start one of the bloodiest Indian wars in history. He also objected to the civil trial of the Apache chieftains on the ground that these men—usually mere figureheads in the anarchic Apache system—were manifestly not responsible for their followers' acts. Furthermore, he urged that the Apaches had no comprehension of the whites' code of justice.

One of the most discussed features of Crook's system was his wide use of Indian scouts in fighting their kinsmen. As employed by him it simply meant furnishing the native auxiliaries with an unfailing supply of provisions and munitions and turning them loose in stronger numbers than the enemy. No effort was made to enforce discipline, since he felt that the efficiency of the scouts depended on their individuality. The general merely showed them that they had his confidence and he left them to fight in their own way. He justified his use of the scouts because the equipment of the hostiles was no longer inferior to that of the military and, since regular troops in the Indian country were now "as helpless as a whale attacked by a school of swordfish," he was certain that the renegades could be run to earth only by members of their own race.

Originally published as Chapter 8 of *Federal Control of the Western Apaches, 1848–1886* (Historical Society of New Mexico Publications in History, vol. 9 [1940]; reprinted Albuquerque: University of New Mexico Press, 1970), pp. 216–23. Bracketed insertions added. All footnotes omitted.

Reservation Life

In the 1868 Treaty of Fort Laramie ending Red Cloud's war, the whites abandoned the Bozeman Trail and the Powder River country, and the Sioux accepted the so-called Great Sioux Reservation, which included all of present South Dakota west of the Missouri River. Red Cloud and many of his band of Oglalas lived near the agency, but Sitting Bull and his followers among the wilder Sioux remained away from the agencies and committed occasional depredations. Warfare broke out when hordes of miners invaded the reservation during the Black Hills gold rush of 1874 and 1875, and in the campaign that followed Lieutenant Colonel George Custer and his command were annihilated on the Little Big Horn in June of 1876. The great concentration of military strength on the northern plains after that battle finally caused the hostile Sioux and Cheyennes to surrender, Crazy Horse in 1877, and Sitting Bull in 1881 after several years in Canada. By 1881 approximately eight thousand Sioux had returned to the reservations.

The 1880s were a period of severe stress for the Sioux. They had been defeated militarily, and now the government was defeating them politically, socially, and economically. The Indian Bureau, with full support from eastern humanitarians and "friends" of the Indians, was determined to civilize the Sioux and other tribes, for the goal of federal policy was the assimilation of Indians into white society. To secure this end the government believed that it was necessary to eradicate native religions and replace them with Christianity; convert the Indians into farmers who would ultimately support themselves; and break the power of the chiefs and destroy the tribal basis of Indian society. These were the general tasks confronting Dr. Valentine T. McGillycuddy, a former military surgeon, when he became agent at Pine Ridge in 1879.

McGillycuddy was a man of strong will, and at Pine Ridge he was confronted with Red Cloud, the famous Oglala warrior, who had an equally strong will. As a result, McGillycuddy's tenure was marked by a continuous series of skirmishes and maneuvers between the two men as each sought to impose his will upon the reservation. The white agent had considerable advantages in the struggle. Change was already evident in the Sioux way of life. Customs associated with warfare and the warrior societies were beginning to disappear, and the old hunting economy had collapsed. McGillycuddy could also bring the full weight of the government to bear on the chief, and he possessed the ultimate weapon in the military units stationed in the vicinity. The clash of wills might carry Red Cloud and his followers to the brink of revolt, but each time the chief retreated. He would not risk hostilities. Instead, Red Cloud tried to maintain his own prestige and to preserve the authority of the office of chief, and he used his position to oppose the changes sought by the government. McGillycuddy, on the other hand, tried to undermine Red Cloud by supporting rivals and by creating an Indian police force to enforce his policies.

The struggle between these two able and colorful men is dramatic and interesting, but it is only one example of the problems that existed on reservations in this period. Similar situations occurred at other reservations, and in each case change was inevitable. The stress of reservation life and the attack on the old customs contributed to the Ghost Dance movement, an attempt to reassert Indian culture which culminated, on the Pine Ridge Reservation, in the Wounded Knee massacre of 1890.

Red Cloud vs. McGillycuddy

JAMES C. OLSON

On New Year's Day, 1879, James Irwin submitted his resignation as agent for the Red Cloud Indians, "to take effect as early as may be convenient." . . . Commissioner [of Indian Affairs Ezra] Hayt, who had been at odds with Irwin for months, lost no time in accepting the agent's resignation and in finding a successor. His choice fell upon Dr. Valentine T. McGillycuddy, thirty-year-old contract surgeon [who] . . . had had wide experience in the West and among the Sioux [and] . . . had been with General Crook in 1876, and as post surgeon at Camp Robinson had attended the dying Crazy Horse. Fearless, hot-tempered, and stubborn, he seemed to be just the man to break the will of Red Cloud and the other recalcitrant old Oglalas, and drive them along the white man's road.

While McGillycuddy remained in Washington to study the Indian Bureau's procedures, Special Supervisor James R. O'Beirne continued to develop the facilities at Pine Ridge. He seems to have won a degree of cooperation from Red Cloud; at least, the chief consented to participate in laying the cornerstone of the agency schoolhouse. O'Beirne regarded this as evidence of "triumph quietly effected over his haughty disposition and inclination to self will," although Red Cloud's brief comments were open to another interpretation. As he placed a gold ring in the box, he said solemnly, "May Almighty God put it into the hearts of the white man not to disturb us in our present home, but allow us to remain here in peace."

McGillycuddy arrived at Pine Ridge on March 10. . . . Trouble with Red Cloud soon followed. McGillycuddy called a conference of the principal chiefs to explain his hopes for their people and to enlist their cooperation. Red Cloud presided, and at first he seemed disposed to cooperate. He passed the pipe to the new agent and advised the Indians to listen to what their new Father had to say. Encouraged, McGillycuddy got out a map of the reservation. He pointed to many fertile valleys. The Indians, he said, should quit living around the agency and go out into those valleys, plow the land, and grow crops. They then would become independent. Red Cloud immediately objected. He rose and said:

> Father, the Great Spirit did not make us to work. He made us to hunt and fish. He gave us the great prairies and hills and covered them with buffalo,

deer, and antelope. He filled the rivers and streams with fish. The white man can work if he wants to, but the Great Spirit did not make us to work. The white man owes us a living for the lands he has taken from us.

After a warning that the time would come when the Indians would have to work in order to live, McGillycuddy dropped the subject and proposed the creation of an Indian police force. He would hire fifty young men, give them uniforms, and organize them as a mounted police force. When they were sufficiently well trained, he would try to have the soldiers removed from the vicinity of the agency. Red Cloud replied that he would be happy to have the white soldiers taken away, but there was no need for a special police force; his own soldiers would enforce the law. The two men sparred verbally for a while and the council broke up, with Red Cloud opposing the idea of a police force and McGillycuddy determined to have one.

A few days later, McGillycuddy went over to the Missouri River to inventory government property that had been left there. While he was gone, Red Cloud concluded that he would be unable to live with his new agent, and on May 1, together with twenty-one other chiefs, including Man-Afraid-of-His-Horse, Young-Man-Afraid, and Little Wound, he signed a letter to the President, asking for the removal of McGillycuddy and the reinstatement of Dr. Irwin. O'Beirne was convinced that Irwin, who was still at the agency, had "been tampering with Red Cloud." He suppressed the letter and warned Irwin that he was violating the law in trying to influence the Indians as a private citizen, and that if violation could be proved he would be arrested. Nothing came of either Red Cloud's request or O'Beirne's threats, but the difficulties increased rather than diminished.

On the day before Red Cloud requested McGillycuddy's removal, Father Meinrad McCarthy arrived at the agency with a letter to McGillycuddy from Abbot Martin, Superior of the Benedictine Mission among the Dakotas, requesting permission to establish a mission at Pine Ridge. Red Cloud, who repeatedly had asked for a Catholic priest, welcomed Father McCarthy and insisted that he stay at the new house which the Government was building for him and which was nearing completion. O'Beirne was friendly enough—he even gave the visitor twenty dollars to further his work—but he saw very clearly that Father McCarthy's objective was in violation of Indian Bureau regulations which gave the Episcopal Church monopolistic control over the souls of the Oglalas. He asked the priest to wait until Agent McGillycuddy returned and hurried off a letter to Washington, requesting guidance.

By the time McGillycuddy got back, word had arrived from Washington that the priest would have to leave, and on May 17 the agent sent Father McCarthy a terse note informing him that his presence on the reservation could not be allowed, "Ecclesiastically or otherwise." Not wanting to make an issue of the matter, McCarthy pitched his tent about two miles south of the reservation border near Camp Sheridan in Nebraska, and settled down to await further orders from his superiors. Red Cloud urged him to return, saying that he had his permission to re-enter the agency and that he was going to send a petition on his behalf to the Great White Father. McCarthy, however, did not want to create a disturbance which might jeopardize Catholic work among the Sioux; so despite Red Cloud's entreaties, he decided to remain off the reservation until given official permission to enter. After four months, he and his superiors concluded that there was no hope, and he was ordered to withdraw.

In denying Father McCarthy permission to work at Pine Ridge, the Government acted against the expressed wishes of many Oglalas, who from the days of Father [Pierre J.] DeSmet's early work had preferred Catholic to Protestant missionaries. In a council held May 26, Red Cloud and a number of other leading chiefs insisted that they be permitted to have Catholic teachers. Red Cloud said:

> The Great Father and also the Commissioner told me that whenever and wherever I selected my place for a home, that there I should have school houses and churches with men in them in black gowns. There is one of those men here now and I want him to stay, and if Mr. Robinson [The Reverend John Robinson, Episcopal missionary at Pine Ridge] wants to stay, I have no objections. We want Black Gown and Mr. Robinson also to teach our children. I want you to write a letter and write it strong to the Great Father and the Commissioner telling them these things.

McGillycuddy transmitted the request in a letter addressed to the President, but Commissioner Hayt stopped it in his office. When Secretary [of the Interior Carl] Schurz visited Pine Ridge during the first week in September, Father McCarthy appealed directly to him but was told in no uncertain terms that he could not work on the reservation. It was this that ended the matter as far as the Catholics were concerned.

Red Cloud used Schurz's visit as an opportunity to repeat his request for the removal of McGillycuddy. Schurz replied condescendingly: "Red Cloud, the Great Father is a very wise man. He knows everything. If there is anything wrong with your Agent he will know it before either you or I know it." Indeed, Schurz seemed unable to take the old chief seriously. Although Red Cloud complained about a variety of things, including the Indian police which McGillycuddy had organized over his objections, Schurz told a reporter that he had heard only one complaint during his visit, "and that was that the school-teacher talked Dakota, and I was requested to urge upon them to confine themselves to English." Obviously pleased with the way in which the Sioux were moving along the white man's road, as he had staked it out, Schurz wrote, in his annual report:

> When I entered upon my present duties I was told by men of long experience in Indian affairs that we would never be able to do anything with the Spotted Tail and Red Cloud Sioux "until they had received another thorough whipping." Since that time they have twice been obliged to change their location. A general outbreak was predicted a year ago. When I visited them this autumn I found their freighting wagons by hundreds on the road with their young warriers on the box, their chiefs with their people making hay and cultivating fields on the bottom lands, many of them building houses for their families; anxious to have their children educated; many requesting that their boys and girls be taken to our schools in the East, and the universal wish to be permanently settled and led on "in the white man's way."

McGillycuddy, too, was pleased with the progress his charges had made in the few months he had been responsible for them—progress which had been achieved despite a history of "bribery, fraud, and corruption on the part of some of the former representatives of the government, in the way of contractors, agents, &c." The only serious obstacle to continued progress was the influence of the chiefs. They opposed all efforts to encourage the Indians to work and support themselves because they saw the development of independence as a threat to their authority. If the Government wanted to continue to maintain the Indians as savages "and feed them until they finally die out," McGillycuddy wrote in his first report, "I would recommend the tribal system as the most feasible one." But if the present program, designed to make the Indians self-supporting, was to succeed, the power of the chiefs must be broken. . . .

McGillycuddy did not mention Red Cloud by name, but it is clear that he had him in mind: the chief had opposed him at almost every turn and had even gone so far as to ask for his removal. This opposition, and—in McGillycuddy's eyes—general obstructionism continued during 1880, both on and off the reservation. In particular, there was difficulty at the Indian Training School at Carlisle, Pennsylvania, where a number of young Brulés and Oglalas had been sent. In June, Red Cloud paid a visit to the school along with several other chiefs. Among them was Spotted Tail, who, despite his long history of collaboration, was developing a reputation for backwardness equal to Red Cloud's. The officer in charge of the school, Lt. R. H. Pratt, complained that both Red Cloud and Spotted Tail made speeches "offensive and prejudicial to the discipline of the school." Further evidence of the obstructionist activities of both chiefs was reported shortly after the delegation returned. Charges that T. G. Cowgill, a licensed trader, had been stealing corn were brought before a grand jury at Deadwood, Dakota Territory. The charges were quashed, but McGillycuddy had to go to Deadwood and testify on behalf of the trader. He complained that the whole affair was "a case of malicious prosecution" directed at him and reported that the Indians were "very much disturbed" because of the prominent part taken by Red Cloud and Spotted Tail in presenting the charges. McGillycuddy further reported that the Indians were "holding councils day and night looking toward the final deposing of Red Cloud as chief."

Four months earlier, in March, McGillycuddy, recommending the purchase of a wagon and horses for Red Cloud, had reported that the chief was "behaving himself in an exemplary manner," but by the end of the summer he had obviously taken all he could tolerate from the head man of the Oglalas. In his annual report, submitted September 1, he wrote:

> I have necessarily met much opposition, notably from Red Cloud, who, with the neighboring chief Spotted Tail, form about as egregious a pair of old frauds in the way of aids to their people in civilization as it has ever been my fortune or misfortune to encounter. When these two old men shall have been finally gathered to their fathers, we can truly speak of them as good Indians and only regret that Providence, in its inscrutable way, had so long delayed their departure.

Two days later he called a council of the chiefs and head men for the purpose of deposing Red Cloud and selecting a new head chief. Sensing what was up, Red Cloud refused to come, even after McGillycuddy had sent the head of the Indian police to tell him that his rations would be stopped if he did not obey the summons. There had long been dissatisfaction with Red Cloud's leadership among those who wished to supplant him—Young-Man-Afraid-of-His-Horse, for example, told a reporter that Red Cloud and Spotted Tail were "not fit to be Agency Chiefs; they don't know how to do business"—but McGillycuddy soon learned that when the chips were down most of the Oglalas would stay with their old chief; of more than a hundred chiefs and head men who were asked to vote, all but five placed their sticks in Red Cloud's pile. American Horse, designated to report the results of the council to the President, wrote: "Red Cloud was chosen almost without opposition. . . . He has been our head chief, he is now and always will be, because the Nation love, respect and believe in him." If there was to be a change, it should be in the agent. "We ask and beg of you to take our present Agent from us," American Horse continued, "and give us another in his place so our people can be at peace once more which they will never be as long as he remains with us."

As far as McGillycuddy was concerned, the chiefs' action had no effect; he always referred to Red Cloud thereafter as "the former chief" or "the deposed chief," and kept insisting that the old man was no longer a power to be reckoned with in dealing with the Oglalas. The realities of situation, however, destroyed much of the force of the agent's insistence, and throughout his remaining years as agent at Pine Ridge, McGillycuddy, in one way or another, was preoccupied with the problem of Red Cloud, who symbolized the old way of life and who seemed at every turn to be blocking his people's progress along the white man's road.

In February Red Cloud tried to stop the census. This was a perennial issue, deriving in part from a deeply ingrained dread of being counted and in part from a belief that the whole process was somehow designed to bring about a reduction in rations and annuities. When [Agent J. J.] Saville had first tried to institute the census among the Oglalas in 1874, he had stirred up unrest almost to the point of an outbreak; in subsequent years the annual counting had always produced a degree of tension, but none of the chiefs had openly rebelled. Why Red Cloud decided to make an issue of it at this time is not clear; more than likely he opposed the census simply because McGillycuddy had ordered it taken. Whatever his motives, however, his efforts were unsuccessful. He sent runners to the villages with orders to stop the count, but none of the chiefs were willing to interfere. McGillycuddy met Red Cloud's own refusal by withholding rations from his village, and after a week Red Cloud relented and permitted himself and his twenty-seven families to be counted.

With the inauguration of President Garfield, Red Cloud made yet another attempt to secure McGillycuddy's removal. He wrote the President, saying that he hoped to see him soon and noting that the agent was on his way to Washington. The agent was not a good man. He had never given Red Cloud the ox-teams and wagons which had been promised him, and he was making the agency "more like a military post than an agency to civilize my people." Red Cloud hoped the Great Father would keep the agent in Washington and not let him return. A short time later, Red Cloud and ninety-six chiefs sent a petition to the President formally asking McGillycuddy's removal:

> We as a people have lost faith in him from his unjust treatment of us in many cases. He says we have no rights on our reservation when we differ from his opinion. He has tried to depose our head chief Red Cloud which the nation does not want and we believe he steals our goods and we know he lies to us.

All this happened while McGillycuddy was in Washington. When he returned to the agency he found that there had been "secret counselling" during his absence and concluded that members of the Dear family were responsible for it. They may have been—the family had had no love for McGillycuddy since he had taken H. C. Dear's tradership from him—but George Stover had signed the petition as interpreter. In any case, McGillycuddy was able to produce the names of seventeen chiefs who swore that they had not authorized use of their signatures, but of these only five appeared on the petition: Little Wound, Red Dog, High Wolf, Slow Bull, and Man-Afraid-of-His-Horse. Whether these men knew nothing of the contents of the petition, had not authorized the use of their names, or simply had had a change of heart, we will probably never know. Little Wound and Red Dog, particularly the latter, had often worked closely with Red Cloud, but consistency was no more an attribute of the red politician than of his white counterpart, and given the complexities of Oglala politics, anything could happen. Moreover, because of the language barrier, it was always possible—and frequently justifiable—for any Indian to say that he did not understand what was in a paper to which he had put his mark.

At the annual Sun Dance on June 22, Red Cloud and McGillycuddy had it out in the presence of many chiefs and several Army officers, including General Crook's aide, Lt. John G. Bourke. Red Cloud made a long speech, protesting his friendship for the Great Father and reciting his efforts to maintain peace; as for difficulties between himself and his agent, they were mostly the result of women's talk. He concluded: "I hope the Great Father will keep us both still." But McGillycuddy was in no mood to keep still. He wanted Red Cloud to explain the letter he had sent to the President, charging the agent with lying and stealing; he wanted Red Cloud to explain why the chiefs had said that their names were put to the letter without their consent, that they had been stolen by Red Cloud and Mr. Dear. Red Cloud replied: "As to the names you say I stole, I'd like to hear them read so I could find what ones I stole. I want to have a talk about that letter as soon as the Sun Dance is over. I don't think I put anything bad in that letter." . . . Actually, the Sun-Dance confrontation, inconclusive as it was, seems to have been accompanied by a temporary thaw in the relations between Red Cloud and McGillycuddy; at least their personal conflict was subordinated to the problem of the Ponca lands along the Niobrara which had been plaguing the Indian Bureau for several years. These lands had been assigned to the Sioux by the Treaty of 1868, and in 1877, when the Government was making an effort to remove the Sioux to the Missouri River, the Poncas had been sent down to Indian Territory against their will. Some of them, including Standing Bear, tried to return; their arrest and ensuing trial created so much public concern that President Hayes appointed a commission to investigate. The Commission recommended that those Poncas who wished to return to their ancestral lands be allowed to do so, and the Government was now anxious to obtain the consent of the Sioux. Accordingly, the Indian Bureau decided to fall back upon the time-honored custom of bringing a delegation of chiefs to Washington, and no matter what agents might say, any delegation of chiefs had to include Red Cloud and Spotted Tail. Since Spotted Tail was killed shortly before the group was scheduled to leave, the Brulé delegation was headed by White Thunder, who was later killed by Spotted Tail's son.

Although White Thunder spoke for the Brulés, Red Cloud clearly dominated the proceedings at Washington. He was in a generous mood; in addition to agreeing that the Poncas should return to their lands, he suggested that if the Cheyennes wanted to leave Indian Territory he would be happy to provide lands for them on his reservation. Red Cloud also looked after a few of his friends, securing permission from the Secretary of the Interior (S. J. Kirkwood, who had replaced Schurz with the inauguration of the Garfield administration) for certain white men who had intermarried with the Indians to remain on the reservation, pending good behavior.

McGillycuddy saw nothing but evil coming of this. In his annual report, penned shortly after his return from Washington, he complained of drunkenness among the Indians as the source of much difficulty and charged that unprincipled white men on the reservation were at the root of the evil. . . . On September 5 the agent reported "several cases of drunkenness among the Indians," and charged that they were getting their liquor "through the medium of white men living with Indian women for whose welfare ex-chief Red Cloud was so solicitious." Pursuing the matter with the bulldog tenacity so characteristic of his actions, McGillycuddy charged later that "many of these white men, or as they are more fitly termed 'squaw men'" were not really married to their Indian women but lived with them or not as their desires dictated, and when "tiring of their squaws . . . purchased newer and fresher ones," with the result that they had "several broods of half-breed children, who are illegitimate."

Although McGillycuddy continued to press his case against the squaw men with his superiors in Washington, in view of Secretary Kirkwood's letter and Red Cloud's solicitude, there was little that he could do about them on the reservation, and apparently during the fall of 1881 he did not try to move directly against the offenders or against Red Cloud himself, who seemed to be reasonably content. . . . In January, he reported: "My people are getting along well. The Agent with us is a good Agent. . . ."

This happy state of affairs was not to last long; on April 5 McGillycuddy warned Commissioner [of Indian Affairs Hiram] Price: "Ex-chief Red Cloud is holding his usual Spring councils with the intention of securing if possible the removal of the present agent." He confessed that "to be eternally harassed by this old man is getting to be somewhat monotonous," and suggested that if Price had any misgivings about the agency, it might be just as well to send an inspector out to investigate. Meanwhile McGillycuddy moved to strengthen his position vis-à-vis the aging chief. He called a council of the chiefs and head men and, according to his report, got a vote of confidence in his administration of agency affairs and of censure of Red Cloud. We do not know just who attended the council, but Young-Man-Afraid, Little Wound, American Horse, No Flesh, and Blue Horse all made speeches, presumably in support of the agent.

Despite this vote of confidence, McGillycuddy viewed the approaching Sun Dance with apprehension. The Indians always worked themselves into a fever of excitement at the Sun Dance, and the ceremony was calculated to arouse visions of the glories of the old way of life. Moreover, there were many Sitting Bull Indians on the reservation and some Northern Cheyennes, and most of these were hostile to the agent and the whole reservation system. Red Cloud could easily use the occasion to stir up ill feeling. Apparently he tried to do so. Rigged out in breech cloth, paint, and feathers, he served as "whipper in" during the ceremonies, and counciled with many large delegations. Nothing happened—for which McGillycuddy credited Young-Man-Afraid and the Indian police—and the agent reflected that it was "merely a question of time, pending the death of Red Cloud and a few more of the ancient that the Sun Dance and other barbarous practices will die a natural death."

It was, indeed, "merely a question of time," but McGillycuddy would not see that time during his tenure as agent, and within a few weeks after the Sun Dance of 1882 he found himself locked in combat with his ancient rival and facing the most serious crisis of his stormy career at Pine Ridge.

On Sunday, August 13, Red Cloud and about fifty followers left the reservation without a pass and went down into Nebraska for a feast at the ranch of Louis Shangrau, a half-breed whom McGillycuddy had evicted for bad conduct. Among those present were He Dog, a Sitting Bull chief; Woman's Dress, an enlisted scout from Fort Robinson; Cloud Shield, who recently had been dismissed as lieutenant of the Indian police; and American Horse, who was apt to turn up in any council, and who had earlier supported McGillycuddy. Also present was William J. Godfrey of Colorado, who, McGillycuddy charged, was purported to be an old personal friend of Henry M. Teller, Kirkwood's successor as Secretary of the Interior. Godfrey had a letter all ready for the Indians to sign. Addressed to Secretary Teller, it informed him of "the many acts of petty tyranny and insults we are daily compelled to endure from our Agent here." Reminding the Secretary that two earlier petitions for the removal of the agent had been transmitted without acknowledgment, this one advised him that

> if the incumbent as U.S. Agent is not removed from this Agency within sixty days, or a proper person sent out in the mean time to fully investigate his gross misconduct here, we will upon the expiration of the above stated time take upon ourselves the responsibility of politely escorting him out of our country, and let the consequences be what they may.

The next day Red Cloud threatened to kill the freighters who were preparing to leave for the railroad station at Thatcher, Nebraska, to pick up some six hundred thousands pounds of freight, including a large quantity of bacon, which had been delivered there. Fearing for their lives, the freighters refused to move, and McGillycuddy suspended the issue of coffee, sugar, and bacon. He also got wind of the council at Shangrau's and arrested Woman's Dress for violating his trust as an Indian scout. On Tuesday morning the telegraph line, which had been out of repair for two days, was put in working order, and McGillycuddy wired Commissioner Price of Red Cloud's threat against the freighters, adding, "It depends on your department whether I am to be agent or chief clerk for Red Cloud." That afternoon he received a telegram from Price assuring him that he would be "sustained by this office as agent against the claims of Red Cloud."

Armed with this, and hearing on Wednesday morning that a copy of the petition had been sent to the commanding officer at Fort Robinson, McGillycuddy decided to summon a general council and sent runners to the villages. Freighting was resumed on the same day, and Red Cloud made no effort to carry out his earlier threat. Also on Wednesday George Sword wrote the Commissioner of Indian Affairs, assuring him that white soldiers were not needed, that most of the Indians wished "to live in peace and enjoy the prosperity which has come to them." "Red Cloud," he added, "has been trying hard to make trouble and I think that any foolish Indians who think he can make trouble should be locked up."

McGillycuddy would soon be saying the same thing. On Friday afternoon the Indians assembled in the general council room. McGillycuddy warned them that unless Red Cloud could be stopped his actions would bring white soldiers. He hoped they would take the matter in their own hands and settle it. Sword, Young-Man-Afraid, and Little Wound dominated the proceedings: the agent could rest assured that they would take care of Red Cloud. Yellow Hair, a common Indian who had signed the threatening petition, made a long speech in which he protested his innocence and his desire for peace. American Horse was on hand too, but McGillycuddy refused to shake hands with him. American Horse was hurt. "I have seen nothing wrong at the Agency," he said. "You have refused to shake hands with me. I don't know what for. I simply wanted to explain the present trouble."

"This is no place to explain," McGillycuddy snapped back. "You should have sent your explanation to the Great Father with the letter you signed threatening to make trouble."

At the end of the session, thirty-one of the Indians signed a letter to the Great Father, assuring him that no troops were needed and deprecating Red Cloud's behavior. Numbers are not particularly significant, but fifty-four had signed the threatening petition.

By this time the country was agitated by the perennial fear of an Indian outbreak, and that night McGillycuddy received telegrams from Price and General Crook asking for an investigation of reports that Red Cloud was about to go on the warpath. McGillycuddy replied that while the situation was in hand and no troops were required for the present, Red Cloud would be "always a source of trouble and should be removed to Leavenworth, and the continual interference and counseling of white cut-throats prevented." He requested power to act as he saw fit. The next morning (Saturday, August 19), while awaiting an answer, he assembled the friendly chiefs and the police, instructing them to go to Red Cloud's village and demand to know his intentions. They returned about two o'clock with an evasive answer from Red Cloud, who denied that he had made any threats. Sword reported that the chief had assembled his young men under arms, and that many of them "had bad hearts." While McGillycuddy was debating what to do, he received a telegram from Price authorizing him to arrest Red Cloud and hold him prisoner, if necessary to prevent trouble. The agent at once told the chiefs that Red Cloud must report to the office and listen to the telegram. Red Cloud's village was only a mile away from the agency, and the runner sent out with the message returned in a short time. Red Cloud was glad to hear from the Commissioner and hoped that he was well, but he could not come in now to listen to the message because he was tired.

McGillycuddy was in no mood to be trifled with. He told the chiefs that either Red Cloud would come in or he would send the Indian police to bring him in. At this point, Yellow Hair volunteered to see what he could do. While awaiting word from Yellow Hair, McGillycuddy scanned Red Cloud's village with his field glasses. He noticed much excitement: "Indians were flying around in all directions, gathering in their ponies, squaws were leaving and bucks coming in, so that things looked like the old business of 1876 when the Army had to handle Red Cloud for his insolence and hostility." There was excitement at the agency too. Many Indians were leaving, and along with them several traders and employees with their families, all heading south to Nebraska. McGillycuddy issued arms to the fifty Indian police; he also opened up fifty additional rifles, a few of which were issued to friendly Indians and employees who had remained at the agency.

After what seemed like a long absence, Yellow Hair returned with word that Red Cloud was coming. When he did not appear after what would have been a reasonable time for the trip, McGillycuddy asked the chiefs what they proposed to do. They went into council among themselves and after a short time returned with their decision:

> Father, send Yellow Hair with these words to Red Cloud. Tell him that we make third and last call. That to prevent bloodshed, if he does not come at once, we will ask our agent to call for troops. We will turn our young men and police in with the troops and disarm and dismount Red Cloud's and Red Shirt's bands. Or, if you say so, we will give you our young men to help your police and bring him anyway. . . .

Yellow Hair went out again, and soon Red Cloud appeared. He was brought into the council room, all arms were laid aside, and McGillycuddy read the Commissioner's telegram. He told the police and the chiefs that he would hold them responsible for Red Cloud's future conduct. Asserting that the Great Father and his government were not to be argued with, he dismissed the meeting without permitting anyone to speak.

Apparently the crisis had passed. Red Cloud went quietly back to his village; the Indian police, except for an agency detail of ten, were permitted to return to their homes. The next day,

Sunday, McGillycuddy reported all serene at the agency—"the Church bell is ringing and the flag still floats"—but he warned Commissioner Price that certain whites and half-breeds around the agency were out to force his removal and that they would continue to center their troublemaking on Red Cloud. To Maj. E. V. Sumner at Fort Robinson he telegraphed: "As far as outbreak is concerned, our own Indians will prevent it and kill Red Cloud if necessary, but as long as Red Cloud remains here we will have more or less disturbances. I shall demand that the leaders in the movement be sent to Leavenworth or the Department stand the consequences. . . ."

The next morning McGillycuddy left for Omaha to meet six women who had been hired to teach in the agency boarding school. Commissioner Price was somewhat disturbed that the agent should leave his post at this particular time, but McGillycuddy was certain that every thing was in hand, and no valid reason existed for changing his plans; besides, as his wife Julia remarked, "Nothing irked McGillycuddy more than to have his plans upset."

With McGillycuddy gone, his enemies at the agency moved to press their case against him. On August 21, T. G. Cowgill, trader; J. G. Edgar, his clerk; James F. Oldham, chief of police; and Fordyce Grinnell, agency physician, wrote a long letter to the Commissioner, warning that the agent's arbitrary and unjust treatment of Red Cloud might well provoke war: "We are not at all afraid that Red Cloud will make any trouble . . . but we are afraid that the vindictive temper of the Indian Agent will bring it upon us." McGillycuddy, who was keeping in touch by means of a field telegraph with which he could cut in on the line, learned of the letter and immediately ordered his chief clerk, John Alder, to arrest Oldham and maintain a close surveillance of the others. Reporting his action to Price, he stated:

> Red Cloud is a tool, but a dangerous one. This is mutiny, the result of cowardice and conspiracy. I demand that to prevent estrangement of friendly chiefs you positively order Acting Agent Alder to remove offenders from reservation at once. Trader and physician defy the Agent as the Dept. appointed them. This is a criminal disgrace to Indian Service.

The complainants responded by sending another letter to Price (signed by seventeen employees and residents), reasserting that the difficulty was largely the fault of the agent, who had provoked a personal quarrel with Red Cloud, and asking that an inspector be sent out to investigate. Grinnell, who also had signed the petition, sent a separate letter denying that he had ever conversed with Red Cloud in regard to the troubles and asking for an investigation.

McGillycuddy's friends were also active. Trader George F. Blanchard and twenty-nine others signed a letter which repeated McGillycuddy's view that Red Cloud was but a tool in the hands of unprincipled whites and urged the Department to sustain the agent. Little Wound, Young-Man-Afraid, and forty-two other Indians also sent a petition testifying to their satisfaction with the agent and pledging their support of his efforts against Red Cloud.

From Fort Robinson, Colonel Sumner wrote: "Red Cloud is cool but determined; has quite a following which I am informed is daily increasing. Something should be done at once to counteract this influence; otherwise trouble will surely follow, the extent of which cannot be foreseen." He thought "a little more strength" at Fort Robinson and at Fort Niobrara would be desirable.

In Washington, Commissioner Price, thoroughly irritated with McGillycuddy for leaving his post, refused the agent's request to come to the capital and ordered him to return from Omaha as soon as possible. He also decided to send an inspector out to Pine Ridge. The inspector, W. J. Pollock, visited the agency in September. McGillycuddy, quite understandably, did not take kindly to the idea that an investigation was necessary—after all, the call for one had been part of the threatening petition—and he gave Pollock only minimal assistance. He warned him that he should pay no attention to Red Cloud and that under no circumstances should he recommend that the old man be restored to the position of head chief; if this were done, the "younger and more progressive element" would send Red Cloud to "the happy hunting grounds to keep company with his compeer, Spotted Tail."

McGillycuddy's fears about Pollock were soon justified. On

the same day that McGillycuddy warned him against Red Cloud, the inspector wrote a letter to Teller, which was to constitute the first part of his report. Red Cloud was by no means blameless, but, in Pollock's judgment, by far the greater share of blame for the controversy lay with the agent:

> It could hardly be expected the old chief would work in harmony with a man who lost no opportunity to humiliate and heap indignity upon him, who called him liar, fool, squaw, refused to shake hands with, deposed him, ordered the Agency employees not to entertain him in their houses, and no doubt sought to enforce a condition of affairs on August 19th that would result in his death.

Nor was that all. Red Cloud had got along with all of the ten agents who had served his people, "excepting only those who have retired from the service in disgrace." The real reason for the present difficulty, Pollock hinted, was that Red Cloud had discovered irregularities in McGillycuddy's management of the agency and had had the courage to protest them.

The second part of Pollock's report, filed from Sioux City, Iowa, on October 14—the day which, incidentally, marked the end of the sixty-day period of grace granted in the Red Cloud petition which had precipitated the fuss—detailed the irregularities: the agent was living high at the expense of the Indians; he had taken credit on vouchers that were not paid; he had unlawfully deprived Red Cloud of rations while giving the Indian police and other favorites more than they could use; he had permitted agency employees to convert government supplies to their own use. On the same day that Pollock wrote to Teller from Sioux City, E. B. Townsend, another special agent who had recently visited Pine Ridge, reported to Price in Washington, providing advance confirmation of what Pollock would write: not only was McGillycuddy fraudulent in the management of the agency, but the fraud was being perpetrated willfully and as the result of collusion which dated back to 1879, when the agent had assumed his post. Also on October 14, S. S. Benedict, still another inspector brought into the case, was holding a council with the Indians at Pine Ridge. His report, transmitted to Secretary Teller a month later, completely exonerated McGillycuddy of any but "technical irregularities" and asserted that "there would be no trouble if the Department would give Red Cloud to understand that he is not Agent at Pine Ridge and that the Agent must be respected and obeyed." McGillycuddy, in Benedict's opinion, was one of the best agents in the service, and he should not be driven from his post by a chief who stood in the way of his people's progress toward civilization.

Apparently the Indian Bureau felt the same way. The charges against McGillycuddy were not pursued, and he was not even reprimanded for his "technical irregularities," whatever they might have been. Viewed from the perspective of the years, and from the evidence available, those charges do seem fairly flimsy (for example, according to Townsend, the trader, with whom McGillycuddy was supposed to have been in collusion was T. G. Cowgill, a leader of the anti-McGillycuddy faction at the agency) and at the same time it seems clear that they are hardly in keeping with McGillycuddy's reputation, which, despite his many faults, was generally high. As George Hyde wrote, "This agent was armed at every point, with not a chink in his armor through which a weapon might be slipped. His bookkeeping was perfection; his probity above criticism; and not a thing could be found that might be employed as a hook on which to hang charges."

McGillycuddy had ridden out the crisis. There was no sign on October 14 that Red Cloud or anyone else remembered the threat to remove the agent by force if he were not removed by the Government. At the end of the month, writing his annual report, McGillycuddy exulted that the prompt manner in which Red Cloud had been suppressed, "and the peaceful and prosperous condition of affairs here, will, I trust, be an example in the future for ambitious chiefs and designing white men."

Red Cloud had indeed been put down, but he would not stay down for long. His arrest apparently had no significant effect upon his influence among the Oglalas. He still remained a symbol of the old way of life which many of the Sioux hoped would be returned to them, the prating of agents about the progress their charges were making toward civilization notwithstanding. Red Cloud probably had no great hope that the Sioux would walk the old ways again, but he was determined to hold his position of leadership, and even as McGillycuddy was writing of the chief's "suppression" events were transpiring which would thrust him once again to the foreground as a leader of his people, and in the end would let him triumph over the hated agent.

Originally published as Chapter 14, "The Struggle with McGillycuddy," of *Red Cloud and the Sioux Problem* (Lincoln: University of Nebraska Press, 1965), pp. 264–85. Bracketed insertions except those in direct quotations added. Ellipses other than in direct quotations indicate editorial deletions. All footnotes omitted.

The Dawes Act

Americans concerned with Indian policy in the 1870s and 1880s talked of civilizing the Indians and preparing them for assimilation into white society, but that goal was about as old as English settlement on the continent. Puritan divines in New England were ambivalent in their attitudes toward Indians, but they did believe that the tribes should be civilized and Christianized and devoted some effort to this end. Henry Knox, George Washington's Secretary of War and a man who was instrumental in the development of federal Indian policy, also desired a program of civilization, and the government financed small attempts in that direction during the first half of the nineteenth century.

After the Civil War, as humanitarian groups turned their attention to Indian affairs, the demand that the Indians should be civilized received considerable impetus from a series of events in the West that publicized the weaknesses of government Indian programs. Fraud, invasions of Indian lands, and the removal of tribes from one region to another were old problems, but the seriousness of these issues in the late 1870s and 1880s aroused public attention on a wide scale. The removal of the Commissioner of Indian Affairs for malfeasance in office in 1879; the invasion of Indian Territory by the Boomers, who wanted to open the area to white settlement; the Ponca removal and subsequent court case; and the flight of the Northern Cheyennes from Indian Territory to their old home in the North had the immediate effect of spawning a host of new organizations devoted to aiding the Indians and reforming federal policy. In time the reformers concluded that the answer to the Indian problem was the allotment of land to individual Indians as part of the broader crusade of civilization and Christianization. It was thought that private property had inherent and peculiar civilizing qualities and that individual ownership of land would provide the incentive for the Indians to adopt the ways of white farmers, and reformers insisted that joint or tribal ownership should not be permitted to hinder Indian participation in American society.

The government had introduced land allotment on a small scale as early as the 1850s by providing for it in treaties with small tribes such as the Wyandots of Kansas. The results of these experiments were disastrous, but proponents of allotment were confident that they could improve the system. In 1875 the homestead privilege was extended to Indians, and after 1878 allotment laws were introduced in every session of Congress. In 1887 a union of West and East developed, as Loring Priest indicates, and the Dawes Severalty Law, sponsored by reformer Henry Dawes of the Senate Indian Committee, was passed. Western support was secured by providing that surplus reservation lands left after allotments were made would be opened to white settlement. A crucial feature of the bill was its mandatory character.

Reformers generally believed that the Dawes Act was the great panacea for the Indian problem, but some Americans did not agree. A few Indian agents argued that the plains tribes, recently at war with the United States, were not ready for land allotment. Indians also protested. The famous Kiowa chief Lone Wolf and other representatives of tribes in Indian Territory went to Washington in an effort to prevent passage of the bill, but they arrived too late. Upon their return the tribes held a series of councils and asked that the act not be enforced. The Five Civilized Tribes, which had been exempted from the Dawes Act, expressed their opposition, too, but in 1898 the Curtis Act authorized the allotment of their land.

The Dawes Act was applied gradually to the various tribes, although some, especially in the Southwest, escaped it. By subsequent legislation Congress permitted leasing of Indian land in 1891 and authorized Indians to sell inherited lands in 1902. The Burke Act of 1906 enabled the Secretary of the Interior to decide when Indians were competent and could therefore receive title to their allotments and manage their own affairs. The effect of these laws was devastating. During Woodrow Wilson's administration Commissioner of Indian Affairs Cato Sells declared Indians competent in wholesale numbers although they actually failed to meet the normal criteria for such a decision, and he contributed greatly to the serious decline in Indian landholding. Donald Berthrong describes the process of allotment on the Cheyenne-Arapaho reservation. He estimates that by 1949 some two thousand of three thousand Cheyennes and Arapahos had lost their land.

The Congressional Decision to Use Force

LORING BENSON PRIEST

Agreement concerning administrative features of the Dawes Act did not solve the important question of how rapidly the new policies should be applied. While a large number of reformers wished legislators to force immediate allotment upon the tribes, many opposed action without Indian consent. As in the case of other parts of the measure, therefore, sections dealing with enforcement were the result of compromise. The attempt of legislators to avoid antagonizing either of two widely divergent groups played a part in the decision that selection of tribes to which the Act was to be applied should be left to the President. Advocates of rapid allotment were more critical of this method than their opponents, but even the most enthusiastic champions of the cause supported presidential discretion in the end because of confidence in their ability to exert pressure upon the Chief Executive. A definite decision as to whether tribes selected by the President should be allowed to reject the change, however, could not be similarly avoided.

While legislators tried to satisfy both the friends and enemies of force, the ultimate effect of the Dawes Act was to require submission to government policies. The measure left no question about the authority of federal officials in the matter of allotment, section two declaring:

> . . . if any one entitled to an allotment shall fail to make a selection within four years after the President shall direct that allotments may be made on a particular reservation, the Secretary of the Interior may direct the agent of such tribe or band . . . to make a selection for such Indian, which selection shall be allotted as in cases where selections are made by the Indians.

Even the four years thus allowed for the choice of allotments seemed too long to many congressmen. Six months had been considered adequate by Representative [Alfred M.] Scales in 1879 and the House of Representatives fought for only a two-year limit until the conference committee capitulated to Senate pressure just before final passage of the Act. If senators and members of the Board of Indian Commissioners had not striven to obtain a period of at least five years, Congress might even have demanded immediate acceptance of allotments. The only important concession to Indian opinion was the provision that unallotted land should not be sold without tribal consent. As surplus land would be of no value after a tribe had been forced to accept individual allotments, however, there was little reason to fear that opposition to white occupancy would overcome a desire to profit from the sale of property which was no longer of use. A forced surrender of land could hardly have been demanded by reformers who were interested in just treatment of Indians. But failure to require abandonment of unallotted areas specifically did not mean that Indians could avoid the outcome. Despite frequent denials, passage of the Dawes Act marked official acceptance of the view of those Americans who had believed that Indian progress would prove impossible without coercion.

The decision of American legislators to effect vital changes in Indian society by forceful methods was perhaps inevitable. The distaste of reformers for gradual advancement has always been a subject of comment, while measures of unquestionable merit have frequently failed because their advocates lacked sufficient patience to prepare the ground for their success. Yet American Indian reformers had been constantly warned that civilization was a matter of gradual growth and not of sudden conversion. For many years, indeed, most Indian friends had followed the advice of the agent who declared that in elevating barbarous nations to a state of civilized life work must proceed upon the principle of "making haste slowly." Such warnings were heeded less often as the movement advanced; and once Indian organizations were formed in the early eighties all pretense of caution disappeared.

While the decision to employ force in the reformation of Indian affairs has been frequently condemned, the number of able men recommending coercion testified to the strength of arguments advanced in its favor in the eighties. Secretary [of the Interior Carl] Schurz believed that compelling unprepared Utes to accept individual ownership would be preferable to allowing their entire reservation to be seized by angry whites; while young Teddy Roosevelt held that Indians were bound to perish as they were and should, therefore, be required to adjust themselves to white life even though all but the best would die. Innumerable other Americans urged speedy allotments among backward tribes in the spirit of an agent who wrote, "Of course in many ways the Indians will be wronged and cheated, but such a condition has got to be met sometime, and why not commence at once, instead of putting off the evil day?" Reformers, who refused to believe that allotment would endanger the welfare of any Indian, naturally urged its adoption even more heartily. Lyman Abbott of the *Christian Union* supported the severalty movement so enthusiastically that he declared any means could be defended that would help attain the goal. The refusal of Congress to tolerate opposition made force an indispensable part of any reform program. But before the effect of this decision can be fully understood, the battle between the advocates and opponents of force must be described.

Indian Opposition to Reform

As force would have been unnecessary if land allotment had been welcomed by the tribes, Indian opposition may be held primarily responsible for the coercive character of the Severalty Act. Some of the more advanced tribes supported the measure in hope that they might prepare for contact with the whites more easily; but in most cases the principle of severalty required too great a revolution in tribal customs to justify the Board of Indian

Commissioners' belief that "no single measure of legislation would give such general satisfaction to the Indians." Petitions requesting the division of a reservation among its residents were more often due to a desire to escape government control or to profit at the expense of fellow Indians than to sincere interest in the merits of allotment. The average red man resisted the change so strongly that there was little hope of success if Americans insisted upon waiting for Indian consent.

The opposition of American Indians to land allotment can not be regarded as mere obstructionism. Although chiefs were unreasoning in their opposition to abolition of a system upon which their influence depended, and although young warriors were unduly resentful of outside interference, there was no question that the race was more securely protected under tribal rule than it ever would be with individual ownership. Maintenance of a tribe's authority not only guaranteed the continuance of long-established customs, but was a vital factor in the conduct of satisfactory inter-racial relationships. Opportunities for robbery, numerous enough under existing conditions, would only increase once united resistance was no longer possible, while all pretense of racial independence would have to be surrendered once tribes were destroyed. Fear of white settlers, distrust of government officials, racial pride and a spirit of freedom were fully as responsible for the unpopularity of severalty as unreasonable opposition to change.

The wisdom of Indian opposition to severalty was never more effectively confirmed than in the answers of forty-nine Indian agents to a Board questionnaire of November, 1885, asking whether individual ownership would prove of benefit to their Indians. To reformers hoping to secure assistance in their fight for allotment, the replies could hardly have been more disappointing. Not only did nine agents question the ability of their Indians to assume the responsibilities of land holders, but nineteen stated that there was not the remotest possibility of success. The refusal of a majority of field officials to support the severalty program is especially significant when the attitude of the tribes under their direction is considered. Strange as it seems in face of the widespread conviction of contemporaries that Indian opposition to severalty was unjustified, not a single agent whose charges resisted allotment believed his Indians prepared for radical social adjustments! Wherever a tribe opposed severalty, an agent was ready to uphold the wisdom of his Indians. Yet in spite of this astonishing circumstance, the enthusiasm of reformers for allotment did not abate. Opposition to the use of force was successful only in cases where unusual conditions rendered allotment extremely dangerous.

Section eight of the Dawes Act, which stated "the provisions of this act shall not extend to . . . the Indian Territory, nor to any of the reservations of the Seneca Nation of New York Indians in the State of New York," was the result of peculiar conditions and not of any desire to extend special favors. If reformers had had a free hand, the Five Civilized Tribes of Indian Territory would have been the first required to select allotments. But while no Indians were better prepared to assume the responsibilities of individual ownership than those of New York and the eastern Indian Territory, allotment was inadvisable because of the existence of large provisional land grants which permitted private corporations to claim possession once tribal title was extinguished. Immediate occupancy of the Seneca reservations in New York had been promised to the Ogden Land Company of Buffalo, in case tribal ownership was abandoned. Soon after the Revolution, investigation revealed, dispute over Massachusetts's right to land occupied by the Indians of western New York had resulted in sovereignty being ceded to New York and a pre-emptive right of purchase to Massachusetts. This right, ultimately obtained by the Ogden Land Company, had been recognized by the United States in the Seneca treaty of 1794. The abolition of tribal title contemplated by the Dawes Act, therefore, would open Seneca land to preferred white buyers before allotments could be made to individual Indians. As title to much of the Indian Territory had been similarly promised to the Atlantic and Pacific Railroad, fear of dispossessing New York and Indian Territory Indians forced introduction of the exemption provision. Popular pressure might easily have caused Congress to force severalty upon all tribes, however, if Indians of the Territory had not strongly resisted the change.

By far the most effective Indian opposition to the Dawes Act was conducted by the Five Civilized Tribes. Believing that their future would prove a determining factor in the fate of other tribes, the five nations hoped to forward the cause of all Indians by advancing their own. Their struggle to preserve their right of self-government, therefore, rested upon arguments of more than local significance. Their frequently expressed apprehension that severalty would result in robbery and subjection was especially convincing when applied to tribes less prepared for responsibilities than themselves. Such a defense of Indian independence was absolutely essential if Indian rights were to be respected, for there was no end to the inroads that might be made once the power of Washington officials over tribal affairs was accepted. As it was, the intelligent arguments of delegates of the Five Civilized Tribes and their ability to cite definite treaty provisions won sufficient sympathy to secure temporary exemption for themselves. In resisting severalty for others, they convinced only a few that force should be avoided.

The Opposition to Force

The decision of reformers to demand acceptance of land allotments was reached only after the implications of such action had been fully considered. Whenever Indian policy was debated, opponents of coercion urged the inadvisability of proceeding without tribal consent. Impatience with Indian backwardness and a conviction that a rapid change was necessary caused reformers to disregard all criticism of compulsion. The failure of the case against force to make an impression provides excellent evidence of the extremes to which advocates of severalty were willing to go to insure adoption of their plan. Even a brief examination of the frequent clashes over the use of force reveals that reformers were fully warned of the danger of acting without Indian consent.

Most opponents of coercion were not fanatics. In nearly every instance, their arguments were exceptionally reasonable. There was nothing irrational in criticizing the inconsistency of reformers who had opposed compulsory removal only to champion forcible allotment, while there was similar logic in sarcastic comments regarding the supernatural insight assumed by advocates of any policy of force. Enemies of coercion were determined that compulsion should not be adopted until every possible means of securing Indian consent had been tried. If severalty supporters argued that immediate allotment was necessary to prepare the Indians for contact with whites, opponents of force replied that successful introduction of any reform would depend upon Indian co-operation. Unless a tribe was convinced of the necessity for change, reformers could hope to accomplish little. Real progress, if ever achieved, must rest on persuasion and conversion, not on compulsion and force.

Although there were but few opponents of force, both their influence and activity helped to compensate for their lack of numbers. No one was more determined to consult Indian wishes than President Cleveland. When a Mohonk [reformers'] delegation demanded immediate action of the newly elected President, Cleveland insisted that justice was more important than speed. This caution was shared, if not inspired, by Secretary of the Interior [Lucius Q. C.] Lamar, who announced in his first report that changes of Indian policy must be both gradual and tentative. But while the President and his Secretary were often able to resist the demands of impatient reformers, the most active critics of force were [Alfred B.] Meacham and [Theodore A.] Bland of the *Council Fire*. Every issue of the Indian magazine stressed the desire of its editors to protect tribes from outside interference. While both men professed to believe that severalty would prove the ultimate solution of the Indian problem, neither wished to have the change instituted without consent. No Americans saw the evils of force more clearly nor publicized their respect for Indian opinion more persistently than Meacham and Bland. If legislators had decided to consult the Indians instead of insisting upon allotment, chief credit for the success would have been due to the *Council Fire* and its editors.

In spite of the failure of the men who opposed the coercive clauses of the Dawes Act, the tactics employed in attempting to prevent passage of the measure are of exceptional interest. Realizing the strength of sentiment in favor of allotment, enemies of force concentrated their energy upon securing as much delay as possible in consideration of the bill. They heartily welcomed, therefore, the interest in establishing a commission to study proposed reforms expressed by President Cleveland in his first annual message. Since transfer of the Indian Bureau to the War Department had been defeated by an investigation less than a decade before, the possibility of delaying severalty by the same process seemed especially promising. The success of the reform program was seriously threatened when Representative [William S.] Holman climaxed the trip of a special investigating committee of the House in 1886 by recommending appointment of a commission of three Army officers and three civilians to provide for readjustment of the Indian question on a permanent basis. Although President Cleveland and Secretary Lamar displayed unusual interest in the suggestion, and although Bland did everything in his power to win support for the plan, the proposal failed by a vote of 68-48. Men interested in speeding reform were not willing to accept a bill which might be used to delay legislation indefinitely. As the Woman's National Indian Association declared:

> The practical effect of the bill would have been, to postpone indefinitely any great and radical legislative action on behalf of Indians, for the authority of such a Commission would be, of course, referred to as a standard, and even its warmest promoters could see no end of its proposed investigations, certainly not for ten or twenty years, it might be for generations, and it might even be a Commission in *perpetuo*.

Such postponement having been defeated, the only path remaining to critics of force was modification of a bill they could not delay.

Attempts to revise the enforcement provisions of the Dawes Act were no more successful than efforts to postpone it. Addition of a clause providing for Indian consent would have been enough to satisfy most critics. Even Bland promised more than once to support a severalty act which outlawed force. Thus an 1884 version of the Coke bill which provided for land allotment only upon request was lauded by the *Council Fire;* and when the House added an amendment requiring Indian consent to the Senate severalty bill of early 1886, Bland hailed the improvement resulting from delay. Pressure for consultation of the Indians nearly succeeded, in fact, during the final months before the Act was passed. In December, 1886, the National Indian Defense Association secured a House amendment to the severalty bill stating that nothing in the act should be construed as authorizing the Secretary of the Interior to abolish any reservation until the consent of a majority of the male members over twenty-one years of age should have been obtained. The Dawes Act would have been acceptable to Bland in this form, as he wrote the New York *Herald* that the action of the House had rendered the bill comparatively harmless. He was exceedingly surprised and disappointed, therefore, when Dawes successfully persuaded the conference committee to omit the Association's amendment. With the bill reported for adoption with its coercive clauses intact, forceful reform seemed unavoidable.

The possibility that sections providing for compulsory allotment might be dropped from the bill still remained even after the conference committee had agreed upon their inclusion. Charges that severalty advocates intended to place Indians at the mercy of unscrupulous whites seriously endangered passage of the conference report. Although a resolution to strike out coercive features of the bill was defeated by 47-13 at the Church-Board meeting of January, 1887, friends of the measure felt it necessary to disclaim any desire to dictate to the Indians. Senator Dawes, in fact, stated both before and after passage of his bill that civilization was "a work of time" which could not "triumph by force." Yet despite his frequently professed dislike for compulsory tactics, Dawes could not deny that forceful methods were possible under his Act only because he had defeated introduction of a specific prohibition. A majority of reformers undoubtedly opposed coercion as a regular practice; but because they felt a show of strength necessary in initiating the severalty program, they opened the way to serious abuse of Indian rights.

The Decision to Use Force

Advocacy of force as a method of solving the Indian problem was not a monopoly of reformers of the eighties. Bishop [Henry B.] Whipple, whose interest in the Indian could not be denied, had recommended the adoption of stringent laws a quarter of a century before the Dawes Act. As long as hostile tribes continued to defy the government, interest in requiring obedience was natural. The outstanding feature of the new movement was a desire to coerce the peaceful as well as the warlike. Yet even during the seventies Commissioner [of Indian Affairs Francis A.] Walker, Colonel [Edward S.] Otis and other prominent students of Indian relations insisted that progress would be impossible unless all red men were made to obey the wishes of the government. As there was no use in enacting legislation if the power necessary for successful administration was omitted, more and more Americans were becoming convinced of the necessity for force as the decade ended. The effect of this growing impatience with Indian opposition was clearly revealed when George E. Ellis concluded a history of American Indian affairs in 1882 by announcing:

> We have a full right, by our own best wisdom, and then even by compulsion, to dictate terms and conditions to them; to use constraint and force; to say what we intend to do, and what they must and shall do . . . This rightful power of ours will relieve us from conforming to, or even consulting to any troublesome extent, the views and inclinations of the Indians whom we are to manage. A vast deal of folly and mischief has come of our attempts to accommodate ourselves to them, to humor their whims and caprices, to indulge them in their barbarous ways and their inveterate obstinacy. Henceforward they must conform to our best views of what is for their good. The Indian must be made to feel he is in the grasp of a superior.

With this uncompromising statement, a majority of the public was in accord. Americans of the eighties were determined to brook no further opposition to Indian reform.

Among the most active champions of force were many Indian agents. Although numerous field officials opposed the severalty program, a large number of others insisted that it was "the duty of the Gov't to *push* the Indians on to civilization, not lead and expect them to follow." Several of the men most closely connected with the tribes, in fact, sprang into prominence because of the vigor of their reports. Thus Agent McGillycuddy of Pine Ridge attracted national attention because of his attacks on Indian independence; while Agent Milroy, who never failed to send a detailed report of the Yakimas, believed that "the whims and wishes of ignorant Indians should not be consulted or permitted to interfere" once proper methods for reform had been decided. Agent Armstrong of the Crows, who had so strongly insisted upon the inalienability of allotments, was equally determined that Indians should not reject severalty. He well expressed the disgust of many Indian workers with any policy of temporizing when he complained:

> I believe the Government should adopt a more vigorous policy with the Indian people. I can see no reason why a strong Government like ours should not govern and control them and compel each one to settle down and stay in one place, his own homestead, wear the white man's clothing, labor for this own support, and send his children to school. I can see no reason why . . . good and true men and women should come to an Indian agency and labor honestly and earnestly for three or four or a dozen years trying to *coax* or *persuade* the Indians to forsake their heathenish life and adopt the white man's manner of living, and then go away feeling they have thrown away, almost, the best years of their lives. The truth is the Indians hate the white man's life in their hearts, and will not adopt it until driven by necessity.

As several other agents were only slightly less outspoken, wholehearted co-operation in a policy of force could be expected from many field workers.

The hatred of caution, which led Armstrong to condemn American Indian policy, was shared by a group of United States senators who became noted for the bitterness of their attacks upon Indian autonomy. No doubt concerning the value of coercion was entertained at least by Senator [John J.] Ingalls of Kansas when he remarked:

> Some races are plastic and can be molded; some races are elastic and can be bent; but the Indian is neither; he is formed out of rock, and when you change his form you annihilate his substance . . . Civilization destroys the Indian . . . and the sooner the country understands that all these efforts are valueless unless they are based upon force supplemented by force and continued by force, the less money we shall waste and the less difficulty we shall have.

Senator [John T.] Morgan of Alabama and Senator [Henry M.] Teller of Colorado were especially active in demanding the exercise of congressional authority over all Indians. Whatever policy was adopted such senators insisted that it must be solely the product of white deliberation. Concessions to Indian prejudices should not be permitted to stand in the way of wise legislation. Certain features of the Dawes Act were the result of sympathy for the red man's interests; but the measure as a whole gave the United States more power over Indian affairs than any previous enactment mainly because a number of legislators had at last decided that the whims of a minority race should dictate American Indian policy no longer.

While the interest of Indian agents and congressmen in strengthening their control over the Indians was not surprising, the enthusiasm of reformers for a drastic assertion of national authority is less easy to explain. Whereas concern for Indian rights might have been expected to cause opposition to the use of force, many leading friends of the race recommended coercion. Lyman Abbott, who exercised a wide influence among American intellectuals as editor of the *Christian Union,* urged Senator Dawes to make allotment both immediate and compulsory. The second conference of Indian friends at Lake Mohonk criticized a Coke bill clause requiring two-thirds consent as an outrageous impediment to freedom of action. Captain Pratt of Carlisle advised that Indians be "so thoroughly conquered as to be convinced of the futility of further resistance." In each case, reformers hoped that the race would benefit from the forceful action of whites who had studied the Indian problem and believed that they had found a way to avoid ultimate racial conflict. Only if all Indians surrendered their right of self-determination did such men feel that annihilation could be averted. No better proof of the strength of this conviction exists than the eagerness with which reformers urged violation of Indian treaties whenever attainment of their end seemed impossible by other means.

Indian treaties had been condemned as obstacles to an effective Indian policy long before the eighties. When the act of 1871 prohibited further negotiations with Indian tribes, abrogation of previous treaties was prevented only because the Senate insisted that nothing should be interpreted as invalidating any arrangement already concluded. As provisions of outmoded agreements rapidly grew more and more embarrassing to the government, the treaty problem attracted increasing attention. A surrender of established rights in return for new privileges was frequently suggested as a solution of the difficulty; but actual abrogation under a higher law appealed much more strongly to the realistic men in charge of Indian relations. Thus Commissioner E. P. Smith asked in 1874 whether the government should hold itself bound forever by bargains which damaged both the nation and its wards; and his successor urged that public necessity demanded the adoption of enforced allotment and sale of surplus land as the supreme law of the land. For a time, this official attitude was reflected only in abrogation of such out-moded provisions as the right to hunt. But the idea spread rapidly that Congress should modify all treaty provisions for Indian benefit. Since legislators had not hesitated to violate treaties for selfish gain, reformers argued, there was no reason why they should not also be disregarded when the future of the Indian was at stake.

In recommending treaty violation, reformers were treading on dangerous ground. Although previous treaties now seemed "absurd" in many instances, there was a strong possibility that the chaos resulting from their abrogation might make matters considerably worse. Legislators could not "make the bargain upon both sides," as a House committee proposed, without exposing American Indian policy to change at the whim of each succeeding Congress. Yet many reformers condemned all who insisted that Indians treaties should be observed. Lyman Abbott, in particular, used his influence as editor of the *Christian Union* to demand that no agreement should be allowed to prevent immediate land allotment. So seriously did Abbott's position threaten the sanctity of Indian treaties that men interested in upholding the honor of the United States became greatly alarmed. Senator Dawes and Secretary [Herbert] Welsh of the Indian Rights Association occasionally displayed an interest in forceful reform; but a report in which the latter described an unsuccessful effort to battle Abbott's views reveals the earnestness with which both men fought treaty violation. Welsh left no doubt that abrogation of Indian agreements was obnoxious to many supporters of severalty when he wrote Dawes:

I am well aware of the views held by Dr. Abbott. I do not think that he has long studied the Indian question or has seen the Indian in his home. I believe that the radical nature of his views as to how the Indian problem may and should be solved would be greatly modified by close contact with the cold facts of the question, which at present do not come within his range of vision. I think he is disposed to look with impatience upon Indian Treaties, and to believe that *they,* rather than *their violation,* have heretofore prevented the solution of the question. I believe he is inclined to give more credit to Western men for honest and just intentions toward the Indian than my short experience makes me think they are entitled to. The more I reflect upon it the more I regret your absence from the meeting recently held at the office of the Christian Union. I of course fully understand that it was unavoidable. The burden rested upon my shoulders of opposing the crude and radical views expressed by Dr. Abbott. Dr. Rhoads who previous to our meeting had spoken to me with extreme dissatisfaction of these views as already set forth in the columns of the Christian Union, remained perfectly silent when the same opinions were expressed by word of mouth. I did my best to show that it was only by an appeal to treaties which were the groundwork of our relations to the Indians that we had so far succeeded in protecting him from fraud and spoliation, and that in cases where a modification of the treaties was necessary a fair appeal to the Indians in the matter would secure the needed change without a lawless violation of our faith. I do not know how far my views had the sympathy of those present. I felt as though I were very much alone.

Welsh's despair was justified. With many reformers becoming so radical that the movement threatened to exceed proper bounds, advocates of severalty had a harder task defeating dangerous proposals than they had winning votes for reform.

While Senator Dawes denied that his act interfered with the fulfillment of treaty obligations, the measure gravely menaced racial independence. Stimulation of a respect for Indian agreements could hardly be expected of legislation obviously constructed on the theory that tribes should be destroyed by being ignored. The continued effectiveness of treaty provisions depended upon preservation of the tribal units which had concluded the agreements. Such a destruction of Indian government could hardly be achieved by voluntary action. "The idea," Senator Dawes explained, "is to take the Indians out one by one from under the tribe, place him in a position to become an independent American citizen, and then before the tribe is aware of it its existence as a tribe is gone." Although responsibility for outright treaty violation was avoided by such indirection, the ultimate effect on established Indian rights was the same. Attempts to under-estimate the coercive nature of the Act by pointing out that ninety of 159 reservations were already subject to executive order were beside the point. The significant accomplishment of the Dawes Act, as realistic students of Indian affairs recognized at the time, was the portion of the measure which brought an end to tribal authority by forcing tribes to allow allotment upon the request of individual members. Thereafter privileges based upon racial dissimilarity were no longer of importance.

Passage of the Dawes Act was a victory for the champions of force. Most reformers only regretted that President Cleveland might not demand immediate allotment. But while presidential discretion could protect the tribes temporarily, ultimate Indian submission was certain to prove only a matter of time. Little chance of delay in forceful application of the Dawes Act remained after such a strong and influential conservative as Secretary Lamar reported in 1887 that the government should no longer rely solely upon the attractive aspects of civilized life to convince Indians of the value of reform. Executive judgment was the sole obstacle to coercive action and popular pressure immediately gave indications of weakening the caution of even Cleveland and Lamar. A new day for the Indians was clearly at hand. Whether it was to be bright or stormy rested with the future.

Originally published as Chapter 18, "The Decision to Use Force," of *Uncle Sam's Stepchildren: The Reformation of United States Indian Policy, 1865–1887* (New Brunswick, N.J.: Rutgers University Press, 1942), pp. 233-47. Bracketed insertions added. All footnotes omitted.

Federal Indian Policy and the Southern Cheyennes and Araphoes, 1887-1907

DONALD J. BERTHRONG

The Cheyenne and Arapaho tribes divided into northern and southern groups shortly after William Bent built his fort on the Arkansas River in 1832. A majority of the tribes came south, leaving their hunting grounds of the northern plains, their possession of the lands north of the Arkansas River being recognized by the Treaty of Fort Laramie in 1851.

Part of these new lands of the Southern Cheyennes and Arapahoes contained gold—the object of the Colorado gold rush of 1859. When the white settlers swarmed into western Kansas territory, these Cheyennes and Arapahoes no longer enjoyed the undisturbed possession of their lands. Pushed into a small, barren reservation in southeastern Colorado by the Treaty of Fort Wise in 1861, the Cheyennes and Arapahoes broke out in a series of raids along the Colorado-Kansas frontier. The loss of their hunting grounds was difficult to accept, and further resentment was created by the Chivington Massacre at Sand Creek in 1864. Proximity to the Whites was now impossible—the young braves demanded the war path which the chiefs knew would lead to vigorous retaliation. At the treaties of Little Arkansas and Medicine Lodge Creek in 1865 and 1867 respectively, the federal government attempted to establish reservations for the Cheyennes and Arapahoes, which they refused to occupy. Campaigns led by Winfield Scott Hancock, George A. Custer, William T. Sherman, and Philip H. Sheridan convinced the peaceful bands among these Indians that further military resistance would lead to extermination. Thus by 1869, the Southern Cheyennes and Arapahoes, though refusing the treaty reservations, had settled on the North Canadian River in the present state of Oklahoma, and in that year President Grant by executive order set aside approximately four million, three hundred thousand acres of land in western Indian Territory. Not until 1875, however, did the Southern Cheyennes and Arapahoes finally cease to be a problem to the military forces in and around western Indian Territory.

Railroads brought settlers, and as the states surrounding Indian Territory became filled, the island of little used land was covetously desired by western frontiersmen. Oklahoma boomers made the virtues of the unused lands known to other land hungry people. After the passage of the Dawes Act in 1887 which provided the means for the final reduction of the Indian reservations and the opening of the Oklahoma lands in 1889, the fate of the tribal lands was sealed. Any honest reflection on the condition of these tribes would have led to the conclusion that the application of the Dawes Act to the Cheyennes and Arapahoes would be a serious mistake. The vast majority of these tribes were totally unprepared to accept citizenship and the individual ownership of land. Captain J. M. Lee, Cheyenne and Arapaho agent, in 1886 conceded that at best after another continuous decade of progress he could class these Indians as "semi-civilized." Lee's description supported his position. ". . . Many adhere tenaciously to their old customs—the plurality of wives, . . . medicine making, holding of property in common, with many other ancient practices and superstitions. . . ." Further, these Indians cultivated only 1,868 acres of land which was divided into some two hundred and eighty Indian farms. Although complete statistics are lacking, one suspects that much of this land was being farmed by inter-married Whites or Indians of mixed blood.

Progress and the program of allotting Indian lands in severalty could not be checked, so Lee was replaced by G. D. Williams, who agreed completely with federal policy. With more imagination than realism Williams reported that eighty per cent of the Indians of the reservation were "industrious and successful workers." By implication, the Cheyenne and Arapaho reservation was dotted with "neatly whitewashed" houses and five to one hundred acre farms, all being successfully worked by the Indians. Charles F. Ashley, Williams' successor, attempted to correct these optimistic statements when he assumed control of the agency's affairs in 1889. He found the agency in a "very demoralized condition," a number of farms abandoned, and more distressing, almost complete opposition to allotment. The bitterest opposition to the federal policy centered in the non-progressive nucleus led by Young Whirlwind, Little Big Jake, Little Medicine, and Howling Wolf who had replaced the old war chiefs such as Stone Calf and Little Robe after their deaths. These Indians in the 1870's located themselves in the western portion of the reservation where they maintained their tribal camps, living on their annuity goods, treaty monies, and such tribute as they could exact from the herds of Texas cattle which passed over their lands to the cattle towns of Kansas.

Despite the obvious fact that the Cheyennes and Arapahoes

were not sufficiently advanced to make the successful transition to citizenship and its implications, the Cherokee Commission arrived at Darlington, Oklahoma Territory, on July 7, 1890, to begin negotiations for allotment and the sale of surplus land. Forty days of negotiation failed to produce an agreement, and a recess was called until the first week of October. When the non-progressives refused to meet at the appointed site, the commissioner easily prevailed upon the progressives to accept the government's terms. Rumor that those who signed the agreement were to be killed did not prevent Left Hand, principal chief of the Arapahoes, from signing and others followed his example. Rapidly gaining the assent of the progressives and padding the list of signatures with those of women and children, the government officials considered the agreement ratified by the middle of November, 1890. Evidence points to the fact, however, that the agents never acquired seventy-five per cent of the signatures of the adult males as required by the treaty of 1867.

The agreement, nonetheless, was approved on March 3, 1891, and each Cheyenne and Arapaho on the rolls was allotted one hundred and sixty acres of land which was to remain in trust for twenty-five years. The surplus lands were purchased by the federal government for one and one half million dollars. One million of this sum was deposited in the United States Treasury to bear five per cent interest, and the remainder was distributed among these Indians on a per capita basis in two separate payments.

Even while the allotting process was taking place, the press of Oklahoma Territory demanded that the allotting agents reserve some of the more fertile agricultural land for White occupation. Pressure was applied to speed up the allotting of lands so that the Cheyenne and Arapaho reservation could be thrown open to settlement. Indian allotments were not selected with reference to their value for agricultural purposes. Some Indians preferred to take their allotments at or near the sites of their old tribal camps, and thus were assigned lands which could not be adapted to agriculture. Few of the Indians located in the western portion of the reservation possessed lands which could support an Indian family by agricultural pursuits. Those Indians, however, residing in the more fertile eastern portion of the reservation still retained enough land to support a family unit if the land was fully utilized.

With the destruction of the institution of communal property, an integral factor in the Indians' culture, and the taking of land in severalty, a critical point in the history of the tribes was reached. By legislative enactment and "mutual agreement" the Indian was forced to assume one of the basic institutions of western civilization—that of private property. This institution demands, however, certain conditions if it is to operate for the benefit of the individual concerned. First, the property owner must have the ability to protect the rights inherent in the possession of private property. Second, he must have the desire and needed knowledge to profit by the ownership of his property. Third, he must either enjoy sufficient cultural similarity to comprehend and attain the ultimate objectives of the surrounding community or he must enjoy a toleration of his differing culture. Since attitudes present on the western frontier clearly ruled out toleration of Indian culture, the criteria then for the judgment of the federal Indian policy should be based upon the success or failure of the Indians to adjust to the problems of the ownership of private property.

A superficial analysis might show that the federal government between 1887 and 1907 did protect the rights of the Cheyennes and Arapahoes, for title of the Indian land was retained without encumbrances, a leasing policy was adopted which contributed money to the Indians' support, and local taxation was minimized by rulings of the Interior Department. As a citizen of the United States after accepting land in severalty, the Indian had recourse to the courts for redress of his grievances, and as a citizen of Oklahoma Territory his right to vote could be used to protect his social and political privileges. Yet, as we view this twenty year period, our judgment must be that the Indian policy of the federal government failed when applied to the Cheyennes and Arapahoes.

Of tremendous significance to the Indian was the retention, protection, continued control, and utilization of the allotted land. As long as the land was held in trust by the government, it could not be encumbered or alienated. Inroads, however, were made on the Indian land. With few exceptions, the Cheyennes and Arapahoes did not possess either the ability or the resources necessary to cultivate the lands of the family unit which averaged about eight hundred acres. At best by 1892 the Indians had planted small vegetable patches and a few acres of corn. Thus, most of the Indian lands would lie idle unless opened to White men for farming and grazing. After inspecting the Cheyenne and Arapaho Agency, J. M. Lee, an army officer and ex-Cheyenne and Arapaho agent, predicted that reduction of the Indian land would be demanded unless it was opened to White use.

Early in 1891, Congress enacted a statute which permitted the leasing of Indian lands, thereby opening them to the farmer and cattleman. The Commissioner of Indian Affairs interpreted this law closely and would not permit indiscriminate leasing. Indians having ". . . the necessary physical and mental qualifications to enable him to cultivate his allotment, either personally or by hired help . . ." were barred from leasing. Still, this freed most of the allotted lands for leasing—only the adult male's lands were restricted. Changes in the leasing rules, occurring in 1894, 1897, 1900, and 1902, confused the agents and hampered a consistent leasing program. But the general tenor of these revisions was more favorable to the White than to the Indian. By 1902 an Indian male was required to retain only forty acres of land for his own cultivation; hence the remainder of his and his family's land could be leased. The length of leasing time varied between one and five years depending on the type of lease, and in general the Indians could lease if they did not benefit from the improvement of their allotments ". . . by reason of age, disability, or inability."

It was the hope of the federal officials to protect the Indian's allotment by leasing the land to Whites. This would quiet the demands for further reduction of Indian lands. In addition, the Indian's unbroken lands would be brought into cultivation, improvement would be placed on the allotment in the form of houses, fences, wells, and orchards which would be of great value to the Indian after the expiration of the lease. Further, the Indian would benefit from the lessons derived by watching the White farmer at work. Rarely, however, was the lease contract of lasting value to the Indian. Improvements were seldom placed on the land, lease contracts were broken with impunity because of the reluctance of the courts to hold in favor of the Indian, trespass could not be prevented, and Whites often refused either to move from the Indian's land once leased or to pay the money due the Indian. If a contract was agreed to, the lessor often removed his crops and left the country without paying the lease money. "Informal leases" were always a source of worry to the agents. Because farmers and cattlemen offered small sums or gifts to Indians for the use of their land without the agent's knowledge, land was thus obtained for a fraction of its value. Indians did not materially gain additional knowledge through the leasing process either. Although complete statistics are not available, undoubtedly more than 2,000 of the 3,293 allotments of the agency were held by Whites by 1901. The agent and his subordinates handled all the details—appraised the land, set the conditions of the contract, collected and distributed the lease money, while the Indian remained an uncomprehending witness to the process. Hence this method by which the Indian was to have been protected in the rights of his property did not ultimately operate completely to his benefit.

For the most part, the Indian remained in the tribal camp or settlement despite vigorous efforts to make him occupy his allotment. The "object lesson" of White agriculture was of little avail and the lease money was used to enjoy the old way of life. Undoubtedly, the White utilization of the Indian allotments by leasing created the desire to purchase this land, and the demand was strengthened by the growth of towns where real estate agents hoped to buy Indian allotments adjacent to the town. Thus, the opening of the reservation and the leasing of agricultural and grazing lands, originally designed to protect the Indian, only stimulated the desire for the additional reduction of Indian lands. Further inroads were made possible after 1902 when Congress enacted legislation enabling the Indian to sell inherited lands.

The problem of the land was certainly the most important example of the Indian's inability to control the disposition of his property, but others can be cited. As a citizen the Indian was placed on the local tax roles and all property not ultimately derived from the federal government was liable for taxes by the local governments. More often than not the Indian's personal property was assessed above its value. Without political influence within these essentially antagonistic local governments, the Indian was at the mercy of the assessors because the over-burdened agency staff could not take the separate actions required in the local courts. Another common injury to the Cheyennes and Arapahoes resulted from the usurious rate of interest charged to the Indians when they borrowed money on personal notes or chattel mortgages. Although interest rates of one hundred per cent or more were charged, the limited staff of the United States District Attorney could handle but few court cases when property was seized for payment of the note or mortgage. One final example will illustrate the Indian's helplessness in protecting his property. When herd laws were passed for Oklahoma Territory, strays could be seized and held until damages were paid for the crops injured or destroyed. White farmers seized the Indians' stock and collected their damages, but few damages were paid to the Indians except where the agency officials could intervene. Clearly, the Indian did not possess the ability to protect his property during the period which we have under consideration.

The obvious profits from the ownership of private property, it was hoped, would stimulate in the Indian the desire to cultivate his land and acquire additional competence. Two different levels of education would provide the Indians with the needed knowledge to engage in gainful employments. Young Indians in day, boarding, mission, and non-reservation schools were educated in basic academic and practical vocational subjects. Adult male Indians were instructed by district farmers who resided among them and demonstrated better agricultural techniques. However interpreted, the educational policies of the federal government depended upon the utilization of the Indians' main source of wealth—land.

Rather than stimulating the desire for further profits, the lease money and funds derived through the sale of inherited lands only provided the means for the Indian to continue his tribal existence. Camps and settlements, despite efforts of the agents, could not be broken up so long as the Indian was not dependent upon the cultivation of his own allotment or engagement in other employment. Education by itself was of little value unless the Indians possessed enough money to buy the tools needed for agriculture. Lease and annuity funds were used to pay debts to local merchants or their agents who gathered at the payments, and the money derived from the sale of inherited lands was for the most part doled out at the rate of ten dollars a month to prevent fraudulent and immediate separation of the Indian from his money. Young Indians educated at Haskell, Chilocco, or Carlisle returned home and quickly resumed tribal life, partly because of the conservative pressure of their elders and also from the lack of funds to buy the implements needed for successful agriculture.

Another critical factor in the failure of the Indian to progress towards self support was the incompetency of the agency personnel. For thirteen years, from 1893 to 1906, the agent or superintendent was a military officer, who, although a conscientious administrator, did not fulfill the needs of the Indian. A versatile and able man, well grounded in agriculture and stock raising, was needed above all. Since the army officers rarely were intimately concerned with agriculture, they could not correct the mistakes of their subordinates, the district farmers. The agents too often relied upon the advice of these district farmers, some of whom were equal to the task of instructing the Indians, but others were too old or were appointed solely through political influence.

As well intended or sympathetic as the federal educational policy might have been, it failed miserably when applied to the Cheyennes and Arapahoes. These Indians possessed private property in the form of ponies, food, and traders' goods but were not vitally interested in the further acquisition of private property. The leasing policy, sale of inherited lands, and education did little to change the Indian's original attitude towards his property. His culture was not dependent upon the acquisition of property but only upon its immediate availability and use. Without establishing the basic relationship between the acquisition of property and continued or increased quantities of useful goods, the Indian policy in this period was doomed to failure.

After the opening of the Cheyenne and Arapaho reservation

on April 19, 1892, the Indian became a minority group surrounded by a hostile and non-understanding majority. By legislative enactments or governmental policy the community tried to remake the Indians' social way of life. Plural marriages were prohibited, communal life in villages was forbidden, old chiefs were replaced by submissive headmen, the Indians' religious practices were discouraged, and medicine men curtailed in the performance of their rituals. These brusque efforts to force cultural change often only resulted in a further withdrawal into protective social mechanisms.

When the Messiah craze reached the Cheyennes and Arapahoes late in 1889, many of the conservatives hoped for a general adoption of this religious manifestation. Some adherents were gained, although the Indian officials discredited the movement through the use of progressives. More serious were the religious practices built upon the use of the peyote button obtained from the Kiowas or from Mexican traders. The Peyote Cult quickly arose in considerable force after 1899 and despite all efforts of the agents it gained converts among the progressives and non-progressives alike. Leaders of the cult were prosecuted in courts, but the Indians, finding refuge in the dreams produced by the use of peyote, showed their antagonism to the religion of Christianity.

Nor did the Whites desire to assimilate the Indians through educational means. When schools were opened in the counties, Whites were outspoken in their demand that Indian children continue to attend their established schools despite the fact that the federal government offered to pay tuitions well above the costs of the Indian pupils. The exceptions to the rule were those children of mixed blood whose parents resided in the towns.

How well did the Dawes Act and subsequent Indian policy succeed to 1907? When the Burke Act of 1906 was enacted enabling the Secretary of the Interior to declare certain Indians competent, thus granting them the right to manage their own affairs and receive the patent to their allotment in fee simple, Charles E. Shell, Superintendent in Charge of the Cheyenne and Arapaho Agency, could only find 115 Indians out of more than 2,700 whom he could recommend for independent status. The effectiveness of the program, however, is further reduced when one finds that many of those included in the 115 were mixed bloods who had lived outside of the influence of the Indian policy for over a generation. Although it is not the object of this paper to discuss Indian policy after 1907, certainly the acts and policy between 1887 and 1907 contributed to the further increase of landless Indians. As of 1949 it has been conservatively estimated that 2,000 of the 3,000 Cheyennes and Arapahoes were without land.

Originally published in *Ethnohistory* 3 (Spring 1956): 138–48. All footnotes omitted.

The Indian New Deal

By the 1920s the condition of Indians in the United States was extremely serious. They were rapidly losing their land, and their culture was still under attack by government officials and reformers who continued to insist that they must be assimilated into white society. Indian arts and crafts were dying out; Indian children were forced to attend schools that represented an alien culture and many were sent to distant boarding schools over parental opposition; and native dances were prohibited because the government judged them pagan ceremonies that hindered acceptance of Christianity. Furthermore, public concern for the Indians had dropped sharply after the passage of the Dawes Act, but that changed radically in the mid-twenties.

The initial stimulus to renewed interest in Indians was provided by the Bursum bill. Introduced into the Senate in 1922, it would have accelerated the loss of land by Pueblo Indians, and it aroused an outcry of resentment by Indians and whites and inaugurated a campaign to reform federal Indian policy that ultimately led to the Indian New Deal under Franklin Roosevelt and his Commissioner of Indian Affairs, John Collier. The bill provoked an organized protest by the Pueblo people and generated a series of organizations devoted to Indian welfare. Led by John Collier, the dynamic American Indian Defense Association sparked the crusade for reform. The General Federation of Women's Clubs cooperated, as did the older Indian Rights Association. Mass meetings were held and investigations were begun, and both stimulated new excitement. National magazines such as Sunset, Survey, Current History, *and* Forum *carried muckraking articles describing conditions on the reservations and indicting the current administration of Indian affairs. The clamor was so great that when Hubert Work became Secretary of the Interior in 1923, he instructed the Board of Indian Commissioners to investigate and organized a National Advisory Committee of one hundred prominent Americans to study the question. In 1926 Work authorized an independent organization, the Institute of Government Research, to prepare an impartial report on reservation conditions and federal policy, and its findings, issued in 1928 as* The Problem of Indian Administration *(also known as the Meriam Report), echoed the criticisms of reformers and recommended changes similar to those suggested by Collier and others.*

Reform began during the administration of Herbert Hoover, who appointed Ray Wilbur, president of Stanford University, to be Secretary of the Interior. Charles J. Rhoads, president of the Indian Rights Association, served as Commissioner of Indian Affairs and J. Henry Scattergood, a Philadelphia philanthropist, became assistant commissioner. The reform movement accelerated quickly when John Collier, the most outspoken critic of federal Indian policy, became commissioner in 1933. Collier selected like-minded men for high administrative positions in the bureau and instituted a series of reforms that led to a radical change in the direction of federal policies. The alienation of land was halted and steps were taken to purchase additional lands for some tribes. Efforts to destroy old customs gave way to acceptance of the unique aspects of Indian culture, and an Arts and Crafts Board was created in 1935 to stimulate the production of Indian goods. Additional funds were secured for Indian education, and the Johnson-O'Malley Act of 1934 authorized the Secretary of the Interior to enter into contracts with state agencies for education and other services. The most significant piece of Indian legislation of the New Deal period was the Indian Reorganization Act of 1934 (sometimes called the Wheeler-Howard Act), which incorporated the principle of self-determination, providing for tribal constitutions and self-government. The act was explained to the tribes and their opinions were solicited before its passage by Congress, and it applied only to those tribes that voted to accept it.

"The Genesis and Philosophy of the Indian Reorganization Act," by John Collier, was presented at a symposium on Indian affairs at the University of Arizona in 1954. It is a defense of his policies but also explains the principals underlying the Indian New Deal and describes the development of the Indian Reorganization Act and other important legislation.

William Zimmerman, who was brought into the bureau by Collier and served throughout the New Deal period, is also favorable to the reforms. His article describes the shift away from New Deal principles after Collier's resignation, and he is critical of the subsequent policy of termination, or the withdrawal of all government support of and control over the Indian people. The reaction of scholars and of a large segment of the Indian community is in accord with that of Zimmerman. Although some Indian groups bitterly resented certain aspects of the New Deal, there is general agreement that the termination policy was a disastrous mistake.

The Genesis and Philosophy of the Indian Reorganization Act

JOHN COLLIER

. . . I ask you to bracket with the IRA the Johnson-O'Malley Act of 1934; the Indian Arts and Crafts Board Act of the same year; the repeal of the so-called espionage acts affecting Indians, and of the regulations governing Indian religious observances; and the arrangements, administrative and budgetary, commencing in 1933, through which the Indian Service and the Department of Agriculture cooperated in ecological and land-utilization research and in soil and water conservation through nearly the entire Indian country outside Alaska. These several other enactments and arrangements were supplemental to the IRA and were "geared in" systematically with the IRA operations. I would even ask that you bracket with the IRA the Indian tribal claims act, formulated by Nathan R. Margold just before the Indian New Deal was launched, though it did not become law (through

Felix S. Cohen and William A. Brophy's efforts) until 1946; for this tribal claims act reaffirms one of the essential affirmations of the IRA, namely, the fundamentally bilateral nature of the Government-Indian relationship. This bilateral, mutually consenting, contractual nature and foundation of the Government-Indian relationship, graven at the very base of Federal Indian law and of Indian relations, is the particular datum which the present Congress and Interior Department, and President Eisenhower himself, have been oblivious to. . . .

Every thinker involved in Indian matters by 1922 recognized that particular ameliorations, and local or even universal defensive actions, within the system which [then existed] must be fruitless. President Lincoln had supplied a phrase: "The accursed system of Indian Affairs." All workers for and with Indians, by 1922, were convinced, obscurely or explicitly, that unless the philosophy in Indian matters could be changed, and the system of Indian affairs be reoriented and reconstructed, the tribes and their members were doomed. Therefore, from 1922 forward, while many particular struggles were waged, by the Indians and their white friends, the controlling preoccupation was that of discovering a new philosophy, and of ingressing a changed orientation and structuring, in the Federal-Indian relation. Effort for and by Indians became, to use an important current concept, problem-centered; and upon this problem of how to achieve a new orientation, first intellectually and then politically and legislatively, the work of the Indians and their friends became concentrated.

The solution was pursued through litigations, particularly those which were related to the Pueblo land situation . . . ; through researches into the history of Indian land tenure and use; researches into the history and the then-status of Indian indebtedness to the Government, totally around $60 million in the 1920's; researches historical and anthropological into the Indian organizations as they had existed, and still existed in limited regions, and into the effect upon Indian social energies of the destruction of the Indian organizations; and researches into the condition of the Indian resource-base and of its wastage, within the concept voiced to Congress by the Assistant Commissioner of Indian Affairs in 1917, that since the Indians were by policy being liquidated, their forest, soil and water resources should not be conserved but liquidated. I mention only two or three names of individuals and groups, the movers in these endeavors. One name is that of Richard H. Hanna of New Mexico, who handled the Pueblo land litigations and, subsequently, researches into aboriginal occupancy in Alaska; Congressman James A. Frear of Wisconsin and Senator William H. King of Utah, who brought genuinely first-rate intellects to bear upon the whole reach of the Indian's problems; the American Indian Defense Association, from 1923 onward; Nathan R. Margold, who studied with profound attention and creativeness the vast subject of Indian claims against the Government; the Senate Investigating Committee in the years 1927 to 1932; and the Brookings Institute, which produced in 1928 the monumental Meriam and Associates Report on *The Problem of Indian Administration*. . . .

I will now try to summarize the conclusions to which all of the 12 years of consultation, research and practical effort tended. Largely, these results had become verbalized into official utterances before the end of the Herbert Hoover presidency and the Wilbur-Rhoads-Scattergood Indian administration, 1929–33.

1. The new Indian policy must be built around the group-dynamic potentials of Indian life. This meant an ending of the epoch of forced atomization, cultural prescription, and administrative absolutism, and an affirmative experimental search for the power abiding within Indians, waiting for release through the enfranchisement or the re-creation of Indian grouphood.
2. The monolithic Federal-Indian administration, with stereotyped programs for all Indians everywhere, must be changed over to become a flexibly adapted and evolving administration, fitted to the cultural, economic, geographic and other diversities of the Indians, which the generations of the steam roller had not been able to flatten out.
3. In place of an Indian Bureau monopoly of Indian Affairs, there must be sought a cumulative involvement of all agencies of helpfulness, Federal, state, local and unofficial; but the method must not be that of simply dismembering the Indian Service, but rather of transforming it into a technical

servicing agency and a coördinating, evaluating, and, within limitations, regulatory agency.

4. Finally, and most difficult to state in a few words, the conclusion emerged that the bilateral contractual relationship between the Government and the tribes (the historical, legal and moral foundation of Government-Indian relations) must no longer be merely ignored and in action thrust aside and replaced by unilateral policy-making. Rather, instrumentalities must be revived, or newly invented, to enable the bilateral relationship to evolve into modern practicable forms—forms through which the "group life-space" of the tribes could shift from the exclusively governmental orientation toward an orientation to the American commonwealth in its fullness. I state this last conclusion rather ponderously and abstractly; but at the very core of the Indian Reorganization Act, precisely, is the revival, and the new creation of, means through which the Government and the tribes reciprocally, mutually, and also experimentally, can develop the Federal-Indian relation, and the Indian relation to all the rest of the Commonwealth, on into the present and future.

. . In the Fall of 1933, the tribes were circularized with questions inviting discussion, the most urgent of these questions having to do with the allotted and fractionated Indian lands.

At the same time, Ward Shepard, then Chief Conservationist of the Indian Service, urged that, insofar as practicable, all Indian legislative proposals by the Interior Department be offered in a single legislative bill. There existed a philosophy, theory, or hypothesis, an integrating core of ideas. Let a single bill contain them, Shepard urged, and let the bill be justified to Congress, the Indians and the general public in terms of the knowledge out of which the bill had grown, and the philosophy it was designed to implement. This suggestion was agreed to, and in the Solicitor's Office, the prime movers were three: Nathan R. Margold, Solicitor; and Felix S. Cohen and Charles Fahy, Assistant Solicitors. The non-legal personnel of the Indian Office participated, and I mention particularly Walter V. Woehlke, Ward Shepard, and Robert Marshall. As introduced in the Senate and House by [Senator Burton K.] Wheeler of Montana and [Representative Edgar] Howard of Nebraska, the bill contained five sections. One section provided statutory authority and procedural direction for Indian tribal courts. This section was eliminated in committee. Another section empowered the Secretary of the Interior to consolidate the allotted lands and fractionated allotments, within limitations which safeguarded all property rights. This section, too, was eliminated in committee. The substance of the remaining three sections became law. Two important provisos, not in the bill as introduced, were added. One of these was a requirement that tribes which should bring themselves under the Act should conserve their vegetative, soil, water, and timber resources. The other proviso, initiated by Representative Howard, Chairman of the House Indian Committee, imported into Federal statute-making a new element; it made the Indian Reorganization Act operative, after enactment, only when a given tribe, at a formal referendum of all its male and female adult members, voted to make it operative.

Senate and House hearings, starting early in 1934, went ahead for more than two months. They were suspended while the bill was discussed at regional congresses of the tribes—congresses fully recorded. The Congressional hearings were resumed, and the bill was passed in July, 1934. I sketch briefly the main features of the Indian Reorganization Act:

It prohibited the future allotment of Indian lands; empowered those tribes which might incorporate under the Act to proceed with the voluntary consolidation of fractionated lands; and established a policy, and authorized the funds, for the purchase of needed lands, titles to be not individual but tribal.

It established a revolving credit fund, in the nature of grants to tribes which then would lend their portion of the fund to individuals and associations within the given tribes; and repayments would stay with the tribe for relending.

It provided that any tribe so desiring could form itself into that which the Supreme Court had defined the New Mexico Pueblos to be: "In the nature of municipal corporations," with home-rule powers in the political and human-relations spheres. A tribal constitution, once adopted, could be annulled or amended only through the tribe's own initiative.

It provided similarly and with like safeguards for tribal charters of incorporation for economic enterprises.

It authorized the incorporated and/or chartered tribes not merely to take to themselves, in advancing stages, the functions of the Indian Bureau, but in addition, to draw to themselves, through contracts, or otherwise, state and local services and the services of unofficial agencies. (The Johnson-O'Malley Act of the same year, 1934, similarly authorized the Interior Department to devolve its Indian Service functions, through contracts and grants-in-aid, to local authorities and unofficial organizations, but not to jettison the bilateral Federal-Indian relationship in the process of development.)

The IRA directed that the yearly Appropriation Requests of the Indian Bureau be submitted beforehand to the organized tribes, for their criticism and suggestions.

It provided for Indian preference in employment in Indian Service; the possibility of an autonomous Indian Civil Service was thus created; and by implication, the establishment within Indian Service of a job-classification system, making possible a career service within tribal or ecological areas.

Finally, the Act authorized the funds requisite for the advanced education of Indians—for their technical and professional training, whether toward careers in their own people's service or in the general community.

. . . I would give this final, as it were "mountain-top" view of the *intention* of the Act and of the acts and policies complementing it.

That intention was that the *grouphood* of Indians, twenty thousand years old in our Hemisphere, should be acknowledged as being the human and socially dynamic essential, the eternal essential, now and into the future as of old. It should be grouphood culturally, as rooted in the past as the group at issue—each group among the hundreds—might desire, and as modern, American-oriented and implemented as the group at issue might desire. Definitely, finally, cultural determination for Indians was not to be a function of governmental authority from this point forth. Cultural determination, by American public philosophy, has been and is the function of all our many thousands of human groups; the IRA only restored this fundamental of mental and moral health to the only groups which officially or governmentally had been denied it, the Indians.

I add: this affirmation of cultural diversity and cultural autonomy did not imply a doctrine or practice of *laissez-faire* either within the Indian group or in Government or the surrounding Commonwealth. It implied, rather, the attractive and permissive way in place of the authoritarian way of swaying the human process. It implied leadership—within and without the Indian group—of the democratic and integrative type, not the regimenting, commanding and "bossing" type. I illustrate by the Indian Arts and Crafts Board, whose authority is only the negligible one of certifying the genuineness of Indian handicraft products. That Board has served, with an extremely minimal budget, as a creative power in the Dakotas, the Inter-mountain country, Alaska, the Southwest, and Oklahoma. I refer to a more massive case, but one equally as relevant to the Indian situation and the purposes of the IRA. That case is the modern soil conservation work, at this writing threatened with demolition from Washington, whose first demonstrations and "try-outs" were among the Indians after 1933; soil conservation work whose problem-areas are whole watersheds or sub-watersheds, whose dynamic is principally social-economic and esthetic and ecological and only subordinately engineering, and whose employment or authority is almost zero; and whose reliance is voluntary effort illumined by science—voluntary yet patterned effort. Of this sort is the principle of action embodied in the Indian Reorganization Act.

Originally published in *Indian Affairs and the Indian Reorganization Act: The Twenty Year Record* (Tucson: University of Arizona Press, 1954), pp. 3–8. Bracketed insertions added. Editorial omissions indicated by ellipses.

The Role of the Bureau of Indian Affairs since 1933

WILLIAM ZIMMERMAN, JR.

. . . When the Indian Reorganization Act was finally approved it was very different from the original bill. Unfortunately there was still much confusion. Many Indians thought that they were voting on the original bill. Some tribes were influenced by their superintendents and other agency employees who saw threats to their security. Others voted against it either because they were distrustful, having in mind a long series of unsatisfactory dealings with the government, or because they saw no quick way in which the Act would help them.

Almost immediately after the Act became law agitation began for its repeal. Yet the Act survived all attacks, and until 1950 it was certainly the foundation of policies formulated by the Bureau and the Department. At the risk of making a sweeping generalization to which everybody can take exception, I should conclude that the policy was beneficial to the Indians. Certain results can be documented. The sale of Indian land was halted, at least temporarily. Substantial additions to the Indian land base were made as the result of outright purchases, exchanges, and restoration of ceded lands. Other sources of money, notably appropriations to the Emergency Relief Administration and its successors, were tapped for the purchase of "submarginal lands"—mostly lands which had been farmed and ought to be restored to grass. Also carrying out the IRA policy of adding to the Indians' land, the Congress in four years added 1,200,000 acres by legislation.

One of the urgent needs of the Indians was capital and credit. The loan fund created by the Act and subsequently enlarged by the Oklahoma Indian Welfare Act was fully as important as the land fund. An outsider's appraisal of this activity in 1952 summarizes its success: "From June 30, 1936, to June 30, 1952, all types of loans by the Bureau totaled $30,911,060, of which $22,797,722 has been repaid, and $91,268 has been charged off. Thus from 1936 to 1952, losses due to charge off amounted to 0.22 per cent. This is an excellent record when operational difficulties, types of loans, and quality of credit bases are considered."

More land and more credit soon meant more extension work, more cattle, and more Indians farming. The control of grazing which had begun in the Rhoads administration was made more effective. For the first time a mass attack was made on soil wastage and bad land use. When the Soil Erosion Service, later Soil Conservation Service, was established in the Department of the Interior its first major operations were on Navaho and other Indian lands.

Conservation of forest resources began in 1911; it received new support from the language of the IRA directing "the operation and management of Indian forestry units on the principle of sustained yield management." In this field of resource conservation, great service was rendered by the Civilian Conservation Corps with its separate Indian unit and by the Public Works Administration. Public works money also made possible a rapid improvement in the medical and educational plants. Some twenty hospitals were repaired or enlarged and at least nine new ones were built.

In education the shift from boarding schools to public or federal day schools followed the recommendations of the Meriam report. The first state contracts for Indian education in public schools were with California and Washington for the fiscal year 1935. Contracts with Minnesota came a year later. New buildings and a new curriculum also appeared. Emphasis was placed on vocational training and on arts and crafts as a factor in Indian life and economy. The Arts and Crafts Board, working closely with the Education staff, labored to raise standards, to increase production and improve marketing; it also started many new enterprises. In the Eisenhower administration many of these programs have been shut down or abandoned, and Bureau support and guidance have been withdrawn.

In March 1944, in presenting his last budget to the House Appropriations Subcommittee, Commissioner Collier, responding in effect to an attack on him by the Senate Committee on Indian Affairs (Partial Report 310), made what turned out to be a valedictory:

> . . . We have tried to energize the individual Indian and the group, and to equip individual and group with knowledge and skills to enable them to go into the white world successfully if they want to or to hold their own and make their way where they are if they want to. That is the meaning of the Indian Reorganization Act and of all other major things we have been working at. . . . In brief, we have quit thinking about assimilation and segregation as opposite poles and as matters of "all or nothing." They are oversimplifications of thinking which do not connect themselves with the dynamic realities. Indians are more themselves than they have been for a long time, and they certainly are more assimilated than they ever were.

. . . With the accession of Dillon S. Myer as Commissioner of Indian Affairs in May 1950, the Bureau began a new epoch. Mr. Myer was not informed about Indians, but he had experience with the Japanese as Director of the War Relocation Authority. He had his own ideas about the administration of the Bureau. There was never a question of Mr. Myer's integrity and ability as an administrator. He was responsible for a general "tightening up" in administration.

According to the Commissioner, his first year saw "a great change in the basic organization of the Bureau." The result of this change was a further delegation of authority to area directors and an increase in their authority over superintendents. Superintendents have become the servants or errand boys of the area directors, for they have no control over funds or personnel.

New emphasis was placed on plans and programs. In particular, first steps were taken to start the Navaho rehabilitation program, which the Congress had approved before Mr. Myer became Commissioner. Other rehabilitation programs, such as the Papago, on which the tribal council had worked for several years, were not pushed. In connection with the Navaho education program, perhaps for the first time there appeared a flat statement by a Commissioner of Indian Affairs that "the Federal off-reservation education of Navahos is directed entirely toward the preparation of these children for permanent off-reservation employment." It is noteworthy that the utilization of the largest of the off-reservation schools, Intermountain School at Brigham City, Utah, was preceded by approval of the Navaho Tribal Council.

In the field of resources Commissioner Myer's own appraisal of his program read as follows:

> Development of the latent physical resources of the Indians throughout the Country is being hastened. Indian land is being brought under irrigation to protect their water rights, as well as to increase yields and convert large blocks of grazing land into productive crops. They are being provided with increased economic opportunities through industrial and agricultural development of their resources and adequate training programs to fit them for employment in skilled occupations off the reservations. There is oppor-

tunity for a wide expansion of cattle herds, establishment of small businesses, initiation of saw-mill enterprises to market Indian timber, and many other methods of increasing Indian income.

Mr. Myer also made one comment which deserves quotation here: "The Indians have demonstrated the progress they can make when financing and technical and supervisory assistance are made available to them."

Under Commissioner Myer came a change in credit policy, which was extended under Mr. Emmons. Intensive efforts were made, Mr. Myer reported in 1952, in his last annual report, to obtain loans for Indians from banks and other types of credit institutions rather than from the Bureau. As a part of this new policy, the Bureau issued regulations permitting Indians to mortgage trust or restricted land, thus reversing both policy and legal opinion which had prevailed since allotment began.

Several years later, some insurance companies expressed doubt as to the legality of this regulation. The Bureau then supported legislation to validate mortgages already made and leave no doubt as to future transactions. If the Bureau follows the same easy policy on mortgages that it has followed recently on land sales and patents in fee, the mortgage will become just one more easy road to land alienation.

The Bureau was also giving much attention to termination or withdrawal. Bills for the Indians of California and of western Oregon were presented to Congress, but were not enacted. Discussions were carried on about Klamath, Menominee, Osage, and other tribes. As to the Klamath and Menominee, Commissioner Myer's summary may stand as a model of understatement:

> Although both tribes indicated some initial reluctance to contemplate the prospect of Bureau withdrawal, a number of consultations were held with them during the fiscal year and efforts were being continued to elicit their active cooperation in the development of constructive programs.

In 1952, in a letter to the Chairman of the Osage Tribal Council, Commissioner Myer made three points about termination, the third of which has been subsequently ignored. As to tribes which desire to assume some of the responsibilities which the Bureau now carries, he was prepared, he wrote, "to work with such tribes in the development of an appropriate agreement, *without termination of the trusteeship relationship.*"

This was in effect a return to the plan proposed in 1947 by the present writer, who was then acting Commissioner of Indian Affairs, when he testified before the Senate Committee on Civil Service headed by Senator Langer. That testimony has since been repeatedly misquoted and misinterpreted. The Committee's announced purpose was to reduce the number of federal employees. The Indian Bureau was only one of many agencies to appear. Testifying under subpoena and replying to a demand from the Committee, the witness said that Bureau services could be curtailed or eliminated as to certain tribes and reservations, by groups. He specified certain criteria which the Congress should consider in such reduction in services, and he indicated that these criteria did not apply uniformly. In fact all four could not be applied to any one tribe.

The witness also submitted drafts of a number of proposed bills whose enactment would permit reduction in Indian Bureau personnel. A bill for Klamath Indians proposed a federal corporation with a life of fifty years and provided that "none of the property of the corporation shall be subject to taxation until otherwise provided by Congress." The Menominee proposal also called for a federal corporation and it specified that the tribal lands should remain in trust, non-taxable, and inalienable for fifty years.

These proposals were very different from the termination bills which the Klamath and Menominee Indians were finally constrained to accept. It was clear then, as it is now, that these tribes cannot survive economically if their tribal property is taxed.

Let us now examine the current situation with Glenn L. Emmons as Commissioner of Indian Affairs. It is not easy to evaluate the present, . . . partly because at so many points the actions of the Bureau are impossible to reconcile with announced policies. There is also disagreement within many tribes, as much disagreement about policies and personalities as there is on the outside. Much of the disagreement is the inevitable result of the ferment of the last twenty-odd years. Indians are more articulate now, and both the majority and the minority speak, vote, and occasionally fight for their opinions. Many Indians believe that the Bureau, instead of going along with a tribal majority, sides with the minority when the minority supports Bureau policy.

Sometimes, too, there is a break in the communication system. A Secretarial letter to a Washington, D.C., attorney made a basic decision about Blackfeet election procedures, but a copy of the letter was not sent to the tribe nor to the tribal attorney. Again, in a controversy at Fort Berthold, after two years of argument, a Departmental decision made possible the holding of an election; but public notice of the decision was apparently not given. One of the tribal factions learned of the decision which called for tribal action within a stated time limit from a private citizen, not from the Bureau. It is easy to argue that such lapses are inadvertent, but it is hard to persuade Indians that they are not all part of a pattern.

In two major fields, health and education, the Bureau has effected far-reaching changes since 1953.

First, in the field of health, on July 1, 1955, it completed the transfer of all medical work to the Public Health Service. The legislation requiring this transfer was sponsored by the Council of State and Territorial Health Officers and by numerous private organizations including the National Tuberculosis Association and the Association on American Indian Affairs. If any one person deserves major credit for this legislation it is the late Dr. A. J. Chesley, of Minnesota. The public record shows that it was initially opposed by the Department of the Interior and by the Department of Health, Education, and Welfare. Not until it became almost certain that the bill would pass did the Department of the Interior reverse its position.

The first result of the transfer was a large increase in appropriations; they rose from $21,000,000 in 1953 to $38,000,000 in 1956. For 1958, the Public Health Service is asking more than $50,000,000. There certainly has also been some marked improvement in medical services. More doctors are on duty, perhaps totaling 100, who are almost all young men subject to military draft. More patients are in hospitals, even though there are no additional nurses. After a year and a half in control the Public Health Service is still side-stepping two basic issues: which

Indians are eligible for medical care and which ones, if any, should pay for services. In a letter written in January, 1957, the Public Health Service comments: "No Indian, either on the reservation or off, has a legal entitlement to medical service under the Indian health program." If the Public Health Service should take the position that medical care for Indians is given as an act of grace, as may be here implied, it is certainly headed for trouble.

The Bureau under Commissioner Emmons claims and deserves credit for getting more children, especially Navahos, into school. In three years as a result of truly herculean efforts by the staff, especially employees on the Navaho reservation, the Navaho school attendance was increased by about 10,000 children. Most of these are in boarding schools at long distances from home. Many are in public schools in the "peripheral" towns of Gallup, Holbrook, Winslow, and others and are housed in Bureau-operated dormitories. The Bureau pays tuition for these children, and the federal government also pays for additional school capacity on the theory that these are "Federally impacted areas."

The Bureau in 1955 launched a pilot program in adult education designed to make five tribal groups literate in English, and it supported legislation for a program of vocational training. Yet, at the same time it has eliminated or curtailed many activities which seem to involve vocational training. Most of the school-cattle herds, beef and dairy, have been abolished or greatly reduced. School farms have been abandoned. The school farm at Flandreau, instead of being turned over to the local Indians, was declared surplus and offered for public sale. Arts and crafts projects have been shut down or left to shift for themselves. Bureau guidance and support have been stopped, as for example, for the Qualla Cooperative at Cherokee, North Carolina; the Sequoyah weaving project in Oklahoma; and the pottery and weaving project at Pine Ridge, South Dakota.

A new program, which may have important results, plans to bring industry to the reservations. About ten small factories are now either in operation or expected to begin operation before the end of 1957. Cheap, stable, labor supply is the lure; although in some places the attraction may be free land or a suitable building. The Navaho Tribe, for example, is paying for the construction of a building to house a children's furniture factory at Gallup. Again, however, a seeming inconsistency exists. Indian-owned enterprises are being liquidated. The Flandreau garment factory, which made a small profit during each year of its existence, was closed. Here was a small plant in a small Indian community whose average family income was less than $1,000 a year. The factory had a pay roll of about $28,000 last year, or an average of nearly $500 per family. On a very different scale is the Alaska fishing industry. After a profitable period of ten or fifteen years, the community-owned, Bureau-financed canneries lost large sums. The Bureau takes no share of the blame for mismanagement, but now plans to lease these canneries to private operators at nominal rentals. Presumably the non-Indian lessee will make a profit.

Two other major aspects or questions of policy remain to be considered; they are the attrition of the land base and the increased emphasis on relocation. The policy in the 1930's assumed a continuing increase in the land base. A real start was made. But World War II and the changes in policy since 1950 put an end to the purchase program. Recently a member of Congress, not himself opposed to wholesale land sales, said to me that if the present policy continued for another five years there would be no Indian reservations in his state, only Indians. In the past four years approximately 1,600,000 acres of Indian land have gone out of trust. This is roughly 12 per cent of the allotted lands. The present Bureau policy emphasizes the right of the competent Indian to take fee title to his allotment. It ignores the fact that the allotment was received because the individual owner was a member of the tribe, and that allotments were often made over tribal opposition. Even if the sale is detrimental to the neighbors or to the tribe, the sale goes through; the Commissioner, however, has said that he will hold key tracts. Even if the wholesale issuance of fee patents is defensible, there is greater doubt about the supervised sale of land belonging to incompetents. The Commissioner's reports disclose that more land has been sold by supervised sales than has been patented. Generally, such sales provide money for living expenses for a period of months, perhaps years;

after it has spent this money the family goes on some form of relief, or leaves the reservation.

To many Indians there seems no alternative to leaving the reservation, either voluntarily as thousands have already gone, as migrants, or now officially as "relocatees" receiving financial and other help. It is now just fifty years since the Bureau first made an effort to find off-reservation employment for Indians. In those fifty years thousands of Indians have left their homes, mostly for urban areas. Rapid City has 4,000 Indians. Nobody knows how many are in Minneapolis; estimates run from 3,000 to 8,000 or more. Seattle, Portland, Los Angeles, and Phoenix are centers of Indian migration. Smaller towns in many states have hundreds. Statistically there is no basis for saying that any certain percentage of migrant Indians will succeed. The same statistical lack exists for the officially relocated Indian. In the years when Dillon Myer was Commissioner of Indian Affairs, the placement service was revived under the new name; this was taken over from the War Relocation Service which concentrated Americans of Japanese ancestry in camps. Relocation in the present administration is being carried out on an increasing scale. Roughly, $1,000,000 was appropriated in 1956 and $3,500,000 in 1957 for carrying on this work. In 1955, 650 family groups and 800 single men and women were relocated, a total of 3,400 persons. Most of these required financial assistance. In 1957 approximately 10,000 persons will be relocated, of whom 80 per cent will need financial help. With increased appropriations, those who need help will receive larger, more nearly adequate sums: for transportation to the job, for a month's subsistence, for clothing, for furniture, and for a year's Blue Cross medical protection. Undoubtedly, some Indians are asking for relocation because they see no hope at home in the face of the current policies on land and credit. The Blackfeet to the contrary, as an example, recently advertised free sites to industries which would locate on the reservation and stated that 1,500 Indians available for work did not want to be relocated.

The history of government-Indian relations seems to be a succession of waves. One generation of Indian administrators seems to learn little from its predecessor. About thirty years passed, a generation, from the establishment of the Union to the beginning of the era of removal. About thirty years thereafter the planners and administrators began to argue for allotment. From 1857 to 1887 every Commissioner of Indian Affairs, except one, urged allotment.

The General Allotment Act of 1887 set a national policy, which reached its high mark just thirty years later, in 1917. At that time, Secretary of the Interior Franklin K. Lane approved the policy of Commissioner Cato Sells of issuing "forced patents" to Indians who were competent in his judgment, even though the Indians had not asked for patents. Today, through an act passed by the Congress in 1956, the Secretary of the Interior has the same power over Indians of the Five Tribes in Oklahoma. The Lane-Sells policy stopped abruptly when Charles H. Burke became Commissioner in 1921. Although Burke had some understanding of the realities of Indian affairs as a result of his service in Congress as chairman of the House Committee on Indian Affairs, he did not move far enough or fast enough to silence bitter critics of his administration. The Meriam Report of 1928, the policies of the Rhoads-Scattergood era, the Collier administration and the Indian Reorganization Act, all moved along the line of greater service, opportunity, and protection for the Indian.

This wave receded with the appointment of Dillon Myer as Commissioner in 1950. Gradually, Mr. Myer eliminated from the Bureau most of the top men who had been close to John Collier. Certainly there was a shift in policy. Since 1950 not one of the termination bills submitted by the Bureau includes a provision for federal incorporation as provided in the Indian Reorganization Act and as proposed by the Bureau in sample bills submitted in 1947. On the contrary, for any tribe organized under the IRA or the Oklahoma Indian Welfare Act, the Bureau's bills have called for revocation of tribal constitution and charter. The Bureau relies, of course, on the declaration of Congressional intent expressed in House Concurrent Resolution 108 of the Eighty-third Congress. That resolution said that certain tribes and the Indians in certain States are to be "freed from Federal supervision and control." It also included general language to the effect that Indians should be subjected as rapidly as possible to the same laws and entitled to the same privileges and responsibilities as other American citizens. The Eighty-fourth Congress gave some indication that it was not too sure about the Myer-Emmons wave. The only termination bills passed were at the request of tribes which specifically asked for the legislation. Not a single termination bill opposed by the tribe affected was passed.

At the beginning of the Eighty-fifth Congress, Senator Murray of Montana, Chairman of the Senate Committee on Interior and Insular Affairs, introduced Senate Concurrent Resolution 3 (the same text he had introduced in the Eighty-fourth Congress as Senate Concurrent Resolution 85). Representative Lee Metcalf, also of Montana, introduced the same language in House Concurrent Resolution 155. If adopted, this resolution would restate Congressional policy, for it directs the Bureau of Indian Affairs to carry out a Point-Four program for Indians and specifies that this program shall be offered "without exacting termination of Federal protection of Indian property or of any other Indian rights as its price."

Until the Congress does act, it is not likely that the Bureau of Indian Affairs will change its present policies. It is distressing, but impossible to ignore the conclusion voiced by employees as they cluster in two's and three's in the long corridors of the Bureau in Washington. They talk about the present "liquidation program." Let us hope that they will be proved wrong.

Originally published in *Annals of the American Academy of Political and Social Science* 311 (May 1957): 31–40. Bracketed insertions added. Ellipses other than in direct quotations indicate editorial deletions. All footnotes omitted.

The history of the Santee Sioux is like that of many other Indian groups. The movement of white population into the Upper Mississippi Valley led to demands for their lands and the eventual establishment of reservations in the Minnesota Valley in the 1850s. A few years later, in 1862, intolerable conditions on the reservations led to the Santee uprising that surprised and shocked the nation, but the hostiles were quickly defeated and the bulk of the tribe surrendered. Some were tried and executed, while the remainder were held as prisoners. In the following year the government conceded to Minnesota demands and began to remove the Indians from the state, placing many of them on a new reservation at Crow Creek on the Missouri River in present South Dakota. Others eventually were located on the Sisseton Reservation in northeastern South Dakota and the Devils Lake Reservation in North Dakota. In addition some managed to stay in Minnesota, and a number gathered at the Flandreau Colony in South Dakota.

The Crow Creek reservation had been chosen hurriedly and was entirely unsuitable. Many of the tribe died, others simply left the reservation, and in 1866 the remainder were moved to better land near the mouth of the Niobrara River in Nebraska. After a period of uncertainty the Santee Reservation was definately established at that location despite opposition from the local white population. Agitation for their removal continued, but the Santees remained and made steady progress, in the eyes of white officials, toward acculturation. Missionaries strove to Christianize and educate them, while the government tried to make them self-sufficient farmers and destroy their old culture. Under the influence of the Indian Bureau, for example, the governmental structure was changed in 1878 to provide for the election of tribal officials. During the following decade land was alloted to individual Indians, but as elsewhere, this merely contributed to the loss of Indian lands.

The history of the Santee Reservation in the twentieth century, writes Roy Meyer, is one of decay and deterioration. Government services were systematically withdrawn, and in 1917 the agency was prematurely discontinued. In the 1920s and 1930s the Indians suffered from drought and depression, and by the beginning of the New Deal they were in difficult straits. The situation at Sisseton, Devils Lake, and Flandreau was generally the same. Meyer describes the relations of the Santees with the federal government after 1934 and records the continued decline of the tribe despite the Indian New Deal and other positive programs.

The Santee Sioux, 1934-65

ROY W. MEYER

The Santee Sioux accepted the Indian Reorganization Act by a vote of 260 to 27 at an election held November 17, 1934. In a way, it is rather surprising that they voted to accept the act, for they had been proceeding in the opposite direction so long that some major psychological reorientation must have been required of them. Furthermore, their recent experience with the Indian Bureau had not been pleasant. Their dissatisfaction with the successive Yankton superintendents was transferred to a new object when, in 1933, the Yankton Agency was abolished and the Santees were placed under the Winnebago Agency. Complaints against the Winnebago superintendent, Henry M. Tidwell, and members of his staff began reaching Representative Howard, including a telegram from the Knox County Board describing Tidwell as "absolutely incompetent" and demanding immediate relief for fifty destitute families. An investigation by the Indian Bureau substantiated the charges, and shortly thereafter Tidwell was replaced by Gabe E. Parker, a man of Choctaw descent and sympathetic to Collier's policies.

Aid to the Santees under the new administration did not, of course, await the appointment of Parker. Federal Emergency Relief Administration funds were made available in 1933, and many of the Indians were set to work building and improving roads that summer. Some were employed in an Indian Emergency Conservation Work project to develop a public campground on the old agency site. The new government farmer, James W. Brewer, encouraged the Indians to grow subsistence gardens, but no attempt was made at that time to get them back into the wheat and cattle business. They were encouraged, however, to devote some of the proceeds from their road work to the purchase of seed. Direct relief in the form of surplus mutton bought from the Navajos, blankets, shoes, and other clothing was also furnished in 1933 and 1934. When about 130 cattle were issued in October, 1934, the Indians were given complete freedom to keep their cows or butcher them.

Important as these various forms of assistance were, they were in the final analysis palliative rather than remedial. The Santees could not achieve self-support by rebuilding roads or constructing a campground, and the land base remaining to them was insufficient for successful farming. The Meriam Report had stressed the Indians' dependence on agriculture in the future as in the past and had proposed methods to retain and make usable the land resources left to them. One of the objectives of the Indian Reorganization Act had been to permit tribes organized under its provisions to undertake land acquisition programs, the land thus acquired to remain in tribal ownership. In response to a circular from the Bureau in June, 1935, the Santee tribal council prepared recommendations for purchases which they felt would give their people an adequate land base. By this time they had only 3,132.29 acres left out of the amount allotted in 1885, plus about 1,800 acres of fee patent land, nearly all of which was encumbered with unpaid taxes and mortgages. The members of the council estimated that only 2,352 acres of this land was suitable for agriculture. The government farmer thought that out of 105 families only 3 had enough land to provide a cash income from farming, and only 15 had enough for subsistence needs; the remaining 87 families were, to all practical purposes, landless.

Land purchases made with IRA funds ultimately came to 3,368.54 acres, mostly in 1936 and 1937. This was far less than the Bureau had planned to buy and fell short of the Santees' needs, just as purchases for other tribes failed to meet their needs. Funds dried up with the coming of World War II and the diversion of appropriations to defense purposes. As late as the summer of 1940 the landless Santees were said to be "anxiously awaiting the acquisition of additional areas in order that further benefits to individuals, families, and the tribe might be realized." They have continued to wait ever since. Pending completion of expected purchases, some twenty-five families were set up on leased, white-owned lands and furnished with livestock and farm equipment. Although they were said to be doing well in 1937, rentals on the land were taking a third of the profits.

Besides the purchase of land, several other measures were

taken to improve the condition of the Santee Sioux. The Indian Reorganization Act had provided for a sum of $10,000,000 to be used for reimbursable loans to tribal groups. The principle of reimbursable loans was not new, but previous experience with it had been discouraging. More intelligently managed, it proved much more successful in the 1930's, although at Santee as elsewhere the amount of money available was never enough for the needs of the tribe. Rehabilitation funds were also obtained for construction of houses and farm buildings, a project that did much to improve living conditions among those families that were able to benefit. In line with the Collier administration's emphasis on encouraging community spirit, a "community self-help building" was completed in 1937, containing a large room with a capacity of nearly two hundred, a kitchen at the rear, and smaller rooms for sewing projects, committee meetings, or a tribal office; in a wing were spaces for weaving and other arts and crafts activities and a carpentry shop.

It is important to note that in all those projects the Indians themselves were consulted and did much of the planning. Though opposed to the withdrawal of government supervision, Commissioner Collier and his allies had no brief for paternalism. Everything was done to encourage the Indians to take the initiative, apparently with good results, for many of the ideas discussed by Indian Bureau officials came originally from the Indians themselves. Superintendent Parker reported after one meeting at Santee, concerned with a plan for subsistence garden plots for the old and needy: "It would do your heart good, as it certainly did mine, yesterday afternoon to sit through long hours of serious expectant and profoundly appreciative attitudes and discussions of the members of the Santee Sioux Tribal Council."

The constitution and bylaws drawn up after acceptance of the IRA were designed to reflect the peculiar status of the Santees as Indians in an advanced stage of acculturation. For example, whereas many tribal constitutions gave the tribe jurisdiction over marriage and divorce practices, such a provision was omitted from the Santee constitution because these Indians "wanted to move in the direction of comprehensive State control over law and order and domestic relations rather than in the direction of tribal regulation of Indian custom marriages and Indian conduct." After being approved by the Department of the Interior, the constitution and bylaws were accepted by the tribe, 284-60, on February 29, 1936. The council elected that year proved a more effective instrument of community policy than the old rubber-stamp body that had been instituted late in the nineteenth century and had existed nominally since then.

Education was a central concern of the Collier administration, though at Santee it was distinctly subordinate, as a government activity, to other objectives, inasmuch as the reservation had long been incorporated into the county public school system. A specialist in Indian education visited six one-room schools and one two-room school in 1935 and found conditions markedly better than a similar tour of inspection nineteen years earlier had found them. Out of a total enrollment of 194 in those schools, 98 of the children were Indian. Their tuition was paid by the government. The rates varied from twenty-five to thirty cents a day at the smaller schools, and was forty cents at the two-room school, that at Santee village, where a lunch of soup, sandwiches, meat, fruit, doughnuts, and cocoa was served. Ten of the nineteen pupils there were Indians, all of whom attended regularly except for four from one family. The teachers all reported that the Indians did as well as the white children. In 1938 the same specialist found a great increase in enrollment, and a higher proportion of absenteeism among whites than among Indians.

In the middle 1930's the Santee Normal Training School was still functioning, under the direction of Rudolph Hertz, who had succeeded Frederick B. Riggs, son of Alfred L. Riggs [the missionary who had established the school], in 1933. Its enrollment was down to seventy-four boarding pupils and seven day pupils, but it employed twenty people, including six teachers, all with college degrees. In the spring of 1936 it ceased its long service to Indian young people and was transformed the following autumn into an institution for adult education, designed chiefly to provide refresher courses to families engaged in missionary work. Its career in this capacity was brief, however, and in 1938 the American Missionary Association disposed of several of the buildings, which were promptly wrecked for the lumber. The tribal council leased the land and some of the remaining buildings for use as living quarters for families who had not been benefited by the housing program.

It would be pleasant to conclude this account of the Santee Reservation by reporting that the aims of the Collier administration were all achieved and the Indians placed in a position of economic security. Unfortunately, such was not the case. Just as the nation as a whole recovered very slowly from the effects of the Depression, so the Santees at the end of the 1930's were still far from self-sufficiency. Superintendent Parker was obliged to report in 1940 that the condition of all the Nebraska Indian groups was "one of almost total dependence upon Federal Government for work and direct relief; Agency allotments and WPA, Social Security, ADC, Old Age Assistance, NYA, and the like. . . ." He attributed the situation to more than ten years of drought and grasshopper infestations, livestock diseases, and lack of available employment for Indians off the reservation.

During World War II the situation was somewhat alleviated because of the availability of work in war plants and the temporary employment of many men in the armed services. Judging from the census figures since 1940, many of the Santees who left the reservation during and after the war never returned. Between 1940 and 1960 there was a 65 per cent loss in the Indian population of the five townships that comprised the old Santee Reservation, as contrasted to a 13 per cent increase between 1930 and 1940. By 1960 there were only 317 Santees still living in the reservation area. In general and with many exceptions, it has been the most industrious and best-qualified who have left, with the result that the Indian Bureau and local agencies have continued to face many problems among those who have stayed behind.

One may wonder why the Nebraska reservation, alone among those occupied by the Santee Sioux, has suffered so extreme a decline in its resident population. Although no definitive answer can be given, certain factors, cultural and geographical, may go far toward accounting for the phenomenon. Cultural variations probably affect the differential rates of population increase or decline on the respective reservations. The people at Sisseton and

Devils Lake are less acculturated than those at the other reservations and hence less likely to leave home and try their wings in the white-dominated society of the cities. The more highly acculturated people at Flandreau and the Minnesota colonies have more employment opportunities in the reservation area or within commuting distance than do those on the Santee Reservation. Santee is the only Santee Indian community that does not have a fair-sized town within reasonable commuting distance. Niobrara, the only nearby town, had a population of 736 in the 1960 census, as contrasted to 3,218 for Sisseton, South Dakota (in addition to Watertown [14,077] and others near the Sisseton Reservation); 2,129 for Flandreau, South Dakota, with its Indian school employing a sizable staff; 6,299 for Devils Lake, North Dakota; 2,728 for Granite Falls, Minnesota; 4,285 for Redwood Falls, Minnesota; and 10,528 for Red Wing, Minnesota. Norfolk, Nebraska, with more than 13,000 people and a number of industries, is over seventy-five miles away—too far for convenient commuting but not too far to draw people permanently. Another factor is that conditions for successful agriculture are probably poorer at Santee than at any of the other locations. Though few Indians on any of the reservations do much farming, those at Santee may be indirectly affected in that they have a harder time making a living by leasing than the other groups do.

At the same time that the reservation population was declining, the alienation of allotted land, halted during the 1930's, was resumed. Although the tribal land purchased with IRA funds has remained intact, the amount of allotted land dropped from 3,252 acres in 1936 to 3,012 in 1952 and to 2,563 in 1960. In the next five years the acreage held almost steady. The land remaining in Indian possession is widely scattered over the old reservation area, though there is some concentration at Santee village and along the streams. Because the topography is sharply dissected by ravines and lightly timbered with deciduous trees and brush, the acreage left to the Indians is not well suited to agriculture, except for occasional patches of bottomland. The scattered tracts of upland prairies are not occupied by the Indians, but are leased to white operators. Even here the land is rolling; and the roads, built on section lines, dip and rise with such frequency as to give the motorist a feeling of riding a roller coaster. Much of the old reservation, both Indian-owned and white-owned, is used only for grazing or is simply wasteland.

In the later 1940's and early 1950's, when there was much talk about "turning the Indians loose," it was inevitable that the Santee Sioux should be caught up in the controversy. Although they do not seem to have been among those most seriously considered for termination, the possibility was discussed. As on other reservations, there have been Indians at Santee who strongly favored such a move. They were usually either people who had themselves adapted successfully to white society and thought their tribesmen should do likewise, or people at the opposite extreme who resented the supervision of the Indian Bureau and wanted to be free to dispose of their land and spend the proceeds.

An early and unsuccessful move in the direction of termination was made in 1941, when several members of the tribal council went to Washington to seek "full citizenship" for the Santees. Again in 1948 the Niobrara *Tribune* carried a bitter attack on the Indian Bureau for not having brought the Indians out of poverty. Despite the "enormous salaries dished out to its many millions of employees," there were still Indians living in poverty. Perhaps, suggested the writer, the Indian Service was able to help the Indians only once every fifteen years. In any case, he concluded, "It is about time that an investigation be made but very secretly in order that not one stone shall be left unturned." The Santees were generally opposed to termination, however, and their opposition, coupled with their poor economic status, kept the proposal from going beyond the talking stage when it was revived in the 1950's.

The condition of the Santees in the mid-1960's remains depressed in comparison with that of the non-Indian population in the same region. Few are trying to farm the small tracts they have left, and it is doubtful that those farms could be made economically productive, even if the needed capital were available. In Knox County, as elsewhere on the Great Plains, there has been a general decline in the rural population in the past few decades. Between 1930 and 1940, when the Indian population of the reservation area was increasing, the *total* reservation population declined by 23 per cent. And between 1940 and 1960, when the Indian population declined 65 per cent, the *total* population dropped by more than 73 per cent. It may be presumed that where white farmers are unable to make a satisfactory living, Indians, with fewer advantages and more handicaps, will also be unable to do so. Though there has been talk of starting a concrete plant on the reservation, no capital for the purpose has been made available. The area appears to have no other natural resources, except for the recreational potential of Lewis and Clark Lake, the reservoir created by the Gavins Point Dam. Most of the shoreline is owned by the Army Corps of Engineers or by the state, however, and the Santee tribe is not in a position to profit, except indirectly, from the tourist trade.

Younger people continue to leave the area for urban centers, ranging from small nearby cities like Norfolk to distant metropolises like Los Angeles. Some of them have found a satisfactory place in American life; others may only have exchanged rural poverty for urban poverty. The resident population at Santee has continued to decline in recent years, dropping from 317 in 1960 to 299 in 1962, and it includes a high proportion of the elderly and unemployable. In this respect, as in others, Santee resembles many other Indian reservations in the country. If the Santees are no worse off economically than most other Indians, this fact is small comfort to them—and slight balm to the conscience of the white man.

Originally published as Chapter 15, "The Twentieth Century: Santee," of *History of the Santee Sioux* (Lincoln: University of Nebraska Press, 1967), pp. 308–16. Bracketed insertions added. All footnotes omitted.

The Indian Claims Commission

In his discussion of the Indian Reorganization Act in a previous selection John Collier indicated that the Indian Claims Act of 1946 was an essential part of the Indian New Deal. He felt that it, along with the Johnson-O'Malley Act and the Indian Arts and Crafts Board, complemented the Indian Reorganization Act. It unquestionably had broad implications, and some lawyers have described it as a new and revolutionary development in the field of jurisprudence.

From 1784 to 1871 some 377 treaties with Indian tribes were ratified, and after 1871, when the practice of making treaties with Indians was discontinued, there were numerous agreements made which were approved by both houses of Congress. Most involved the transfer of land, but often at an unconscionably low price. The tribes had also lost lands through other means and as a result had many grievances, but they had no recourse under United States law. Indeed, as Wilcomb Washburn has pointed out in Red Man's Land/White Man's Law, *the mechanisms of white man's laws either were incapable of recognizing the cultural and legal separateness of the Indians or were deliberately designed to destroy that independence.*

Under an 1863 law Indians were forbidden to sue in the Court of Claims, and thus they could not bring claims against the government without a special act of Congress. Although some Indian groups did seek such legislation, as Glen Wilkinson indicates, it was an entirely unsatisfactory solution to Indian grievances against the government.

Congressional efforts to establish a review board for Indian claims cases began in 1930 and continued through the decade. The Indian Claims Commission Act of 1946 created a three-member commission appointed by the President with the advice and consent of the Senate. At least two members had to be admitted to the Bar of the Supreme Court of the United States, and no more than two could be from the same political party. Nineteen fifty-one was set as the deadline for the commission to receive claims, and it was to finish its business in ten years. Supplemental legislation has prolonged the commission until 1972, and a bill has been introduced to extend its life until 1977. In addition, the membership was increased from three to five commissioners in 1967.

The Indian Claims Commission is unique. The act authorizing it broadened the government's consent to be sued and conferred special privileges on Indian claimants because of the peculiar nature of government-Indian relations. Intended to clear the nation's conscience for past wrongs to the Indian people, the law, as Dr. Washburn notes, was also motivated by a desire to eliminate the Indian as a separate factor in American society.

Although Congress did not establish the commission as a court, it has acted as such, and tribal attorneys and Justice Department staff members present evidence. Expert witnesses are used to determine tribal occupancy of lands in question and the dollar value of those lands at the time of white acquisition. Using these procedures the commission is slowly dealing with the numerous claims filed before the 1951 deadline.

By 1951 370 petitions had been filed. The 1971 annual report of the commission indicates that they have been broken down into a total of 610 dockets (Wilkinson lists approximately 850 claims) and as of July 1, 1971, a total of 161 dockets had been dismissed and 176 had resulted in final monetary judgments totaling more than $391,000,000. Others are on appeal to the Court of Claims. It is evident therefore that the conscience of the nation has not yet been cleared, if indeed it can be cleared by monetary payments for past wrongs.

Indian Tribal Claims before the Court of Claims

GLEN A. WILKINSON

Perhaps the most fascinating aspect of the jurisdiction exercised by the Court of Claims is its jurisdiction over Indian tribal claims against the United States. The Indian tribes have not always had the right to present their grievances to a judicial tribunal. The first judicial remedies came in the form of special legislative grants of jurisdiction to the Court of Claims to hear Indian tribal claims. Eventually, in 1946, Congress passed the Indian Claims Commission Act, which was designed to provide a uniform remedy for all Indian groups having grievances against the sovereign. Presently, the Court of Claims has original jurisdiction over claims accruing after August 1946 and appellate jurisdiction over cases decided by the Indian Claims Commission.

The following is a survey of cases litigated in the Court of Claims, before and after the establishment of the Indian Claims Commission, which have caused significant and, for the most part, beneficial changes with respect to Indian tribal rights against the federal government.

Litigation under Special Jurisdictional Acts

Early Difficulty in Obtaining Right to Sue

The Act of March 3, 1863, which gave the Court of Claims the status of a court with authority to render judgments, specifically excepted from the court's jurisdiction "any claim against the government . . . dependent on any treaty entered into . . . with Indian tribes." As a result, Indians with grievances were required to petition Congress for redress. Unfortunately, it was rather difficult for a tribe to persuade Congress to enact the necessary legislation. In the sixty-five years between the first special jurisdictional act in 1881 and the passage of the Indians Claims Commission Act in 1946, 142 Indian claims were litigated. This may seem like a fairly large number, but it pales in comparison with the number filed during the five-year period between August 1946, when the Indian Claims Commission Act became effective, and August 1951, the cutoff date within which claims could be filed. During that five-year period, 370 petitions involving approximately 850 claims were filed.

The difficulty the Indian tribes encountered in obtaining permission to sue is well illustrated by the experience of the Turtle Mountain Band of Chippewa Indians. In 1892, the Government and the Band negotiated an agreement for a cession to the Government of land thought to contain ten million acres in exchange for one million dollars. This was sardonically dubbed the "ten cent treaty" by many of the Indians and others who were opposed to the agreement. They attempted to prevent its ratification by Congress, but were successful only in delaying ratification until 1904. Having failed to prevent ratification of the compact, the Band began to petition Congress either to improve the terms of the agreement or to provide for an adjudication by the Court of Claims. Although the Band persisted in its efforts, it was not until 1928 that anything was accomplished. In that year a favorable Senate committee report on a bill to vest jurisdiction in the Court of Claims was adopted, and by 1933 the Band had convinced committees in both Houses that its claims should be heard. Congress passed the bill in 1934, but it was vetoed by President Roosevelt. After what were thought to be the objectionable features were removed, Congress passed another bill. But again the President vetoed it. Favorable congressional committee action continued through the 76th Congress, but no bill became law. Finally, the claim was filed in 1951 under the provisions of the Indian Claims Commission Act; it is still pending.

High Mortality of Early Tribal Claims

Most claims filed by Indian tribes pursuant to special jurisdictional acts have been unsuccessful. One reason many of these claims were treated harshly by the court was that the relief which it might grant was inexpertly defined by the jurisdictional act. For example, in *Northwestern Bands of Shoshone Indians v. United States*, the Bands sought to recover damages for an unlawful taking of their lands in violation of the Treaty of Box Elder. Although the court held that the evidence established that the Indians had exclusively used or occupied all or a portion of the area they claimed and had been deprived of that use through action of the United States, it dismissed the claim because the jurisdictional act authorized recovery only on a claim growing out of a treaty; and the court found that the Indian land involved in this case was held by aboriginal title. It is possible that if Congress had been able to predict the judicial interpretation of the Box Elder Treaty, it would have authorized the court, as it did in four other jurisdictional acts adopted during approximately the same time, to determine liability based upon aboriginal title.

Another case in which the Indians were unsuccessful because of limitations in the jurisdictional act was *Klamath & Moadoc Tribes v. United States*. This was an "unconscionable consideration" claim based on the allegation that the Indians were paid 108,750 dollars for land which the court later found was worth 2,980,000 dollars. The claim was dismissed because the tribes had signed a release demanded by the government negotiators at the time of the negotiations, and the court held that Congress did not waive the release in the jurisdictional act. After the dismissal, however, the tribes returned to Congress and obtained an amendment to the act which waived the release and enabled the court to make an award.

A second reason for the high mortality rate of tribal claims was the often narrow construction applied to the jurisdictional acts by the Court of Claims and the Supreme Court. An illustrative case is *Western (Old Settlers) Cherokee Indians v. United States*. In this case the jurisdictional act instructed the Court of Claims to inquire into past transactions between the United States and the Western Cherokees, granting the court "unrestricted latitude in adjusting and determining the said claim, so that the rights, legal and equitable, both of the United States and of said Indians [might] . . . be fully considered and determined." This broad jurisdictional grant was held insufficient to allow an inquiry into allegations of fraud and duress by United States representatives in procuring the treaty. The court said that Congress had not granted and lacked the power to grant authority to question the validity of the treaty, since reformation of a treaty was a legislative function. Furthermore, it stated that although Congress could delegate extrajudicial power to the Court of Claims, it could not alter the character of the Supreme Court, which tribunal was limited by the Constitution to strictly judicial matters; hence, where the Court of Claims action was subject to review by the Supreme Court, its jurisdiction was likewise constitutionally limited.

In 1923, commenting that the language of the jurisdictional act involved was not as broad as that in *Western Cherokee*, the Court of Claims, in *Sisseton & Wahpeton Bands of Sioux Indians v. United States*, held that a jurisdictional act authorizing the court to hear "all claims of whatsoever nature . . . under any treaties or laws of Congress [and to] . . . settle the rights, both legal and equitable, of said bands of Indians and the United States . . ." was too narrow to allow consideration of the question whether by mutual mistake of fact the United States obtained eleven million acres while bargaining for a tract thought to contain eight million. Likewise, in *Creek Nation v. United States*, the court held that jurisdiction, both legal and equitable, "arising under or growing out of any treaty or agreement" did not authorize setting aside a treaty alleged to have been made under duress or procured by threat. The court concluded that the claim could "not be asserted at once as a claim under the treaty and a claim against the treaty." Similarly, in *Osage Nation v. United States*, the court held that its authority "to hear and determine, as right and justice may require, and as upon a full and fair arbitration the claim of said tribe against the United States" did not allow it to go beyond the actual language of the treaty. The court was constrained to reach this result even though it was convinced that the Indians did not understand the treaty and that part of the consideration to be paid for an Osage cession of land was to be used for the education and civilization of Indian tribes other than the Osage tribe.

Judgments Decreased by Setoffs

In those cases where Indian tribes were successful in persuading Congress to pass jurisdictional acts and where the Court of

Claims was able to find sufficient authority therein to allow it to examine the claims, at least one more serious hurdle impeded the tribal litigants. Most jurisdictional acts directed the court to set-off against any award the gratuitous expenditures made by the United States for the benefit of the tribe.

The effect of this type of deduction was demonstrated in *Blackfeet v. United States.* The Blackfeet Nation, which originally inhabited northern Montana, sued under a jurisdictional act which allowed the Court of Claims "to consider and determine all legal and equitable claims . . . for land . . . alleged to have been taken from the said Indians by the United States, and also any legal or equitable defenses, set-offs, or counterclaims, including gratuities, which the United States may have [had] . . . against the said Nations . . . ." The court determined that the United States through an Act of Congress of 1874 had deprived the tribe, without the payment of compensation, of ownership of more than twelve million acres of land which had been reserved to the tribe by a treaty of 1855. It found that the tribe was entitled to damages in the amount of 6,130,874.88 dollars. But it also determined that the United States was entitled to setoffs resulting from gratuitous expenditures on behalf of the Blackfeet Nation in the amount of 5,508,409.31 dollars, thus leaving the Blackfeet Nation with a judgment of 622,465.57 dollars. Similarly, in *Shoshone Tribe v. United States,* the court held the petitioner entitled to recover 2,483,467.99 dollars, against which the United States was found entitled to setoffs of 1,689,646.50 dollars, leaving a net recovery of 793,821.49 dollars.

The practice of allowing such deductions was considered during the hearings before the Senate Committee on Indian Affairs in 1935. One witness, an assistant solicitor of the Department of the Interior, viewed the deductions as being "grossly unfair" to the tribe. He noted that between 1929 and 1935 "in every case but two where the jurisdictional act allowed set-off of gratuities and where a recovery [had] . . . been won in the court the petition [had] . . . been dismissed because the recovery was exceeded by the set-offs." Furthermore, he pointed out that Congress not only discriminated by allowing unlimited setoffs in some acts and limited setoffs in others, but permitted some tribes to avoid setoffs entirely. Shortly thereafter, Congress adopted legislation which included standard setoff provisions in the various jurisdictional acts.

Indian Claims Commission Act

It was against this background of inequity, inconsistency, and uncertainty that Congress beginning in the 1930's sought to create a uniform procedure for handling the claims of all the Indian tribes. One question for Congress during the time it was considering such legislation was whether all cases should be instituted in the Court of Claims or referred to an administrative agency with limited authority to investigate and make recommendations to Congress. It compromised by creating an administrative agency—the Indian Claims Commission—to make final determinations on all claims, and by granting jurisdiction to the Court of Claims to review the Commission's decisions. Furthermore, the determination of questions of law by the Court of Claims was made subject to review by the Supreme Court on application for writ of certiorari. Under the appeal provisions of the act, there have been at least ninety-one appeals decided by the Court of Claims.

Court of Claims Review of Commission Decisions

Despite what appears to have been the intention of Congress—to provide a forum in which all Indian claims with merit might be adjudicated—the Indian Claims Commission construed its function narrowly. In light of this default, a more objective Court of Claims, already seasoned in Indian matters, took up the responsibility of achieving the congressional intent. For example, in *Western (Old Settlers) Cherokee Indians v. United States,* the first case adjudicated by the Commission, a motion to dismiss as res judicata a petition alleging mistake in the writing of a treaty was granted. On review, the Court of Claims held that its prior decision, involving the same parties and the same subject matter, did not bar the claim because the Indian Claims Commission Act had created causes of action the court did not consider justiciable in the prior action.

The Commission dismissed two other early claims on the

ground that the evidence was inadequate to support the claims alleged. The Court of Claims, in *Osage Nation v. United States,* proclaimed its intention to scrutinize the facts of record on appeals from the Indian Claims Commission. It acknowledged that its inquiry under section 20 of the Commission's enabling act should be (1) whether the Commission's findings of fact were supported by substantial evidence and (2) whether the Commission's conclusions of law were valid and supported by the findings of fact. After searching the legislative history of the Indian Claims Commission Act and prior judicial determinations to ascertain the agency's obligations, the court concluded that the Commission's jurisdiction did "not embrace matters of a technical or highly specialized character" and that the issues brought before it concerned matters in which the court was as expert as the Commission. The court then proceeded to undertake an exhaustive review of the evidence and reached the conclusion, buttressed by facts of which it felt it could take judicial notice, that the treaty involved should be revised on the ground of unconscionable consideration, and remanded the case to the Commission for such revision.

In *Pawnee Tribe v. United States,* the court advanced one step further along the path it felt Congress had intended. It criticized the Commission for making ultimate findings without first making explicit findings of primary or evidentiary facts, commenting that the Commission's drawing of inferences from material contained in excerpts without reference to the documents as a whole made its findings "speculative in character." Faced, as the Commission had been, with a woefully inadequate record, the court pointed out that the enabling legislation contained a grant of investigatory power which authorized the Commission to take judicial notice of historical facts and official published and unpublished government documents in the archives of the various government departments. The court then reviewed the material which it believed the Commission should weigh on reconsideration of the claims. Following the taking of additional testimony on remand, the Pawnee Tribe emerged with an award of more than 7,325,000.00 dollars. If the Court of Claims in this and some of the other early appeals had left the interpretation and determination of the Indian claims to the process of strictly adversary proceedings, it is doubtful whether the Pawnees would have been successful to any extent.

Another landmark case which had a major impact upon tribal claims was *Otoe & Missouria Tribe v. United States.* The claims asserted by the Indians were based on allegations that the United States had acquired, by payment of "unconscionable consideration" and through negotiations which did not measure up to "fair and honorable dealings," lands to which the Indians had held "aboriginal Indian title." The opinion of the Indian Claims Commission was based upon the premise that the Indian Claims Commission Act provided a remedy for the taking of such lands. On appeal, the Department of Justice argued that a taking of aboriginal Indian title land by the United States is compensable only when Congress expressly authorizes payment for such a taking and that there was no such authorization in the Indian Claims Commission Act. The court, in an opinion by Judge Littleton, reviewed the background which led to the enactment of the Indian Claims Commission Act, particularly the inclusion in the act of remedies for claims not cognizable in courts of the United States under existing rules of law or equity. It concluded that Congress had intended the act to cover claims based upon aboriginal Indian title.

Identifiable Groups

Section 2 of the Indian Claims Commission Act authorizes suits by "any Indian tribe, band, or other identifiable group of American Indians . . . ." One of the difficult problems in interpreting the act has involved the meaning of the phrase "other identifiable group." For example, in *Thompson v. United States,* the Government was sued by a statutory group entitled the "Indians of California," for lands in the present state of California to which various bands and groups of California Indians held Indian title at the time the United States acquired sovereignty over the area in 1848. The Indian Claims Commission dismissed the petition for lack of jurisdiction on the ground that the "Indians of California" were not a single group, had no common claim, and were, therefore, not "an identifiable group" within the meaning of the Indian Claims Commission Act. This interpretation was reversed by the Court of Claims which held that Section 2 of the Indian Claims Commission Act was intended to cover "any group of American Indians that could be sufficiently identified as having by inheritance a claim or claims of the character specified," and that section 10 of the act "expressly recognized that there would be claims coming before the Commission which could not be presented by a tribe or band having a common claim at the date of the filing of the petition." In reversing the Commission, the court asserted that Congress, by adding the phrase "other identifiable group," intended to "enlarge the category of groups of Indians entitled to present claims," not to limit this right to only those groups existing when the claim arose and having at the time of suit a common group claim.

A similar problem was involved in *McGhee v. United States.* There the claim arose out of an injury to the Creek Nation as it existed in 1814. During that year, the federal government took steps to move the Creeks from their homelands in Georgia and Florida to the Indian Territory, which became Oklahoma. Some Creeks refused to move, and their descendants became identified as Eastern Creeks. The suit was brought by the Creek Nation of Oklahoma. The Eastern Creeks, who had maintained no political organization, attempted to intervene, but were denied intervention by the Commission on the ground that they were not an "identifiable group of Indians" because the government had always, since the relocation of the tribe, recognized the Oklahoma Creeks as the tribal entity. The Commission interpreted the motion to intervene as a request by the Eastern Creeks that the Commission determine the individual Indians who might participate in any award, not a "common claim" over which the Commission has jurisdiction, but a "common suit for individual claims" over which the Commission has no jurisdiction. The Court of Claims ruled in favor of the Eastern Creeks holding that the claim belonged to the tribe as it existed at the time the claim arose; that the organized tribe could not prevent the participation by another identifiable group having an interest in the claim and that the Eastern Creek group, although no longer organized, qualified as such because it was capable of being identified.

Payment of Just Compensation

On the surface it may seem that Indian tribes have done quite well before the Court of Claims. However, some judicial interpretations have prevented the American Indians from collecting what could be considered just compensation. For instance, a different result on one issue—whether the United States is obligated to pay interest as a measure of just compensation on Indian claims—would add more to tribal treasuries than would victory on all other claims combined.

The first cases in which payment of interest was in issue were litigated under special jurisdictional acts, and dealt with appropriations of Indian lands by the United States. The Court of Claims was confronted with this problem in the 1933 case of *Creek Nation v. United States,* which involved an 1866 cession to the United States of land previously owned in *fee simple* by the Creek Nation. The Government provided a survey to determine the boundary line of the cession, but by error included a part of unceded Indian land. As a result of this mistake, the unceded land was sold by the United States in 1891. The Creeks brought suit in 1926 to recover compensation for the appropriated land. The Court of Claims held that the Indians should be compensated in an amount equal to the value of the land, without interest, as of the date the suit was brought. The Supreme Court, in reversing, held that the lands had been taken by the sale in 1891, and that just compensation was the value of the land at the date of taking plus "such addition thereto as may be required to produce the present [1926, the date of suit] full equivalent of that value paid contemporaneously with the taking." The Court determined that a reasonable rate of interest would be an appropriate means of ascertaining the amount to be added.

Several months later, the Court of Claims again denied an award of interest, this time to the Shoshone Tribe, who had held land by *recognized Indian title*. The jurisdictional statute did not provide for payment of interest, and the court said that interest was not allowed on any claim against the United States unless specifically authorized by statute or contract. The Supreme Court reversed, however, holding that when there is "an appropriation of property within the meaning of the Fifth Amendment . . .

the right to interest, or a fair equivalent, attaches itself automatically to the right to an award of damages."

Finally, in *Alcea Band of Tillamooks v. United States,* which involved *original Indian title,* the Court of Claims followed the Supreme Court rulings in *Creek* and *Shoshone.* The court determined the date of taking and awarded interest from that date as a measure of just compensation. But the Supreme Court reversed, holding that a fifth amendment taking was not involved, and that the jurisdictional act did not contain the necessary authorization for payment of interest. Thus, the principle was established that interest was not to be included as just compensation for the appropriation of land held by *original Indian title.* This brought unhappiness to the many tribes who had been hopeful that they would receive some compensation for the delay in payment, such as interest on their old claims. Under the Indian Claims Commission Act, however, except for two cases, the Indians have failed to receive interest for several different reasons. In *Pawnee Tribe v. United States,* interest was not awarded since the suit was held to involve a "purchase," not a taking. The court reached this determination even though the Commission had found that the loss of land resulted from an erroneous omission by the United States, that the "sale" was involuntary, and that the consideration provided by Congress sixteen years after the omission was "unconscionable."

Another case, *Confederated Salish & Kootenai Tribes of the Flathead Reservation v. United States,* involved the Government's use of tribal funds for a purpose for which the Government was bound by treaty to use its own funds. The petitioners contended that this was a fifth amendment taking. The court held that the wrongful use of tribal money was not a "taking"; it was a breach of the treaty promise, a taking away of *contractual* rights, not *property* rights, and thus interest was not included in the damages.

In *Osage Nation v. United States,* a case in which the Indians were entitled to judgment on the basis of either a "revised" treaty or unfair and dishonorable dealings, the court refused to provide interest as a measure of just compensation, noting that neither theory presented a fifth amendment taking and that there was no contractual provision for an award of interest. Later, in *United States v. Kiowa, Comanche & Apache Tribes,* the court interpreted and followed *Osage* as an unqualified holding that interest may not be assessed on awards arising from revision of a treaty or agreement or under the fair and honorable dealings clause of Section 2 of the Indian Claims Commission Act. It made no attempt to determine whether there was a contractual basis for awarding interest.

In *Nez Perce Tribe v. United States,* the tribe sought a revision of an agreement on the ground of unconscionable consideration. Interest was claimed as compensation on the ground that the agreement directed that the consideration be placed in a trust fund which paid five per cent interest for the benefit of the tribe; and that this provision was applicable not only to the consideration paid under the agreement, but also to the additional sum which would have been paid if the agreement were revised to provide for adequate consideration. Even though the court agreed that the compensation was unconscionable and that the difference in price probably would have been deposited in the trust fund, it held itself bound by the "well established" rule that "interest does not run on claims against the United States unless there is an express statutory or contract provision to the contrary or unless there is a showing of delay in payment for lands 'taken' in contravention of the Fifth Amendment." The result, of course, is that a tribe is found, in 1966, to have been deprived of the use of a sum of money due to unconscionable conduct by the United States, yet it is unable to recover damages for the deprivation of the use of the money since 1894. At best, the result is only partial relief for the wrongs committed.

Future of Indian Claims

The Indian Claims Commission Act, as it was passed in 1946, provided for a five-year period during which claims might be filed and a five-year period thereafter during which all claims would be finally adjudicated. Congress has twice amended the act to provide additional time to complete the involved claims. Statistical data recently supplied by the Indian Claims Commission to the Senate Committee on Interior and Insular Affairs show that of approximately 850 claims filed with the Commission by 1951, 123 claims have been dismissed, 92 have been decided in favor of the tribes, 25 are in the advanced stages of decision making, 19 are on appeal before the Court of Claims, approximately 50 have seen very little activity, and more than 250 are in various stages of trial.

The history of our Government's treatment of the indigenous Americans has been one of gradual progress. Congress enacted special jurisdictional acts which varied in substantial respects. Those acts provided limited relief and were subjected to narrow construction. Congress then created an expert administrative agency to finally decide the claims. The Court of Claims was designated an appellate court in a field in which it had developed considerable expertise over several decades. Progress has been made but considerable work remains before the time-worn Indian tribal claims will be finally adjudicated.

Originally published in *Georgetown Law Journal* 55 (December 1966): 511–28. All footnotes omitted.

Termination

As William Zimmerman noted in a previous selection, the period after World War II was marked by a retreat from New Deal principles in Indian policy and a growing disinterest in the Indian people and their problems. Appropriations for the Bureau of Indian Affairs were reduced. Bureau responsibilities in the fields of health, education, and law were shifted to other federal and state agencies, and there was talk of abolishing the Bureau of Indian Affairs. Under congressional pressure the bureau instituted studies and drew up plans for the termination of federal responsibilities for the American Indians.

Although termination was implemented under the Eisenhower administration, plans for it were prepared during the Truman administration, indicating the bipartisan nature of the policy. In 1953 House Concurrent Resolution No. 108 was passed by Congress with almost no debate or opposition and established the policy of termination by ending the wardship status of American Indians and withdrawing federal responsibilities to the Indian people. Thereafter congressional forces, led by Senator Arthur V. Watkins of Utah, chairman of the Senate subcommittee on Indian affairs and the driving force in the termination movement, secured the passage of legislation to apply the policy to specific tribes. In language reminiscent of that of reformers who supported the Dawes Act of 1887, Watkins described termination as a cure-all to the Indian problem and as a policy designed to aid the Indians. He talked of emancipation and freedom for the Indians and of granting them all the rights and prerogatives of American citizenship; termination was, he said, "the Indian freedom program."

During 1954 six termination bills were passed for the Menominees, Klamaths, and other tribes. The result has been disastrous. Gary Orfield's study concludes that termination was based on a series of false assumptions and that the policy could not achieve its goals. Evidence of its failure, coupled with the opposition of the National Congress of American Indians and most other Indian groups, has led to a growing rejection of termination, and in 1970 President Richard Nixon called for a Congressional repudiation of the policy. This will not, however, be of any consolation to the Menominees and other terminated tribes.

The Menominee Termination Act was passed in June, 1954. Although termination was scheduled for 1958, it quickly became apparent that this deadline could not be met, and the operative date was postponed until 1961. By that time a tribal corporation, Menominee Enterprises, had been created and the reservation had been established as Menominee County.

Under great pressure the Menominees reluctantly accepted termination, but as Orfield explains, the cost has been great. Termination has been a divisive issue among members of the tribe, and there have been several attempts to have it repealed. The Menominees soon lost control of their property to outsiders, and they face heavy tax burdens and the possibility of bankruptcy. Moreover, state and federal expenses have increased rather than declined under termination.

Termination in Retrospect: The Menominee Experience

GARY ORFIELD

. . . A fundamental goal of termination was to give the Indian people control over their own property. Indians already possessed full legal recognition as citizens, but the legislation proposed to add the economic right to fully control property which had previously been held in trust. The achievement of this objective, it was asserted, would stimulate both personal initiative and group development of resources. The people were thus to be given greater economic freedom, but they would also receive the economic responsibility of tax-paying. Members of Congress argued that only the selfishness of the Indians could lead them to oppose a measure making them responsible for the support of a government they helped select.

The evidence is clear. The Menominees have been given more than ample responsibility, but they have gained no significant new freedoms. The inefficient and outmoded sawmill and the poverty-stricken homeowners must now take full responsibility for financing community services. Costs have risen sharply as burdens have been shifted from the state and federal governments to the county. It has been necessary to modify facilities and procedures to meet state requirements. The burden is too heavy for the sawmill, and it will increase as federal subsidies are phased-out. Already, reserve capital has been virtually exhausted. No funds are available for essential capital investments.

The individual Menominee is also faced with ponderous new responsibilities including the payment of taxes set at the highest rate allowable under state law. He has also been forced to absorb a range of new expenses formerly carried by the community. Now he must pay for health care, for utilities, and for other services. For a number of people, water and electricity services have already been discontinued. More than 300 families have not paid property tax since termination. At least 1,000 bonds have been wholly or partially assigned for land or welfare payments. Some Menominees stand in danger of losing their homes if they cannot make payment for the land and taxes. Termination has, indeed, demanded of tribal members the full responsibilities of citizenship, but it has done nothing to provide them with the level of prosperity which enables most Americans to meet these responsibilities. The price of "responsibility" may be bankruptcy.

Freedom was the fundamental objective of the termination act. The failure to extend the real freedom of the tribe has been almost total. The goal of the legislation was to give the tribe full control over both personal and collective property. This policy, however, was rapidly modified, and virtually no trace of this intention remained by termination.

Over the protest of the Interior Department, Congress acted in

1956 to require permanent sustained-yield management of the tribal forest. This action reduced the market value of the Menominee forest by more than 60 percent. The practical effect of the amendment was to limit tribal freedom in two important respects: liquidation of the forest was made far less attractive, and the tribe was forbidden to take the option of clear-cutting the forest for a quick profit at some future date. Later, the Interior Department further limited the tribe's choices by informally notifying the tribal negotiating committee that a plan for sale of the forest would not be considered approvable. Finally, the Wisconsin legislature refused to enact the legislation required by the tribe until delegates finally accepted a 30-year restrictive covenant, forbidding the sale or mortgage of tribal property without state consent.

Tribal control was not only limited by law, but was also curtailed by the plan for business organization. In no sense can it be said that the tribe made a free choice in favor of this plan. Tribal political institutions proved fully inadequate for the job of planning the tribe's economic future. It became necessary to abdicate a great deal of authority to one man called in from outside, and to a lawyer hired by the tribe. The plan was presented to the general council shortly before the deadline, with inadequate explanation, and with no time to prepare an alternative. The tribe did not decide that this was the best plan, but only that it was better to submit a plan than to be placed under a trustee by the Secretary of the Interior. Later, this same argument was used in the election of the Voting Trustees.

The complicated document, which few began to understand, provided no chance to revise the initial decision. Control of the business was to be completely out of the hands of Menominee stockholders for at least 10 years. The First Wisconsin Trust Company was given full control of a decisively large bloc of stock. In the end, tribal members had far less control than before termination. Under federal trusteeship, the elected advisory council and the people in the general council exercised control over budgetary decisions and decisive influence over the tenure of business managers and reservation superintendents. Today, these decisions are made by a Board of Directors controlled by non-Menominees.

Termination has failed to provide real ownership or to stimulate individual initiative. The arrangements devised for personal property combine virtually all the disadvantages with but few of the advantages of ownership. People who own homes are now forced to buy their lots at market value. Almost a third of adult Menominees have used their bonds for this purpose. Although they are required to buy the land, they are not allowed to freely sell it. Menominee Enterprises is given the option of first refusal. Similarly, people have been given bonds for which there is no commercial market, and stock which they are not yet allowed to sell. The bonds are considered a personal asset, however, and must be surrendered to obtain the same welfare assistance to which the people were previously entitled. To obtain services previously received, the Menominees must now give up their one capital asset, their hope for a future financial return, and their stake in tribal property.

The ultimate goal of the legislation was not merely to grant control of property, but to stimulate economic development. From all indications, however, the transfer of tribal assets to a strictly regulated form of private ownership has succeeded only in undermining the precarious basis of the tribal economy and in seriously damaging the economic self-sufficiency of the Menominee people.

State and Local Government. In 1949, the Hoover Commission recommended that primary responsibility for government services to Indian tribes be transferred as rapidly as possible to the state and local levels. Wisconsin was already providing some education and welfare services to Indian tribes. In 1953, Congress passed Public Law 280, transferring federal civil and criminal jurisdiction in several states to the state government. In fact, Bureau officials and some members of Congress assumed that most of the governmental functions relating to the Menominees had already been transferred to the state. Transition was thought to be a matter of little difficulty. The state government could surely provide better treatment because they were so much closer to the situation.

At the time the Menominee Termination Act was under

consideration, the problem of local government was treated in a similarly cavalier manner. Since the tribe had financed local services, the support of local government was thought to present no problem. . . .

The tribal economy was seriously depressed. More than half the population met the standards of eligibility for surplus commodities, and 25 percent were unemployed. Even the men who were employed by the mill received an average income of only $56 per week, to support a typical family of eight persons. Each worker now had to assume the additional burdens of taxation, medical expenses, electricity, water, and other costs. . . .

Menominee Enterprises literally owned most of the county, and the county board was reluctant to oppose the corporation executives. The company was the only important source of employment and of tax revenue. Of the seven members on the 1964 board, six are directly dependent upon Menominee Enterprises for their livelihood. Some of these men are in debt to the company $80,000–$90,000. The county, observes one board member, is "pretty much like any other company town." Most board members, he says, "do not dare to oppose the Enterprise." One member who has opposed the company claims that corporation officials actively supported one of their employees in a race against him. He has faced harrassment both from the company and from the county board. . . .

The termination legislation envisaged the transfer of residual governmental functions to the local and state governments. Responsibility had indeed been given to the county, but it is a responsibility far beyond the resources of the community. The county can only function by further depressing the living standard of the people through taxation, and by dangerously burdening the one local industry. Even then, the county remains chronically dependent upon subsidies. . . .

Assimilation. The Menominee tribe was considered an advanced, self-confident group in need of few special protections. A central goal of termination was to promote the rapid integration of the tribe into American society. It is, of course, too early to judge the long-term effect of the policy. To the present, however, the impact has been to substantially decrease Menominee self-confidence while greatly increasing hostility toward whites. As Menominee attitudes favorable to successful assimilation have changed, so too has the outside view of the Menominees. The tribe is no longer seen as a prosperous and self-sufficient group, but rather as a poor community threatening to become a major welfare drain on the state. . . .

Reduction of Government Expenditures. A final objective of termination was to save the taxpayers' money. The first proposal for Menominee termination came in 1947, as a means to cut BIA personnel expenditures. Obviously, this objective must be ranked as a monumental miscalculation. While federal expenses on the Menominee reservation before termination had been nominal, expenditures began to skyrocket after the law was passed. Since 1954, more than $3 million has been appropriated by Congress, but none of the fundamental problems has been solved. Funds have not been provided for the capital investments required to give the county a chance for self-sufficiency.

The economic position of the tribe was clear long before termination. Through per capita distributions of tribal funds, reserves had declined dangerously by 1956. As the lumber market entered a long decline in 1958, the tribe's position became increasingly precarious. Well before the termination date, it was obvious that only the most optimistic projection of corporate income could show economic viability for the new county. Menominee Enterprises fell far short of this goal, and the tribe now faces economic disaster. The one personal asset of most Menominees is now being consumed in welfare payments. The state government has only postponed the day of reckoning with a very large direct relief burden. Clearly, there is no possibility of realizing this fourth goal.

It is now three and a half years since termination of the Menominee tribe. The years have been full of hard decisions, disappointments, and growing bitterness. The story is not yet over, but it may end soon. Unless new legislation is passed, Menominee stock goes on the open market in 1965, and control of the corporation may pass from the tribe. Unless the record of the business improves dramatically, Menominee Enterprises may face bankruptcy. Unless the legislature finds that the new county has been functioning effectively, the provisional establishment of Menominee county may end next year.

In the ten years since passage of the termination act, none of the major goals has been realized. Even if the objectives of assimilation and tax responsibility are eventually realized, the cost will be exorbitant. Taxes will be taken from people unable to pay, and the process of integration will be begun by people with neither confidence nor skills, at the bottom of the urban slums. Termination was based on a series of false assumptions, and the policy cannot achieve the goals so convincingly set forth in the subcommittee hearing room. The Menominee tribe is dead, but for no good reason.

Originally published in Chapter 6, "Termination in Retrospect," of *A Study of the Termination Policy* (Denver: National Congress of American Indians, n.d.), pp. 15–23.

Recommended Readings

The following books and articles treat broad aspects of the selections in this volume.

TREATIES

Athearn, Robert G. *Forts of the Upper Missouri*. Englewood Cliffs, N.J., 1967. Reprinted Lincoln: University of Nebraska Press, 1972.

Berthrong, Donald J. *The Southern Cheyennes*. Norman: University of Oklahoma Press, 1963.

Hafen, LeRoy R., and Francis Young. *Fort Laramie and the Pageant of the West*. Glendale, Calif.: Arthur H. Clark, 1938.

Jones, Douglas C. *The Treaty of Medicine Lodge*. Norman: University of Oklahoma Press, 1966.

Meyer, Roy W. *History of the Santee Sioux*. Lincoln: University of Nebraska Press, 1967.

THE BATTLE OF THE WASHITA

Berthrong, Donald J. *The Southern Cheyennes*. Norman: University of Oklahoma Press, 1963.

Hyde, George E. *Life of George Bent: Written from His Letters*. Norman: University of Oklahoma Press, 1967.

Leckie, William H. *The Military Conquest of the Southern Plains*. Norman: University of Oklahoma Press, 1963.

Stewart, Edgar I. *Custer's Luck*. Norman: University of Oklahoma Press, 1955.

Utley, Robert M. *Frontiersmen in Blue: The United States Army and the Indian, 1848–1865*. New York: Macmillan, 1967.

GRANT'S PEACE POLICY AND QUAKER POLICY

Beaver, Robert P. *Church, State, and the American Indian*. St.

Louis: Concordia, 1966.
Ellis, Richard N. *General Pope and U.S. Indian Policy.* Albuquerque: University of New Mexico Press, 1970.
Fritz, Henry E. *The Movement for Indian Assimilation, 1860–1890.* Philadelphia: University of Pennsylvania Press, 1963.
Mardock, Robert W. *The Reformers and the American Indian.* Columbia: University of Missouri Press, 1971.
Priest, Loring Benson. *Uncle Sam's Stepchildren: The Reformation of United States Indian Policy, 1865–1887.* New Brunswick, N.J.: Rutgers University Press, 1942.
Rahill, Peter. *The Catholic Indian Missions and Grant's Peace Policy, 1870–1884.* Washington, D.C.: Catholic University of America Press, 1953.
Tatum, Lawrie. *Our Red Brothers and the Peace Policy of President Ulysses S. Grant.* Philadelphia, 1899. Reprinted Lincoln: University of Nebraska Press, 1970.
Utley, Robert M. "The Celebrated Peace Policy of General Grant." *North Dakota History* 20 (July 1953): 121–42.

THE PEACETIME ROLE OF THE ARMY OF THE WEST

Athearn, Robert G. *William Tecumseh Sherman and the Settlement of the West.* Norman: University of Oklahoma Press, 1956.
Carpenter, John. *Sword and Olive Branch: Oliver Otis Howard.* Pittsburgh: University of Pittsburgh Press, 1964.
Crook, George C. *General George Crook: His Autobiography.* Edited by Martin F. Schmitt. Norman: University of Oklahoma Press, 1946.
Ellis, Richard N. "The Humanitarian Generals." *Western Historical Quarterly* 3 (April 1972): 169–78.
King, James T. *War Eagle: A Life of General Eugene A. Carr.* Lincoln: University of Nebraska Press, 1963.
Leckie, William H. *The Buffalo Soldiers: A Narrative of the Negro Cavalry in the West.* Norman: University of Oklahoma Press, 1967.
Wallace, Ernest. *Ranald S. Mackenzie on the Texas Frontier.* Lubbock: West Texas Museum Association, 1964.

THE PACIFICATION OF THE SOUTHWEST

Bourke, John G. *On the Border with Crook.* New York, 1891. Reprinted Lincoln: University of Nebraska Press, 1971.

Crook, George C. *General George Crook: His Autobiography.* Edited by Martin F. Schmitt. Norman: University of Oklahoma Press, 1946.

Goodwin, Grenville. *Western Apache Raiding and Warfare.* Edited by Keith H. Basso. Tucson: University of Arizona Press, 1971.

Kelly, Lawrence. *Navajo Roundup.* Boulder, Colo.: Pruett, 1970.

Moorhead, Max L. *The Apache Frontier.* Norman: University of Oklahoma Press, 1968.

Thrapp, Dan L. *The Conquest of Apacheria.* Norman: University of Oklahoma Press, 1967.

Underhill, Ruth. *The Navajos.* Norman: University of Oklahoma Press, 1956.

Utley, Robert M. *Frontiersmen in Blue: The United States Army and the Indian, 1848–1865.* New York: Macmillan, 1967.

RESERVATION LIFE

Hyde, George E. *Red Cloud's Folk.* Norman: University of Oklahoma Press, 1937.

———. *A Sioux Chronicle.* Norman: University of Oklahoma Press, 1956.

———. *Spotted Tail's Folk.* Norman: University of Oklahoma Press, 1961.

Hagan, William T. *Indian Policy and Judges: Experiments in Acculturation and Control.* New Haven, Conn.: Yale University Press, 1966.

Meyer, Roy W. *History of the Santee Sioux.* Lincoln: University of Nebraska Press, 1967.

Mooney, James. *The Ghost-Dance Religion and the Sioux Outbreak of 1890.* 14th Annual Report of the BIA. Washington, D.C.: G.P.O., 1896.

Neihardt, John G. *Black Elk Speaks.* New York, 1932. Reprinted Lincoln: University of Nebraska Press, 1961.

Walker, Deward E., Jr. *Conflict and Schism in Nez Perce Acculturation.* Pullman, Wash.: Washington State University Press, 1968.

THE DAWES ACT

Berthrong, Donald J. *The Southern Cheyennes.* Norman: University of Oklahoma Press, 1963.

Debo, Angie. *And Still the Waters Run.* Princeton, N.J.: Princeton University Press, 1940.

Fritz, Henry E. *The Movement for Indian Assimilation, 1860–1890.* Philadelphia: University of Pennsylvania Press, 1963.

Gibson, Arrell M. *The Chickasaws.* Norman: University of Oklahoma Press, 1971.

Hagan, William T. "Private Property, the Indian's Door to Civilization." *Ethnohistory* 3 (Spring 1956): 126–37.

Leupp, Francis E. *The Indian and His Problem.* New York: Scribner, 1910.

Meriam, Lewis. *The Problem of Indian Administration.* (Baltimore: Johns Hopkins Press, 1928.

Schmeckebier, Laurence F. *The Office of Indian Affairs: Its History, Activities, and Organization.* Baltimore: Johns Hopkins Press, 1927.

THE INDIAN NEW DEAL

Collier, John. *From Every Zenith.* Denver: Swallow, 1963.

———. *Indians of the Americas.* New York: Norton, 1947.

Downes, Randolph E. "A Crusade for Indian Reform, 1922–1935." *Mississippi Valley Historical Review* 32 (December 1945): 331–54.

La Farge, Oliver. *The Changing Indian.* Norman: University of Oklahoma Press, 1942.

Meriam, Lewis. *The Problem of Indian Administration.* Baltimore: Johns Hopkins Press, 1928.

Parman, Donald L. "The Indian and the Civilian Conservation Corps." *Pacific Historical Review* 40 (February 1971): 39–56.

Philp, Kenneth. "Albert B. Fall and the Protest from the Pueblos." *Arizona and the West* 12 (Autumn 1970): 237–54.

THE INDIAN CLAIMS COMMISSION

Annual Report of the Indian Claims Commission. Washington, D.C.: G.P.O., 1946–

Barker, Robert. "The Indian Claims Commission—the Conscience of the Nation in Its Dealings with the Original American." *Federal Bar Journal* 20 (Summer 1960): 240–47.

Barney, Ralph A. "Legal Problems Peculiar to Indian Claims Litigation." *Ethnohistory* 2 (Fall 1955): 315–25.

Gormley, Donald C. "The Role of the Expert Witness." *Ethnohistory* 2 (Fall 1955): 326–46.

Le Duc, Thomas. "The Work of the Indian Claims Commission under the Act of 1946." *Pacific Historical Review* 26 (February 1957): 1–16.

Lurie, Nancy O. "The Indian Claims Commission Act." *Annals,* May 1957, pp. 56–70.

Manners, Robert A. "The Land Claims Cases: Anthropologists in Conflict." *Ethnohistory* 3 (Winter 1956): 72–81.

Washburn, Wilcomb E. *Red Man's Land/White Man's Law.* New York: Scribner, 1971.

TERMINATION

Brophy, William A., and Sophie D. Aberle. *The Indian: America's Unfinished Business.* Norman: University of Oklahoma Press, 1966.

Cohen, Felix. "The Erosion of Indian Rights, 1950–53." *Yale Law Review* 62 (February 1953): 348–90.

Deloria, Vine. *Custer Died for Your Sins: An Indian Manifesto.* New York: Macmillan, 1969.

La Farge, Oliver. "Termination of Federal Supervision: Disintegration and the American Indians." *Annals,* May 1957, 41–46.

Stern, Theodore. *The Klamath Tribe: A People and Their Reservation.* Seattle: University of Washington Press, 1965.

Van DeMark, Dorothy. "The Raid on the Reservations." *Harper's,* March 1956, pp. 48–53.

Washburn, Wilcomb E. *Red Man's Land: White Man's Law.* New York: Scribner, 1971.

Watkins, Arthur V. "Termination of Federal Supervision: The

Removal of Restrictions over Indian Property and Person." *Annals,* May 1957, 47–55.

General Works on American Indian History

Debo, Angie. *A History of the Indians of the United States.* Norman: University of Oklahoma Press, 1970.

Driver, Harold E. *Indians of North America.* Chicago: University of Chicago Press, 1961.

Hagan, William T. *American Indians.* Chicago: University of Chicago Press, 1961.

Levine, Stuart, and Nancy O. Lurie, eds. *The American Indian Today.* Baltimore and Deland, Fla.: Everett Edwards, 1968.

Owen, Roger C., et al., eds. *The North American Indians: A Sourcebook.* New York: Macmillan, 1967.

Prucha, Francis Paul. *American Indian Policy in the Formative Years: The Indian Trade and Intercourse Acts, 1790–1834.* Cambridge, Mass., 1962. Reprinted Lincoln: University of Nebraska Press, 1970.

Spencer, Robert F., et al. *The Native Americans.* New York: Harper, 1965.

Spicer, Edward H. *Cycles of Conquest: The Impact of Spain, Mexico, and the United States on Indians of the Southwest.* Tucson: University of Arizona Press, 1962.

———. *Perspectives in American Indian Culture Change.* Chicago: University of Chicago Press, 1961.

Steiner, Stan. *The New Indians.* New York: Harper, 1968.

Underhill, Ruth. *Red Man's America.* Chicago: University of Chicago Press, 1953.

Washburn, Wilcomb E. *Red Man's Land/White Man's Law.* New York: Scribner, 1971.

———, ed. *The Indian and the White Man.* Garden City, N.Y.: Doubleday, 1964.

Two important guides to periodical literature on American Indian tribes are:

Murdock, George P. *Ethnographic Bibliography of North America.* New Haven, Conn.: Human Relations Area File Press, 1960.

Winther, Oscar O. *A Classified Bibliography of the Trans-Mississippi West.* Bloomington: Indiana University Press, 1961.

List of Contributors

DONALD J. BERTHRONG is professor of history at Purdue University.

JOHN COLLIER (dec.) was Commissioner of Indian Affairs in the Franklin D. Roosevelt administration.

RICHARD N. ELLIS is associate professor of history at the University of New Mexico.

GEORGE BIRD GRINNELL (dec.), naturalist and ethnologist, was the author of twenty-eight books, many about the plains Indians.

ALVIN M. JOSEPHY, JR., is vice president of the American Heritage Publishing Company and author of a major government-sponsored study of the operations of the Bureau of Indian Affairs.

JAMES T. KING is professor of history at the University of Wisconsin, River Falls.

ROY W. MEYER is professor of English at Mankato State College.

RALPH H. OGLE (dec.), whose study of the Apaches grew out of his Ph.D. dissertation at Columbia University, was head of the history department of the Phoenix Union High School.

JAMES C. OLSON is Chancellor and professor of history at the University of Missouri, Kansas City.

GARY ORFIELD was associated with the University of Chicago at the time he wrote his study of Menominee termination.

LORING B. PRIEST is professor of history at Lycoming College.

ROBERT WHITNER is professor of history at Whitman College.

GLEN A. WILKINSON is a lawyer specializing in Indian legal problems.

WILLIAM ZIMMERMAN, JR., (dec.) was Assistant Commissioner of Indian Affairs during the New Deal period and later served as Associate Director of the Bureau of Land Management.